D1362060

MANSTOPPER!

Training a Canine Guardian

by
Joel M. McMains

HOWELL
BOOK
HOUSE

Howell Book House

New York

Howell Book House
Published by Wiley Publishing, Inc., Hoboken, New Jersey

For general information about our other products and services, please contact our Customer Care Department within the United States at (800) 762-2974, outside the United States at (317) 572-3993 or fax (317) 572-4002.

Wiley also publishes its books in a variety of electronic formats. Some content that appears in print may not be available in electronic books. For more information about Wiley prod-ucts, visit our web site at www.wiley.com.

Library of Congress Cataloging-in-Publication data:

McMains, Joel M.
Manstopper! : training a canine guardian / by Joel M. McMains
p. cm.
Includes bibliographica: references and index.
ISBN 0-87605-144-1
1. Watchdogs—Training. I. Title.
SF428.8.M36 1998
636.7'0886—dc21   97-35213
                                         CIP

Printed in the United States of America
5   4

Book Design by Rachael McBrearty—Madhouse Productions

DEDICATION

For Jo Sykes, trainer and teacher, who told me six books ago as I stared at my third rejection slip from as many publishers and pondered punching the *Delete* key, "Keep writing!"

And for Joyce Guerrero, who told me many other things.

Like construction workers who walk narrow beams at dizzying heights and cops who race through darkened doorways against armed suspects, the work of guard dog trainers is high-risk. That designation should not be a revelation—it's common sense.

Still, be forewarned: The training methods presented in this book carry high potential for danger to owners, trainers, helpers and dogs. *Given the work's nature, you, the people assisting you and your dogs are at great peril and may be seriously injured.*

People aren't supposed to be perfect. Neither are dogs. Mistakes and accidents happen, and the less experienced you are, the greater the risk. As a trainer-friend from Germany once said, "You get bit; that's part of it, too."

This book is not for children. Hide it from them. There is no great mystery about protection training. A child can learn it. A child can also be shredded trying it.

As can an adult.

The canine training techniques described herein are intended for stable canine temperaments only and are not intended for any dog whose lineage or temperament makes him clearly unsuited for protection work.

Neither the Author nor the Publisher shall be liable for any claim, made by any person, trainer or owner, that arises out of the use or implementation of the various training methods presented in this book.

CONTENTS

PART I
Preludes

PART II
Training

PART III
Extras

ACKNOWLEDGMENTS

This page is always my favorite. It gives me a chance to thank those people toward whom Providence has nudged me. They have helped shape the person I am and, therefore, the books I have written.

Bud Swango, Jim Robinson, Robert McKie, Joanna Walker, Roger Davidson, Ron Flath, Lawrence Zillmer, Carol Lea Benjamin, Nancy West, Karen White, Steve and Suzanne SeRine, and most cherished, H.P. Many of you are dog knowledgeable, each of you have shown me love and patience. No one could ask more of friends.

Years ago Sean Frawley and Seymour Weiss of Howell Book House recognized the substance of what I call the *Dog Logic* series and took a chance. The debt I feel toward those gentlemen exceeds my ability to repay.

Beth Adelman, editor, thank you for your gentle, insightful touch that encouraged and allowed.

Jeanne Kuntz, photographer, without your artist's compassion and patience, this book would only strain at the bit.

And a special "Bless you" to the dogs, for their acceptance and for what they've taught me.

Of course, some folks' contributions would have been negative, had I accepted them. Such shadows fall across every life, perhaps for contrast. They are distractions that are better ignored.

We need another and a wiser and perhaps a more mystical concept of animals. Remote from universal nature, and living by complicated artifice, man in civilization surveys the creature through the glass of his knowledge and sees thereby a feather magnified and the whole image in distortion. We patronize them for their incompleteness, for their tragic fate of having taken form so far below ourselves. And therein we err, and greatly err. For the animal shall not be measured by man. In a world older and more complete than ours they move finished and complete, gifted with extensions of the senses we have lost or never attained, living by voices we shall never hear. They are not brethren, they are not underlings; they are other nations, caught with ourselves in the net of life and time, fellow prisoners of the splendour and travail of the earth.

Henry Beston
The Outermost House

PREFACE

This is a book about training man's best friend to be an assailant's worst nightmare, a canine protector who defends his human partner by threat or bite, according to command.

Manstopper is not just for protection buffs. Even trainers ill-disposed to guard dog work can profit from this book's insights into canine nature and motivation, which can be adapted to enhance responsiveness in many areas of training. Moreover, obedience fans unschooled in protection work still have much to learn about obedience specifically and canine potential generally.

This guide operates beyond the genre's typical "Do this, do that." Though I've provided an extensive Glossary, the book uses a minimum of technical jargon, yet its style requires concentration and thought. This is appropriate, because guardian training demands concentration and thought. How much? Well, one does not sneeze when handling nitroglycerin.

By design, the book develops gradually; the first chapter does not open, "Start your pet's protection training by. . . . " Beginners often wish to hasten the learning process; and while enthusiasm is understandable, even commendable, to race through bitework's principles is like sticking your finger in a wall socket to study the nature of electricity. There is much you must know before ever attaching a leash.

In some instances the text is harsh. That's because you and I are examining some harsh realities. No, it isn't all serious. A sense of humor maintains perspective (and preserves sanity). Still, if certain passages make you wince, remember we seek neither show-ring trophies nor performance titles. Our focus is combat. Successful combat.

We are teaching *Canis familiaris* that, on cue, he must unleash his fighting attributes—teeth, nails, cunning, intensity, speed and raw power—against *Homo sapiens*. Not just against padded sleeves but against people. Polite niceties are not coefficients in that equation.

Action scenes abound in *Manstopper*, to provide word pictures of guard training rather than just string together declarative sentences. Q&A sections are provided to fill in anticipated blanks.

Every other photograph doesn't depict a dog biting someone, a proclivity among many protection books that teaches little. I'd rather allocate photo space to subtler aspects of training and handling, because to the dog they are not subtle; they are as important as what occurs during bite practice.

Further, I don't waste your time with captions like, "This is a German Shepherd Dog." Anyone whose experience doesn't enable them to recognize a German Shepherd (or Doberman Pinscher or Rottweiler) at a glance is not ready to try guard work.

People who have never owned or trained a dog, or possess but a vague awareness of the species, should first master obedience. They should not start in protection. One does not begin an education about cars or driving by entering the Indy 500. Dogs are pack animals from another age, not inarticulate children in furry costumes. They respect physical and mental strength, and submit to human domination only if their owners clarify expectations.

In the first chapter you will meet Greta, a German Shepherd who will show you what a manstopper is. And is not. But for now, take a look at perspective, a crucial element. As a professional, my outlook is different from that of competition trainers. Not better—different. Because training is my livelihood, not a hobby, my reputation rides on every dog I teach. Either I produce reliable, confident workers or I'm not only out of the ribbons, I'm out of business.

That said, this book is appropriate for German *schutzhund* and French ring sport trainers. (*Schutzhund* and *ring sport* competition have nothing to do with the vile practice of pit-dog fighting.) That it teaches neither sport implies no slight of either. Some very tough dogs participate in both arenas. But contests measure success in points and titles, not survival, and I've seen competition trainers joke with agitators ("bad guys" the dogs confront) in the animals' presence. To a guard dog, a bad guy is a bad guy, not an actor but the real McCoy.

Police-dog trainers may also gain from *Manstopper*'s training and reinforcement methods. An important distinction, however, is that while police K-9s are trained to defend, they also know to chase and search. Our goals include neither pursuit nor investigation. We're targeting defense. Period.

I presume your dog is a house pet, one who eats in the home, sleeps on or near the bed and knows he is a genuine member of the family. How important are these elements? Well, it's no accident that police K-9s and military dogs often share the home of their handlers and families. A canine outsider, either in perception or location, or one who lives on a chain (please excuse the oxymoron), should not be protection trained. To guard train a dog trapped in such indifferent circumstances is to expect full-time work from part-time help. It is also to construct a time bomb that can explode in the owner's face.

A common question of beginners is, "Since the animal cannot be forced to protect (in the same sense that he can be made to sit, for example), how can an owner be certain the dog will defend on command?" As you should expect, the book answers that question and many like it.

Read the entire text before starting training. Don't just skim. Study. Indeed, go through it more than once, until you have internalized—not just pondered—its concepts. To do guard work with an air of, "Well, I sort of see what Joel means," is not just careless, it's dangerous. It increases the risk to you, your dog and your assistants in an already hazardous endeavor.

Sure, memorizing various steps and procedures may be necessary, but understanding the precepts that support the training's mechanics is vital. Otherwise you are working in the dark, and in this undertaking you need all the light you can get.

The second point to contemplate is outlook. Yours. The German term *schutz* (as in *schutzhund, hund* meaning *dog*) translates as "protection; cover, shelter." Add the notion that my approach to all training centers around a profound human-canine relationship, and the foundation of *Manstopper's* ideology takes form. As I wrote in *Advanced Obedience—Easier Than You Think,* "By the time a person reaches this level, either he has something going with his dog or he never will without considerable restructuring."

As in human relationships, if appreciation, commitment and trust underlie the attraction between you and your dog, all else follows naturally. Should any be conditional, haphazard or absent, surely chaos will ensue.

PART I

PRELUDES

CHAPTER 1

COMMAND PERFORMANCE

At a year old, Greta was a study in curiosity. Excited to be alive, eager to learn, each day offered the black-and-red German Shepherd too brief an adventure. Now in her autumn years, though time has frosted her muzzle and dulled her spark, she can still take your breath away. Greta's loveliness and grace are the stuff of poetry, outshone only by her capacity for affection, which she gives openly and without barter.

But don't misunderstand—Greta is no mouse. Her intensity in guardian work can chill the blood. I've seen it age more than one veteran bad guy. As a wizened trainer-friend once hooted while watching her in action, "*Gott im Himmel!* She works so efficient!"

On Location

Backdropped against a gray, winter-flecked spring all those years ago, Greta flowered in guardian training, sparkling in bitework like fireworks on the Fourth. Truly, she was platinum, a canine bundle of latent promise; the kind of dog who can make a trainer seem more skilled than he is.

Her education complete, the dozing animal's head warmed my leg as I drove through a dense morning fog to a vacant schoolyard where her owner awaited us. He hadn't seen his pet in nearly two months and had fretted on the phone, "Do you think she's forgotten me?" Sensing my car braking, Greta raised her head, stood, yawned, stretched—saw Tim and almost came unglued.

"Yipe!" She flew to the back seat, spun around twice, fixed on Tim—"Yipe! Yipe!"—hurdled to the front seat, tap-danced against the dashboard, did another 360 turn, riveted once more on her human—"Yipe! Yipe! Yipe! Yipe! Yipe!"—then wailed and tried to tunnel under me to get at the door, all in the time it took to shift to *Park* and switch off the ignition while the car rocked like a small boat in violent waters.

"Yes, fickle one, I see him. Just let me get my door open."

Her ballistic exit led to a stream of joyful yips and hops (by both owner and dog, incidentally), and while Greta washed Tim's face, he hugged and petted her and told her how beautiful she was.

All reunions should be like that one.

Once man and dog had returned to Earth, Tim and I reviewed various basics about handling a guard dog. We'd had several such talks before, but today would mark his first time at the helm. I described situations soon to occur and verified that he knew Greta's commands, especially her go and stop words: "Action" and "Out."

Tim nodded, patted the Shepherd's neck once more and heeled her through the mist toward the school's football field. During the next several minutes the pair would twice walk its length, first along one sideline, then the other, as assistants emerging from behind the bleachers created scripted incidents to evaluate Greta as a manstopper. I took a seat to watch the show.

Lights! Camera! . . .

An old man strode through the haze. Clearly in a fog of his own, he carried a cane and jabbered to himself in loud, gruff tones. Jerky hand gestures punctuated his pronouncements as he poked at the fog with his stick.

Mindful that Greta might misread the moment, Tim altered their route so as not to intersect Mr. Strangeways' path. The young dog looked the old man over, curious about his eccentric behavior, but otherwise paid him little mind as he faded into the vapor, still ranting like a politician in search of a podium. Tim and Greta continued their walk.

Soon a young woman rushed up to Tim and breathlessly rattled that she was lost, late for an urgent appointment and "WherecanIfind?" a local business. After Tim gave directions, the woman thanked him, shot a hand toward Greta, petted her, said, "She's sure easy on the eyes," and flurried away.

Several yards later a group of children approached. "Mister, can we pet your dog?" Tim smiled. "Sure. She'd like that."

The youngsters were as taken with Greta as she was with them. Her tail at full wag, she sniffed hands and licked faces. "She's pretty." "Her fur's so soft." "She likes me best, I can tell."

The kids were still chattering about Greta when they departed. "It tickled when she licked my nose." "I wish I had a dog like that."

Tim and Greta went on their way.

A Toy Poodle raced onto the field. Tim stopped, Greta sat. The Poodle halted several yards distant and barked in outrage at the twosome. Fascinated by the tiny creature, Greta craned her head forward but made no move to leave Tim's side. In a twinkling the wee dog departed and disappeared among the bleachers. Tim heeled Greta to the goal line, where they crossed to the other side of the field.

In each instance the German Shepherd showed no aggression, just curiosity, as one would expect of a stable, intelligent, friendly dog.

Then an inebriated panhandler lurched onto the scene. Tim stopped and spoke a word to Greta. "Listen."

The dog switched channels. She showed no hostility, just intense interest as the man drew close and extended a begging hand. Tim ordered him away, but the derelict persisted, waving his arms above his head while cursing the fates in general and Tim in particular. Tim said, "Watchim!" Greta rumbled like summer thunder.

The moocher resembled Ichabod Crane but did a W.C. Fields double-take, as though noticing Greta for the first time. He exited stage left, sprinting across the field with remarkable animation and purpose, blowing hard, really getting his knees into it. Tim and Greta stood transfixed, watching the performance through the breaking fog. Then he told her that she had done well and commanded "Out"—settle down. In commentary Greta puffed a low "Smerf!" at the retreating scarecrow. Tim chuckled as he patted her neck. They journeyed on.

Moments later the indigent returned. "I don't know what came over me," he said. "I'm sorry for the way I acted."

Tim smiled and offered his hand, then commanded Greta, "Stand, stay," and told the stranger, "You may pet her now, if you wish." The dog remained calm yet watchful during this second encounter, and when the vagrant said "Nice doggy, nice doggy" and offered a tidbit from his pocket, she refused it, turning her head aside. The man sighed, shrugged and shuffled off. The team resumed their outing.

Soon a well-tailored gentleman approached, all smiles and stares of awed admiration. "What a beautiful dog!" Tim stopped and grinned, pleased by the compliment. "Truly magnificent!" the newcomer added, smiling broader. Lulled into complacency, Tim had forgotten that appearances are just that. He later said Greta seemed passive but I read her as skeptical, staring at the smiler's face, her head cocked to one side, air scenting more than usual.

Earlier I had directed the well-tailored gentleman, "Send it through the eyes," which he knew to mean that he should appear diplomat friendly in stance and speech, but his gaze should radiate the warmth of a crypt. A good actor can do that, and though Tim had missed the incongruity, Greta had not. Dogs are eagles at detecting anomalies like lying eyes.

I had told Tim that when this person disappeared, an assailant would emerge. That's what happened, but not in the manner Tim expected. Had I been more specific, he might have inadvertently telegraphed a set-up cue to Greta, which could have clouded my evaluation of her responses.

The man moved closer. His smile died. Greta stood, tense, her stare locked onto the intruder. Muted sunlight glinted on a knife. "Let's see some money, sucker."

Tim recovered in a blink. "Action!" Things kicked into fast-forward as a roaring black-and-red blur flew at the assailant. Greta hit like a battering ram. Her bite was a vise. Her impact slammed the man to the ground as she nailed a forearm full-mouth, almost to her back molars.

The weapon fell away, forgotten as the onslaught's ferocity and suddenness disrupted the crook's mental processes. His world spun to ice as the pain took him, his liquid shrieks hideous in their counterpoint to the dog's howling fury.

"No, dog! No! Out! Out!" the man screamed, writhing, but Greta hung on, driven. The mugger swung his free hand at her, but she just bit harder, her ancestors' savage cheers echoing along the darker reaches of her mind. A dreadful intensity raged in her pitiless eyes, now inches from his.

In seconds the thief went from fear to terror to hysteria. "I quit! I quit! Get it off me! Please! Call it off!"

Tim shouted, "Out! Back!" Greta released and backed to Tim's side. Saliva flew as she clacked her teeth together, her muzzle stabbing toward the robber as she bounced on her front paws, quivering in anticipation, ready for another rush. She wanted more of him, and he knew it.

"Get up and get gone!" Tim said.

"Get hold of that dog. K-k-keep it away from me."

"Last chance—git!"

In slow, uncertain stages the man hauled himself to his feet, looking as harmless as he now was. Clutching his damaged arm, he shook his head as if to clear it. Dazed, swaying, his reality in disarray, he stared again at his arm, then at Tim, then at aftershock images only he could see.

His gaze snagged on Greta, on foam bubbling from her jaws. She leaned forward and growled deep in her throat. He heard her counsel and stepped backward. The mugger stumbled. He turned and ran.

Greta whined and raised a forepaw, her fire still smoldering as she stared after the figure shrinking into the distance. The mist had all but cleared as Tim knelt beside the German Shepherd, awestruck. He hugged and petted her, saying, "That was great, Greta! You're fantastic!" Shaking his head, he also said, "I'll be damned!" a lot.

From my vantage point, I thought *Cut!* This was a take. Greta was ready to go home.

Review

No one was hurt. The protagonist, a professional bad guy, known in the trade as an agitator, wore concealed protective gear. Moreover, everyone Tim and Greta encountered was a trainer (save the children, of course, who were sons and daughters of the trainers). All were acting and any could have played the bad guy's role.

This was a dress rehearsal—serious business to the supporting cast but real only to the star, Greta.

And real to her it was. Know this about dogs: Play-acting is not of their world. To them, all moments are real. Think: Have you ever seen a dog or puppy chase a fuzzy toy, grab and shake it? "How cute," I've heard owners say, and, "Isn't that darling?"

Right.

As pooch breaks the prey's back. In the dog's mind, that's what she's doing. It's as though she can hear the vertebrae snap.

"My dog isn't like that at all. When she shakes her furry toy she wags her tail." Most dogs do during a kill.

Sure, an element of play may operate, but realize that your perception of reality differs from your pet's. *Play* means one thing for us, something quite different for dogs.

Canis familiaris lives at once very near our world yet eons from it. The dog still has a paw or two in the wild. The closest we come to guard training of humans involves badges and military uniforms. Even then, we lay out rules with lawyerly precision. The dog follows but one rule: Win. Or, more accurately, don't lose.

Casting

The bedrock of protection is selecting an able dog. Very few qualify as guardians. The animal must be keen, fearless and sound while being stable, intelligent, friendly, a people dog, one children intuitively trust—"Mister, can we pet your dog?" These qualities are not universal among any breed.

Q. You don't want a suspicious, hot-tempered animal?

A. No! Such a dog can fire, but often at innocent occurrences, and shutting her down can be a whole other story.

Ethical training neither produces nor tolerates viciousness. Tim hugged and petted Greta just after she fought a man. Do that with a mean, fear-driven or unstable dog, one whose mind is nibbling on a fight's leftovers, and you may lose face—literally.

We don't want a distrustful biting machine that views every person as a potential target. Witness Greta's disinterest in the old man who made strange, quick gestures with his club (the cane). Notice, too, her unconcern about the frantic soul who dashed up to Tim for directions. A dog with faulty temperament, or one trained with liberal doses of paranoia, might have reacted with violence to either person's behaviors, or those of the Toy Poodle.

Greta keyed on the beggar only after Tim cued her, "Listen." Though she ran the moocher off, she later accepted his touch because Tim's manner said the man was okay—Tim offered his hand.

Even so, Greta would not take food from the stranger, a decision she made without coaching from Tim. Rejecting treats from outsiders is peripheral yet basic to guard dog training. Sick, vengeful minds can target your pet by lacing edibles with poison (or ground glass, or metal shavings or . . .).

The Script

The program entails five commands.

- *Listen*   Alert; focus on the person.

- *Watchim*   Threaten by growling, barking, snapping jaws and/or showing teeth. The command is a contraction of "Watch him!" As it should be spoken so rapidly that it becomes one word, "Watchim!" is used throughout this text.

- *Action*   Bite and hold the target's nearer arm.

- *Out*   Cease aggression but remain alert. This command cancels any of the preceding three and also halts responses to provocation.
- *Back*   Hurry to the handler's left side while keeping an eye on the bad guy.

As you see, *Listen*, *Watchim* and *Action*, the work commands, each contain two syllables. *Out* and *Back*, the shut-down cues, have one. Accident prevention and clear communication underlie this structuring: It takes two sounds to send the dog, one to stop her.

"That's backwards," some trainers say. "Triggers should be a single syllable," their thought being expediency during a hot situation. Regarding effective use of a guard dog, the trainer part of me agrees; but the survivor part disagrees, given our society's addiction to lawsuits and loopholes. Ergo, all my commands are one syllable, except the three protection cues. This provides something of a safety valve that allows me to say, "Everything's okay," with every command I give, except for words with two sounds. They launch the animal's mind onto a different plane.

Notice Tim did not preface commands with the dog's name, a common practice for many trainers but a no-no at my kennels. Speed and safety underlie my preference. While it's obvious that omitting the name halves the words needed for ignition, safety elements may be less apparent. First, a bad guy using the dog's name could obtain a measure of control, because name-linking sets up the dog's mind to respond to the user. A real assailant, hearing the name, could throw it back and cause a blink of hesitation, which might make all the difference. Second, protectors often come to enjoy their rough-and-tumble work. Heartily. Repeated linking of the dog's name with the go word can develop a response where the dog goes target shopping upon hearing his name. Its sound can switch the animal's mind to cross-hairs mode.

Q. Canine mental processes are that fast?

A. Believe it. Dogs aren't encumbered with decision filters like moral? ethical? legal? or the lending of gravity to the absurd, such as political correctness. Dogs accept. Some humans try to make the concrete abstract, but canines no more question reality than fish question water. The dog asks only, "Where lies my advantage?" The instant an answer becomes available, the animal reacts. She doesn't second-guess herself. She knows that second thoughts always come too late.

Regarding technique, note Greta "nailed a forearm," not a leg or the torso. In reaction to a dog's charge, a person runs or raises his hands near chest level.

The latter response puts arms at convenient targeting height. Leg-bite training has use in pursuit work, when an arm would be harder to get at; but, as mentioned in the Preface, chases are not for us.

Consider, too, that a frontal leg strike doesn't just expose the animal to harm from above, where the hands are, perhaps clutching a weapon, it can also get a dog's head kicked in.

Besides, a waist- or chest-high rush intensifies intimidation. It brings flashing teeth closer to the self—the heart, the eyes, the mind. A wrongdoer doesn't ponder all this at the time, of course, but the human brain's feral element, the part that never sleeps, recognizes the fact and responds with fear. Since fright exacerbates pain, an arm bite more overwhelms and thus more inhibits. Sensations arrive quicker, too, as the impulses travel a shorter distance than from a leg.

Greta bit "full-mouth, almost to her back molars." A manstopper does not nip, she engulfs, thus generating pressure across a larger area and stimulating more nerve endings. A related component is bite-and-hold training—"Greta hung on"—not the rip-and-slash or "typewriter" variety (rapid bites along a limb). We want an effective bite, but one that causes as little damage as possible—a conceptual spin off from police use-of-force guidelines.

Did you catch that the assailant twice screamed "Out" at Greta? Sure, few hoodlums know traditional guard dog commands, like "Out," but since some do know such *stop* words, I train my dogs to ignore cues not given by me or a family member.

Finally, Tim did not tell Greta to pursue the mugger. Her role is to shield her human from scoundrels, not to chase or apprehend them. That's the cops' job. Since someone on the run cannot threaten the dog's owner, a private citizen sending a Greta after a fleeing troublemaker not only increases the risk of injury to the dog, but the act could be alleged as battery upon the lawbreaker and a violation of his civil rights. True, rational folks would not suffer insomnia from news of an assaulter having been assaulted. But the fact remains that injuries, real or fancied, resulting from pursuit and "action" could leave an owner vulnerable to criminal and civil charges.

Previews

You've read insights about what a manstopper is and isn't. Of course, all this begs the question of how to train at this level. I'll show you, but not until we lay groundwork rooted partly in another question, posed in the next chapter's title.

Reflection

*If you don't like dogs in general, or if you've never owned
or wanted to own one, don't even think about a guard dog.
The attack-trained animal is not a machine. Like all dogs, he needs
time, effort, and love. Deprived of these, he will disintegrate.*

Jerrold J. Mundis

CHAPTER 2
IS THIS TRIP NECESSARY?

In Columbia Pictures' timeless film *The Karate Kid*, an aged Okinawan teaches a California teenager karate. Several weeks into training they exchange insights.

> *"Miyagi hate fighting," the instructor said of himself.*
> *"Yeah, but you like karate," the student, Daniel, said.*
> *"So?" Mr. Miyagi said.*
> *"So karate's fighting. You train to fight."*
> *"That what you think?"*
> *Was it? Daniel wondered a moment.*
> *"No."*
> *"Then why train?" The old man challenged.*
> *The student thought before answering. Then he grinned.*
> *"So I won't have to fight."*

Deterrence

As the dialogue suggests, a martial arts master may never have to do battle to be effective. The same holds true of a guard dog. He must be trained against the eventuality that his demeanor may not discourage an antagonist, yet in many instances the dog's presence alone may be deterrent enough.

Why? Because of the psychological impact of canine physiognomy, a nine-dollar word referring to facial features, expression and size. Even people unfamiliar with dogs know that the species is controlled by different urges than those of humans. "The dog always lives in the here and now and is unable to understand the reasons for his own actions."[1] To be confronted by a skillful

[1] *The Police Service Dog*, Johannes Grewe, page 27.

12

guardian is to be cornered, because a human, no matter how fleet, cannot out-run a dog, and knows it.

Native canine alertness, the unmistakable loyalty toward his human part-ner, that riveting stare, those sharp, bone-white teeth, the fact that his tail just quit wagging—any of these can trigger primordial dread of the predator, espe-cially among humans who predicate their existence upon predation. Fear has never been the strongest emotion, but for some it's the only emotion. Their histories have taught them to worship fear, chiefly their own.

That's why few sights shut down a genuine bad guy faster than an able dog unimpressed by human bluster. The dog not only yawns in the face of menace, he radiates, "To get at my friend you have to go through me, and I don't take pris-oners!" Result? A sharp intake of breath as psychological handcuffs snap on and a malefactor's menace is mirrored back at him with stun-ning force. With a glance a dog can say, "I see you at your core, and you're running on the rims."

Two outstanding state-certified police K-9s I trained were Chattan and Smokey, a Doberman Pinscher and a German Shepherd who

Physiognomy—the face reveals the character.

shared my days and nights for too few years. Friendly and affectionate, each was always on simmer and could kick up to full boil in a flash. Including my years in law enforcement, how many times do you suppose I flipped either dog's *action* switch? Excluding training sessions, how many times did I command Chattan or Smokey to use teeth?

Once? Twice? Half a dozen? More? Take a guess.

Answer: Never.

Chattan's roar "I'm here!" once froze a memorable bar fight, and one night I cued Smokey to growl at a drunken prowler (who miraculously achieved

Would you reach for Nick's toy? Physiognomy, part two.

instant sobriety and an unwavering allegiance to law and order). Each instance pumped a psychological shotgun, and both were as close as I've come to setting a dog on anyone.

How many times did Chattan or Smokey's presence forestall trouble? I have no way of knowing, but *lots* comes to mind as I write this. Further, more than one incarcerated burglar has told me that he wouldn't touch a home with a dog in it; that he and his peers presume all house dogs bite.

Though I would never recommend using an untrained animal in a hot situation, all you may ever need to ward off evil intentions is a sizable, responsive dog at your side. Watchers noting that your canine buddy is under your control may reconsider the wisdom of finding out what other tricks he knows.

All this comes back to the chapter's title. Do you need a guard dog? Not *want—need*?

Liability

Do you know what a good-sized dog can do to flesh? And how fast? Ponder words like *ripped*, and *fractured*, and *hemorrhaging*. Imagine savaged meat and the

This is something of a Rorschach test— pick out the Doberman that's not guard trained. (You'll find the answer in Chapter 21.)

coppery smell of congealing blood. Add gray-white hues for exposed bone, and the sound of cartilage and tendons tearing, a sound like wet newspaper ripping.

By nature, dogs don't do anything halfway. And, like you and me, they can make mistakes. What if your pet should fire on an innocent? Do you realize how severely someone could be injured, how deep the scaring might go and the amount of civil damages you might have to face, as well as criminal charges?

Make no mistake: A bite-trained dog can be a frightful liability, for several reasons. Certain breeds' bite compression is awesome. Doberman Pinscher and German Shepherd jaw pressure can exceed 750 pounds per square inch (psi). Double that for Rottweiler force. (For reference, the bite power of a great white shark approximates 1,000 psi.) Those numbers may seem startling until you remember that in the wild, the dog's natural home, canines not only need to splinter the bones of prey to get at the marrow, but they must do so fast, lest they themselves become the hunted.

Canine jaws move up, down and sideways. They can grind. Imagine 42 teeth behind that crushing force and its effects applied in a twisting motion to arm or hand. Loss of either, or at least of fingers, can well result— in less time than it takes you to read this sentence.

Skeptical? A professional show dog handler once tried to stop a fight between two German Shepherds. Although the dogs were not guard trained—that is, their biting power was breed typical; it had not been built up through strenuous bite training—one of the man's arms was instantly broken. In three places.

At a vaccination clinic a friend tried to restrain a scared, medium-size cross-breed. The dog snipped off a finger—and swallowed it!

I know a Doberman who can clamp a two-by-two with such power that, if you have the strength (and the nerve), you can hoist him from the ground by it.

Species capabilities comprise one basis of the liability inherent in owning a manstopper. Others are slipshod breeders and inept trainers, both as common as weeds. Preying upon an unsuspecting public, the former pass along genetic junk that should never be bite trained, and certainly not by the latter, whose interests center around status and the almighty dollar.

The court system also looms large in the liabilities column. Judges and lawyers have scant personal contact with crime scenes, their fields of expertise being laws and the courtroom. Their knowledge of dogs or training often derives from what they're told by the media, whose dearth of knowledge about any subject has never precluded making authoritative pronouncements.

Thus, if you send a dog at someone, you damn well better be able to justify your action to a skeptical judiciary, one perhaps whose only personal involvement with crime is watching reruns of *Murder She Wrote*. If that indictment seems too stinging, ponder a passage from *Obedience & Security Training for Dogs*, a 1967 book by Tom Scott, then with the London Metropolitan Police Dog Section. Consider, too, that precedents in American civil law—the kind where people sue each other—have become more liberal, some would say loonier, since the 1960s.

In security training, care must be given to the choice of commands so that they do not confuse with other words that might at some time give offense. This is of special importance if an appearance in the police court may be necessary, since the expression used by a handler might influence a magistrate. For instance, directions to a dog to "Seize him," "Do him," or even "Get him" are frowned on. . . . A person who is being charged might say you told the dog to "Attack him," when actually you said "At him." I well remember explaining to a magistrate that the name of a dog I had at the time was Caesar, and that I had not directed my dog to "seize" the prisoner.

For any educated adult to purport that dogs attach judgmental nuances to words is nonsensical, but it happens. You and I know that when a dog hears a command, he reacts to a sound he has learned to associate with a specific behavior on his part. In psychological jargon, the stimulus elicits the response. No canine could understand that *seize* encompasses such disparate concepts as *appropriate, grab, confiscate, steal, lock, apprehend, catch, possess* and *understand*. Whether a trainer prefers a cue of, "Get him," "Action," or "Lamp shade" makes no difference to the dog. He responds to whatever verbal trigger you teach.

But the reality you have to live with is that, as Mr. Scott implies, judges have the power, nonsensical or not.

History and culture also affect the liability of guard dog ownership. Setting a dog on someone has seldom found favor in America, owing to excesses in the way police dogs have been used for crowd control, principally of minorities, which often has been grossly overdone. Someone chanting "Freedom, now!" has never been legitimate cause for releasing a K-9.

Appropriately last on the liability list is the legion of so-called animal lovers who really just love the sound of their own voice proclaiming that nothing justifies bite training. They're as wrong as they are out of touch, of course, but they get plenty of air time nonetheless.

A Liability Scenario

Suppose you set your dog against someone, let's say a mugger. The animal defends you, the robber flees, and you deem the time, effort and costs of training as sound investments. In a sane world such training would never be necessary, but we both know how the world is. Still, consider how much nuttier things can get.

A cop sees the thief. Noticing the man is injured, the officer questions him. Of course, the nefarious one won't say, "I tried to rob someone but things went awry." Instead, having no compunction against lying and beginning to see a ray of sunshine, he claims your dog bit him without provocation, or that you unjustly set the animal on him. The cop senses deceit but feels bound to investigate.

The felon empties his pockets, showing he carries no weapons. That he could have tossed an arsenal into a dumpster before encountering the officer doesn't occur to anyone. His hefty criminal record seems irrelevant. The cop spots you and your dog. The nightmare begins.

You find yourself under investigation. The thief sues you, having engaged a lawyer more amoral than himself. Things go against you in court, as the carefully coached crook, camouflaged by a decent haircut and a new suit, appears the epitome of respectability. After weepy recountings of his terrible injuries, the court orders you to make a huge cash settlement and to foot the creep's medical and trauma-counseling bills.

Your insurance company refuses to support you. The court, in its infinite "wisdom," after a proceeding that seems little more than a forgone conclusion, directs that your "dangerous" pet be put down—killed. And a prosecutor with an eye toward furthering his or her career may see mileage in charging you with God knows what.

Think it can't happen? Don't bet against it. I could tell you horror stories. Review the newspapers and court records. Talk to lawyers, cops and K-9 handlers. It can happen.

Many insurance companies refuse to sell homeowner policies to guard dog owners. Others decline coverage to owners of certain canine types; and cities and counties have enacted ordinances prohibiting ownership of specific breeds or requiring that the animals be muzzled when in public. At least one state court has likened the protection dog to a deadly weapon.

Understand well a primary concept: A manstopper does not prance up and woof at or daintily nip a target. He overpowers. He becomes a *tsunami* with teeth. He overcomes force through greater force. Compassion does not cloud canine reckoning.

I repeat: Do you need a protection dog?

How to Lose Readers

Insult them. Or break a promise to them (which is a sideways insult). Either can cause a reader not just to set your book down but to pitch it across a room, perhaps out a door.

I don't wish to lose readers. Equally important, I have no desire to hurt anyone's feelings. So please understand I intend the following observations as cautionary, not derogatory.

This chapter has suggested you reexamine your need for a protection dog from a legal standpoint. Now consider another aspect: Are you up to it? I intend no slight by that question; rather, it's a concern for your welfare.

Manstopper ownership requires full-time attention and implies a team effort. The dog's part is obvious: He protects you. How you defend *him* may be less apparent. Sure, you provide room, board, and are his health-insurance agent, but you must also shield the animal from himself by always being aware of his potential. He can view innocent circumstances as threatening. Remember, "Mindful that Greta might misread the situation, Tim altered their route so as not to intersect Mr. Strangeways' route."

Know, too, that while uncertainty and lack of practice might cause an untrained dog to hesitate, thereby allowing an owner to settle the animal, a guard dog has forgotten what *hesitate* means. He moves at the crack of the bat.

Some people may have what it takes to own a guard dog but not train one, for two reasons. First, training can entail greater dangers than ownership, just like combining volatile chemicals can be riskier than handling the stabilized compound. Second, few folks have ever done it. They may have read how-to books and watched training videos, but the paradox is that until a person has had considerable practice, his knowledge of the art is dangerously shallow. As a trainer-friend remarked, "It's a Catch-22: Until you've done it a lot, you've got no business trying it. Otherwise, you don't know enough to know what you don't know. That can get someone hurt. Bad."

All this may raise the question, Why have you written this book? The basic information is already out there. It has been for a long time. *Manstopper's* For Further Reading list contains 22 titles, and there are many more I did not include. My contributions are a clear statement of training principles and mechanics, a writing style of show as well as tell, several training techniques I have not seen published and a shift in perspective—less machismo, more safety, a less-romanticized view of guard dogs and a dispelling of myths.

And warnings like this one, which I hope you don't find insulting.

Corollary

This one is as vital as it is brief: Don't acquire a dog you cannot control physically when he is full grown. Some are a powerhouse when the heat's on, and an overmatched owner can be at risk in high-stress situations.

And finally, as you know, governmental bodies in their benevolent omniscience incrementally try to save us from ourselves. With that comforting thought in mind, find out if local laws restrict training or ownership of a protection dog. Making inquiries now may save you—and your pet—much grief later.

Reflection

The nature of a security dog's training is a factor which imposes on its owner a degree of vigilance greater than that required over an ordinary house pet.

State of New York Court

PREFERENCES

The ideal protection breed is the _____ (insert your personal favorite). That is, the best guardian type is a matter of opinion and taste.

Breed

Of course, some breeds are unsuitable. Size matters. Many Pomeranians and Miniature Schnauzers have watchdog courage and intensity, but either breed could be punted by a fifth-grader (a watchdog is trained to bark at an outsider's approach but not trained to bite). In a force-against-force situation with a smaller dog, one well-placed blow by a human attacker would terminate the fight, possibly the dog.

Irish Wolfhounds are large enough, but manstopper work goes against the breed's temperate nature. I'm not saying one couldn't be guard trained, but that breed would not be my first choice. The role isn't right for many of these gentle giants, and training antithetical to canine nature can spawn disaster.

Rather than burn pages in rating every breed that could be guard trained, know that I prefer German Shepherds, Doberman Pinschers and Rottweilers, in no particular order. These breeds have proven themselves over a broad span of time and each has a high recognition factor: Most people can identify a Shepherd, Dobe or Rotty on sight and realize that these dogs seldom indulge human foolishness.

Ask owners of those breeds to categorize their pets as small, medium or large; many will choose large, but in truth, the animals are medium. *Large* applies to Saint Bernards and some Mastiffs, who outweigh Shepherds, Dobies and some Rotts by two to one. Owners who pick *large* subconsciously append their breed's reputation and visual impact.

My friend is a male Alaskan Malamute. Intelligence? Yes. Size? Obviously. Willingness? In spades. Guard-dog temperament? Not even close.

Q. These three are the only breeds you train?

A. Heavens, no. These are just the breeds I prefer, but I'm an equal-opportunity trainer. Owners have brought me 40-some breeds for protection training. If a dog has sound temperament, adequate size and can do the work, school is in session.

Q. Will I have to spend a fortune on a dog?

A. My current canine companion came from the pound.

A caveat: I would not own a blue-, fawn- or white-coated Doberman. Blues and fawns represent dilutions who tend toward severe coat problems as they age. Whites are mutants hustled by the make-a-buck crowd, and the temperaments of white Dobermans and white German Shepherds are often suspect at best.

Consider eye color, too. While not an absolute, light eyes in a breed that is normally dark-eyed suggest less than solid temperament.

Q. Must Doberman ears be cropped?

A. No. The breed's ears were originally snipped to little more than pin-points to prevent assailants from grabbing them. Present-day long crops negate this defense, so cropping is merely cosmetic and as such constitutes nothing more than mutilation—which is why so many countries have outlawed the practice.

A second caution: Many American breeders of German Shepherds, Dobes and Rotts have done a remarkable job of flushing the working structure, courage and toughness (and, in many cases, the brains) out of their lines.

Q. So not just any German Shepherd, Doberman Pinscher or Rottweiler is a good protection candidate?

A. Right. Fewer than 10 percent of American purebreds can handle the work. They lack the stability, courage, toughness, intelligence, trainability or physical soundness.

Q. What about acquiring an imported dog?

A. That may be a sound option. If you don't have a practiced eye or know a reliable importer, however, consider that some foreign breeders dump their inferior dogs in the States. If imports are new to you, know also that many cost big bucks and are unduly sharp—they ignite like flash paper.

What we're coming up to, of course, is the notion of the right dog, protection training's foundation. That creature already knows about being an effective guardian. She was born with the proper balance of instincts and drives.

Please, don't underestimate the urgency of the right-dog concept. A wrong dog not only presents numerous training problems, she's a disaster on hold. She either riles too easily or will back down when you need her the most.

Q. What characterizes the right dog?

A. A combination of size, a sound and willing dominant temperament, good health, emotional and physical toughness, friendliness and trainability. Greta had these attributes. So did Tank, a Rottweiler you'll meet in a later chapter. After reading about them and other dogs I'll introduce, you should have a pretty fair image of the right dog.

Purebred Versus Crossbred

One purebred edge is that bloodlines can be screened for undesirable traits. Another is the recognition factor, discussed earlier. I've seen some crossbreeds whose lineage was anybody's guess. These dogs were identifiable more by their behavioral tendencies than by any physical characteristics. Many could have been trained as suitable guardians, but their phenotypic genetics didn't provide them with the right look—they weren't believable in appearance, another right-dog quality.

But so long as a crossbreed has right-dog attributes, there should not be a problem in training her for protection. Still, that *should* word can be troublesome.

Suppose you train a Doberman Pinscher-German Shepherd crossbreed. She is a great companion and does admirable work. Now suppose circumstances necessitate she defend you, and a court proceeding ensues. The odds are the plaintiff's lawyer will whistle up some self-styled expert to assert that non-purebred dogs are improper as guardians. Opinions will be presented as facts, and commonplace will be statements like, "The genetic linkages between breed A and breed B often produce (whatever the lawyer wants the expert to say it produces)."

In defense of hybrids, however, consider that the dogs I've trained, together with those who have been through my obedience classes, number in the thousands. Of those, there has been about one guard-size crossbreed for every five German Shepherds, Dobes or Rotts. Fully a third of those mixed-breed dogs could have been trained as protectors. Compare that with, "Fewer than 10 percent of American purebreds can handle protection work."

Q. Why the disparity?

A. Chase-the-dollar backyard breeders, puppy mills and pet store avarice have drastically damaged popular breeds—pushing quantity over quality every time—as has the American Kennel Club's emphasis on conformation showing, where appearances are everything and breed-appropriate temperament receives lip service but little else. I've met Champion German Shepherds, Dobermans and Rottweilers with temperaments as fragile as a snowflake and others who were gasoline waiting for a spark.

I've also seen structure so extreme as to invite hosts of physical problems. I'm referring to Shepherds whose extreme toplines and angulation made them appear crippled, Dobermans with hind quarters so out of sync with their fronts that they appear to have been borrowed from another dog and oversize Rottys whose skeletons were never intended to carry such a load.

At the same time, if you're ever hauled into court over your dog's actions, the phrase "AKC-registered" may well have a positive influence on your defense. True, it's an immaterial consideration in terms of temperamental stability, but many judges and jury members, not being dog knowledgeable, may be swayed by such documentation.

Gender

Male or female? Or, in canine terminology, dog or bitch? Dogs of a given breed are usually larger and thus can appear more imposing. Bitches are often swifter, more agile and—though not a universal truth—quicker to fire. As a friend once put it, "You want to see instant ignition? Mess with a bitch with pups." Maternal and protective urges function in dams with young, yet both operate in many bitches before their first estrus.

Training Age

What's the best starting point for you? Puppy, or more mature dog? Do you have the time, patience and facilities to rear a pup, or would you rather take on an older animal, one who may harbor the effects of former human-canine relationships (or the lack thereof)?

Starting with a puppy enables quicker, deeper bonding. A pup can develop as a family member—an important consideration, especially if you have children or animals toward whom an older dog might be aggressive.

Of course, raising a puppy necessitates dealing with such joys as housebreaking, chewing and digging. Risks attendant to a less-developed immune system are higher, and the pup may not grow into a suitable protector. Often an older dog's temperament is easier to evaluate.

Q. Can a dog be too old for guard training?

A. Sure. An aged animal is not only too set in her ways to take on new attitudes, she doesn't have enough days left to justify the time, effort and costs of training. Besides, it's inconsiderate to throw a radically new mindset at a dog who has already come to grips with life and living.

Q. How old is too old?

A. As a general rule, I won't start a dog beyond life's midpoint, which often depends on the breed—the larger the dog, the briefer the life span. If you are unsure about the statistical longevity of your dog, consult a veterinarian, breeder or breed book.

Another consideration relative to training older dogs is that some dogs, especially those that have lived in kennels most of their lives, have never been properly socialized to humans. Such dogs may be aloof, fearful, nervous, aggressive or all of these things. They are seldom sound candidates for protection work.

Q. But would not such a dog respond well to TLC, having been starved for it?

A. The sad truth is that the creature may not know how to handle it. It's too foreign and comes too late. While there are always exceptions, consider that if a breeder has a single dog left unsold from a litter, it's not likely that she's still around because she is an all-star.

Temperament

Regardless of your preferences for breed, gender or age, a primary guard dog attribute is stable temperament. A steady canine reacts normally to the environment. That's another way of saying she does not over- or underreact. A protection candidate is inherently tough, yes, but she doesn't live to instigate (or avoid) fights, and would rather be petted than bite someone.

Now, don't misunderstand: I'm not saying a canine who lacks guard dog temperament has bad character. Not at all. The animal just has the wrong psychological makeup for the work at hand.

Most dogs' temperaments are a mixture of dominant, submissive and independent tendencies, but some lean toward extremes. A submissive animal is not a sound prospect. A guardian should be a study in dominance, but not so much that she is aggressive toward humans in general and you specifically. At least, not more than once. If your pet fires toward you, perhaps she is just trying to determine pack status and limits. Once you've clarified these points, that should end the matter. A stable dog doesn't need constant reminders not to chomp the hand that feeds and pets.

An independent dog, one who clearly can take or leave human companionship, though she may make a good sentinel (a dog who guards an area and works without a handler), is not personal protection material. Recall from the Preface that a manstopper is "a genuine member of the family." Independent dogs could care less.

Two psychological quirks to watch for are *species aggressive* canines and those who exhibit a pronounced *gender conflict*. Species aggressive refers to dogs who live to fight others of their kind. More common in males, I've seen dogs with this trait who would break off from dealing with a human aggressor to challenge a nearby dog. By gender conflict, I refer to a dog who prefers the company of a man over a woman, or vice versa, sometimes to the extent of hostility toward the other. Neither condition is acceptable in a guardian.

Personality

Some trainers view temperament and personality as inseparable. Others see them as night and day. For me, the concepts are candle and flame, dependent yet distinct. A dog is born with temperament, but personality accrues from environmental effects on her temperament.

A key to developing a sound personality is socialization, which must occur during puppyhood. In general, this means taking your pet with you whenever and wherever circumstances permit. Let her meet only amicable people and encourage them to pet her. These are essential "training techniques" for raising a confident, friendly dog. Moreover, don't guard train a dog who shows effects of improper human socialization.

Q. What do you mean by "effects?"

A. I'm referring to a dog who is improperly aggressive, withdrawn, skittish or downright fearful. My overall word is *spooky*. The animal might have been the right puppy, but was prevented from developing into the right dog.

Professional Trainers

Should you do the training or hire a professional? A pro won't make any mistakes (at least that's the theory), and although professional services can shrivel the pocketbook, doing the work yourself may require considerable sums for equipment and helpers.

Also, regarding the question of who should do the training, reread the warning in the front of this book. Then consider that while *Manstopper* can take you through the steps of protection training, this book (or any of the genre) cannot infuse a novice with reflexive knowledge of the jillion and one things that can go wrong with blinding swiftness during and after such training. Only experience can spawn that depth of awareness.

You must be able to read your pet, to know at a glance what she is thinking, feeling and likely to do. Many people can intuit what is happening in a dog's head and heart and can perceive trouble before it starts. Others could no more interpret canine intent than they could decipher hieroglyphics. I imply no denigration of folks in the latter group; they just have no business training (or owning) a guard dog.

Buying a Trained Dog

An offshoot of "Who should train my dog?" is "What about acquiring one already trained?" Pluses: You start with a finished product, the dog's training is complete, her health is ascertainable.

Downside: Although many trainers are as honest as God, some are as crooked as a pig's tail. Their forte is selling, and I've met some who could peddle additional jail time to a convict. These charlatans content themselves with passing along marginally trained, genetically flawed misfits, often at whimsical prices.

Before buying a trained animal, request names of several people to whom the trainer has sold dogs. If the trainer balks, verify you still have your cash and get gone. Presuming your request is encouraged, contact owners and request their evaluations. Ask, "Would you buy another trained dog from this person?" Also, contact veterinarians and seek their impressions of the trainer's work. Listen for what the owners and vets do *not* say—that can be a statement in itself—and beware when issues are sidestepped. If you often hear variations on, "Oh, he's okay, I guess," keep looking.

Get it in writing. Handshake contracts are all very well, but protect yourself by obtaining written guarantees as to the dog's health, training, total costs to you and so on.

Reflection

I have a dog of Blenheim birth,
With fine long ears and full of mirth;
And sometimes, running o'er the plain,
He tumbles on his nose:
But quickly jumping up again,
Like lightening on he goes!

John Ruskin

CHAPTER 4

GROUNDWORK

Before initiating protection training, your dog must reliably follow obedience commands to heel (walk next to you on a loose leash), sit, lie down, stay (don't move) and come when called, all amid real-world distractions.

Q. What does "reliably" mean?

A. A command given just once elicits the correct response. Every time. Commands don't have to be repeated.

Since *Manstopper* is not an obedience text, I refer you to my book *Dog Logic—Companion Obedience* (Howell Book House).

Obedience Versus the Edge

A popular trainer once cautioned, "Doing obedience before protection lowers the dog's advantage in bitework." The reasoning goes that because obedience training teaches the dog that a human (the trainer) can dominate him, the animal may doubt his ability to fight a person, and thus may be a less effective guardian if obedience training comes before protection training rather than after it.

The doctrine has its share of adherents, and while the theory may seem reasonable, it's only part of the truth. The rest of the story is that if the dog has sound temperament and if his obedience training is conducted properly, any loss of canine fire is negligible—the decrease being comparable to a dog having a 20-foot run at a bad guy versus the same animal's striking power when charging from 19 feet. Besides, your pet learns the person who can dominate him is you, not all of humanity.

Fact: Obedience restricts. It controls and directs another being's behaviors. Further, obedience is only semi-compatible with canine nature. Precision heeling is no more native to a dog than is the conventional automatic sit (whenever the handler stops walking). Observe dogs during the first moments of a first-week obedience class and you will see they forge ahead by nature and that when they halt, they tend to stand, not sit. It is for our convenience that we teach dogs lessons like the automatic sit. That the animals learn such lessons—that they put up with them—attests once more to the concept "Man's best friend."

Protection training allows *Canis familiaris* to be who he is, to slip back into the caves, to heed ancestral urges when challenged. Guard dog work unleashes the animal within.

When obedience deflates attitude, it denotes faulty training methods, spooky temperament, an unhealthy human-canine relationship or all of the above. Consider each impediment.

First, draconian training methods are all too common. More about this in a moment.

Second, off-center temperament disqualifies a dog for protection work. Just as training can't cause a dog born with three legs to grow a fourth, it cannot salvage defective genes that regulate temperament. All training can do in that case is create illusions that vanish when confronted by reality.

Third, under the heading of a defective relationship between owner and dog, no good can come of that. Ever.

As a corollary to number three, there is another reason to teach obedience first. A dog can become disoriented during protection training, and I don't ever want one I'm training to spin around on me. True, it's a remote possibility—I've never experienced it—but I know it could happen. A trainer can misread the dog or the moment, and the animal could slip into a momentary frenzy wherein the handler might seem an opportune target. When obedience training precedes protection, a side effect of the trainer defining human-canine boundaries is that the dog internalizes an absolute: Teeth on the owner is never an option.

Through proper obedience, you establish communication—rapport—with your pet. He learns you have things to show him, tasks to share with him. Initiating formal training through obedience also provides a framework on which to hang new commands, especially protection cues that cannot be fortified via force. The training process becomes a circle: The dog learns from obedience a mindset of "I must," and this transfers to guardian work and heightens the animal's drive to succeed; manstopper training, which is more fun for the dog than "Lie down," has a splash-back effect that increases the animal's enjoyment of obedience specifically and working generally.

Look at it this way: How would you like to have tried to pull Greta off the bad guy in Chapter 1, had she not first learned via obedience to respect your authority?

History Lesson

Let's return to the topic of draconian training methods. Indulge me a brief digression and we'll do a bit of debunking, and perhaps pop the tops off a few of cans of worms while we're at it.

Common sense took a major hit in the 1960s as dog training techniques that would gag the Marquis de Sade were heralded as the Revealed Word. There was a great bowing to self-absorbed preachers of fear-based training systems. For these people the dog was little more than a thing to be controlled.

The pendulum tried to swing back in the late 1970s when Little, Brown published *How To Be Your Dog's Best Friend*, by The Monks of New Skete. This heartening trend was furthered a few years later when Howell Book House released *Mother Knows Best*, by Carol Lea Benjamin. Both works proposed a return to sanity and, not incidentally, offered far more effective training approaches.

Still, much damage had occurred. Many trainers cut their teeth on philosophies born in the 1960s that rationalize training methods as brutal as they are unwarranted. Why have I told you these things? Read on.

Obedience Classes

You say you plan to enroll in an obedience class? Good for you! That's a good idea. *As long as you're careful.*

Careful because not all obedience class instructors are knowledgeable, caring folks who like and understand dogs and do not tolerate abusive or ineffective methods. It's those "instructors," the ones with that '60s twitch, that you have to watch for. The kindest word I can find for them is *inept*, and they have no business being around dogs.

A key to spotting such people is their extremism, which in any form is harmful to you and your dog. In one camp lurk the power trippers. Intimidating to dogs and owners alike, these righteous yo-yos are drunk with their own imagined power and can scar a canine psyche for life. They instruct for one reason: It makes them feel like they are *somebody*. They may have read a train-ing book or two and attended seminars conducted by and for the like-minded, but they see what they want to see and hear what they expect to hear. As you might expect, they view their own pronouncements as Holy Writ. The results are self-sustaining ignorance and canine abuse.

In *How to Be Your Dog's Best Friend*, The Monks of New Skete write, "There are some instances when you should simply quit class and walk out. If an instructor 'hangs' a dog, swirls a dog around on the end of a leash, kicks a dog (except to stop a real dog fight), insults a handler, consistently refuses to answer questions, or derides the dogs, quit."

At the continuum's other end are the food treaters. For them, the notion that obedience means "Dog, thou must!" is anathema rather than axiomatic. Sure, food has a place in training, but not as a focal point. Then it's no better than fear training, as it links compliance with the stuff of survival. Food, which should serve neither as bribe nor paycheck, becomes both. And a barrier as well.

Unlike a veterinarian, obedience trainers and instructors are seldom re-quired to be licensed or certified. (Even when they are, things can go horribly wrong.) Yet, like a vet, an incompetent trainer can mark a dog with long-lasting, deleterious effects.

AKC Groups

Obedience classes offered by dog clubs that are affiliated with the American Kennel Club may be just what you're looking for. Be aware, though, that the AKC does not teach, test, endorse or certify trainers or instructors. That means the teacher may or may not possess great knowledge and wisdom about dogs. Sometimes the teacher is merely the group's dominant personality.

No, I am not knocking classes or instructors from AKC-affiliated groups, per se. Many are top-flight and their concerns center around valid education. Some spend too much time on a limited slate of material and focus too in-tently on the comparatively simple obedience routine required to earn the Companion Dog (CD) title, but these are minor objections. Just realize that "AKC-affiliated" does not guarantee that the group knows any more about *Canis familiaris* than you do.

Before enrolling, ask to observe a training session. Your request should be encouraged, but if the sponsors don't seem ready to comply, go elsewhere. Moreover, if the trainer's philosophy is "My way is the only way!" grab your dog and get gone. Fast.

Regardless of whose class you attend, be very, very selective before handing your leash to anyone. You are *never*—repeat: *never*—obligated to do so, regardless of the setting or the "rules." If in doubt, don't. Follow your own rules. Listen to your inner voice. Respect it. Your dog does, and he's counting on you.

How Young?

A dog should be 10 to 12 months old before beginning formal protection training. Lest that alarm knowledgeable trainers, note the modifier "formal." Evaluation and drive stimulation of puppies can be started as soon as the little ones can puppy-run and show interest in bump-crash play with one another.

Since the minimum age for *Dog Logic's* five-week obedience program is six months, a dog may be just over seven months young at graduation. While he then knows a good deal of obedience, he is yet unpolished because he's still equal amounts puppy and dog. Much proofing lies ahead before the animal will be reliable and mature enough to begin structured guard dog training. Some obedience reinforcement lessons, in fact, occur during protection work, as you'll see.

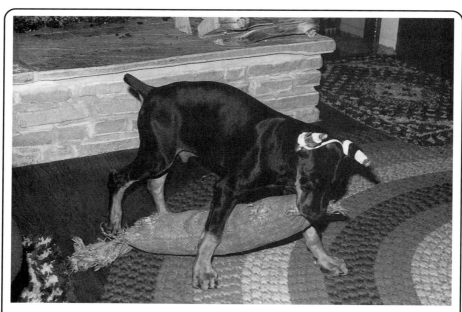

This Doberman is learning at a young age that it's fun to bite burlap shaped like an arm.

Another consideration relates to the nature of guard dog training. It makes great demands of both body and mind. I want the dog to be past his puppy emotions, his skeleton to be firm and his coordination closing in on that of an adult's.

Though it may seem odd, if obedience begins at a more mature age, say a year, often the dog's protection training can be run concurrent with obedience work. This presumes that the animal's obedience schooling is done privately, as it's too dangerous to let a dog undergoing guard training into an obedience class.

Q. Would you take a fully trained protection dog to an obedience class for brush-up obedience work?

A. With the instructor's approval, of course. My protectors often participate in my obedience classes.

Health Considerations

Is your dog in good physical shape? Does he get sufficient exercise? Is he overweight? How is his muscle tone, his wind, his stamina?

Has he had a recent veterinary exam? Did it include a heart evaluation and checking his joints? Is he free of hip dysplasia?

Is he current on all shots, especially rabies?

Before subjecting your best friend to the rigors of guard training, make sure your answers are yes, yes, no, good and yes to the rest. Bring an out-of-condition dog to an ethical trainer and you'll be told to return when the animal is in acceptable shape. At my kennels I won't touch a dog not in top form, or who has not passed a recent vet exam or is not vaccinated against common canine diseases.

A guardian not in peak shape is incapable of peak performance. He's at risk, physically and emotionally. If your pet needs firming up, don't institute a crash program; build steadily and with consistency, not in haste or erratically. Not only will this produce more enduring results, your dog will live longer and happier.

Reflection

She had no particular breed in mind, no unusual requirements.
Except the special sense of mutual recognition that tells dog
and human that they have both come to the right place.

Lloyd Alexander

CHAPTER 5

SLIGHT SHIFTS IN PERCEPTION

Many readers of *Manstopper* are familiar with obedience training. For a budding protection trainer, an obedience background can be a leg up or a liability. The determinant is trainer perspective, a recurring theme in my books.

Understand, protection work is at once a subset of obedience and a realm apart. When a dog sits on cue, obedience occurs. Defending on command is likewise an obedient response. In both instances a dog does as ordered.

But there the similarity ends. A correct response to "Sit" is light-years from fighting a human. One act is calm, the other a raging storm; one command restricts, the other frees.

Ponderables

Two less apparent differences involve attitude and approach. Consider attitude first. President Jimmy Carter, in his inaugural address, said he expected to make some mistakes, being new to the job and all. History has proved him correct, as his hugely successful second term attested. Moral: Expect things to go wrong and they will. A trainer's attitude should be, "I can forgive myself honest errors, but I'll try to avoid them anyway." True, no one bats a thousand in any endeavor, but in guard dog training, you want to get it right the first time and every time. It's sort of like the porcupine approach to love making: You can't afford mistakes. If a trainer goofs when teaching "Sit," life goes on. But a miscue during protection work can necessitate a 911 call, a fast trip to an emergency room, even hospitalization. And your health insurance company may decide that such dangerous endeavors as guard dog training exceed your policy's coverage.

Now look at approach: Unlike obedience methodology, force is not an option. You can make a dog sit. But should a dog not defend on cue, prying the animal's jaws open and hurling her at whomever is not acceptable technique. An obedience cornerstone is domination, gentle to firm, depending upon the dog's nature. In guardian training a key is license, balanced with unwavering control.

Protection training's no-force aspect can cause aspirants grounded in obedience to smack into the legendary brick wall. The problem evolves from what I call the *forced reliability illusion*, the fallacious notion that training not based in compulsion cannot produce reliability, that a dog not force trained will never be dependable. That fuzzy reasoning can blind trainers to the light of common sense.

Canine intelligence, willingness and endurance being what they are, a person can train passable obedience—heel, sit, lie down, stay and come—without having a profound understanding of dogs or training. But while appropriate pressure can play a role in obedience training, force alone has yet to produce reliability. That statement may cause squawks of "Heresy!" in some obedience camps, but the notion that no force equals no reliability is notable only in the number of dogs' spirits it has broken. Like many rules, it's a generality that propagates more trouble than it suppresses. Force philosophies ignore the veracity of insights like "man's (or woman's) best friend." Not merely inhumane in concept, insisting upon force in training says more about some trainers' frail confidence than about their supposed wisdom in the ways of *Canis familiaris*. Dogs trained under such attitudes learn to fear their own fear, and to avoid the feeling by compliance. They are reliable until they encounter something scarier than the trainer.

The better rule for guard dog trainers is—as a friend once put it—"If you don't understand rapport obedience, you've got no business fooling with protection work." Her point was that someone who has ascended no further than force-only concepts of obedience cannot grasp how beyond-force training speaks to a dog. Therein lurks the ultimate danger, because comprehensive understanding of canines and training is crucial in protection work. Otherwise, trainers don't understand what is happening right in front of their noses. They can't see trouble coming until it's too late. Way too late.

Trainers and agitators read the dog and react from second to second, to preserve their well-being and to train the animal. Things happen very fast in this line of work, and a flawed understanding of dogs or training principles could result in not just teaching a faulty lesson but in not even knowing it had been taught. In this pursuit, that can be catastrophic.

Aggression? Or playfulness? I have the time it takes this Doberman to explode toward me from a sitting position to decide.

Domination Meets Trust

The need for unwavering control in protection work should be obvious from Greta's Chapter 1 performance. Equally evident is the notion that you don't want to have to argue the point when commanding "Stay" during a boiling situation. This is where the stand-stay's relationship to guard dog training comes in.

Recall that in Chapter 1, after the panhandler returned Tim "commanded, 'Stand, stay,' and allowed the stranger to pet Greta." Use the stand position when an outsider will touch your pet during a stressful situation. (Exception: A veterinary procedure. No dog should be commanded during medical treatments. Trust in you should be the settling influence.)

Q. Why not use "Sit" or "Lie down" to facilitate a stranger's touch during a questionable moment?

A. Safety. Of the three positions, sitting is the most dangerous in terms of a dog's edge in potential speed and power. The stance not only aims her upward, she already has her standing balance and her rear legs are coiled springs.

The stand-stay.

Lying down is the most submissive posture, and I don't want my pet to associate contact by strangers with submission.

To break a stand-stay the dog need only move a paw, while to violate the sit- or down-stay the animal must effect significant movement. Thus, the stand-stay confers more handler control, as to sustain it requires more canine concentration. The stand-stay preoccupies the dog's thoughts at a moment when I don't want her considering external factors.

In teaching a manstopper the stand-stay, never trigger your dog in practice right after, "Stand, stay." True, during training the dog may be standing just before "Action!" or "Watchim!", but she will be in that position by her choice, not your command. You don't want short-fuse readiness during the stand-stay, and one way to communicate that message is by never linking the stand-stay command with "Action!" or "Watchim!"

A key here is your pet's trust in you. Over time she learns that you will never put her in a predicament she can't handle. This is another reason for never using the stand-stay during potentially explosive situations.

Puppy Conditioning

Teach the stand-stay during puppyhood by using treats.

Q. You teach a manstopper to bait?

A. A manstopper, no. A puppy, yes. Baiting is a breed ring technique for capturing and holding a dog's best attention. The stand-stay places the animal in something of a show stance, comfortably balanced with her feet placed squarely (except for German Shepherds, who position a rear foot under the midsection).

Never use force to teach a puppy. Use pleasant repetition and smooth-variety peanut butter. When a pup blows the stand-stay, just reposition her and go again. Puppies take time. That's just a given.

Ease one hand under the pup's chest, the other under the gut. Lift the puppy a few inches for a two-count, then set her down in one smooth move (lowering her very slowly can cause anxiety). Owing to canine structure, most pups will reflexively place their feet correctly. Immediately touch a peanut-butter coated fingertip to the young one's lips while using your other hand to make minute adjustments in her foot placements, starting with the front paws. Don't grasp legs suddenly or tightly, but smoothly and gently.

Always work from the pup's right, to put you at the heel side and establish the command position at a young age.

Gently stroke the pupper's back and softly repeat, "Good stay," as she maintains position.

Q. Shouldn't I command, "Stand, stay?"

A. Don't command pups; praise them. We seek to condition, not train. Puppies don't have the attention span for formal training.

When the pup moves, as she will at first, flick your peanut-buttered finger upward and out of range (not level and away, as that would induce forward movement). Then lift the puppy and place her again. Remember, pleasant repetition is a key, as are patience and never allowing the little one to win treats when she's moving. She may lick the peanut butter from your fingers only when she is stationary.

Mature Dogs

Food rewards are okay when teaching an older dog, but as inducement, not reinforcement. Extend stand-stay obedience by positioning each foot as needed, starting with the front legs. Once you've set the dog, command "Stay," but

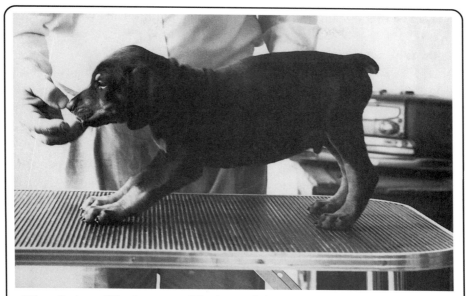

When first conditioning a pup, if he is not sitting or lying down consider him to be standing and tell him how well he's doing. Before-the-fact praise leads to success.

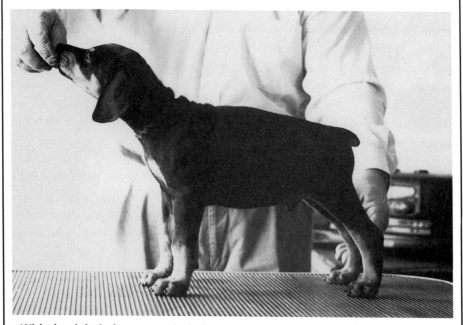

With the right inducements, including your encouragement and approval, very soon the pup begins to gain confidence and stand more properly.

don't leave the animal. Remain with her, stroking her back while repeating "Good stay."

Q. Why say "Stay" if I'm not going to depart?

A. "Stay" means *don't move*. It has nothing to do with whatever you do next. Again, the stand-stay's purpose is control during the approach of an individual who seems iffy to the dog.

Biggie: Never—*never!*—leave a guard dog at such a moment! That can get someone hurt.

During training, block any initial movement by walking your pet a step or two into the stand-stay position, then placing her legs as needed. Once the dog gets the idea (and not before), should she move appreciably, say "No" and firmly reset her.

Q. "Move appreciably" meaning . . . ?

A. Stepping forward, sitting, or lying down.

Q. And "firmly reset" means . . . ?

A. The initial correction is to finger-tap, not hit, the chest. If the dog needs a second correction, tap harder. Should she continue moving, comment "I said 'Stay,'" and flick—don't yank—the pinch collar sideways and toward yourself (not upward or forward, as that angle would make the dog sit). If further correction is needed, the dog is either showing defiance or is playing with your head. In either case, turn toward the animal's posterior and encircle her neck with one arm as you put the other under her gut. Lift her off her feet, hoisting her butt a tad higher than her head, and set her down firmly. Don't grab the dog's fur or skin; use your arms to hold her body and accomplish the lift with your legs. Accompany any correction with "No—stay!", then reset paw placements as needed.

Q. Isn't that rough treatment?

A. No. I didn't say to slam the creature about. This is a quick lift-and-set move, effective in its suddenness and the fact that the dog is being carried backward. Canines, like felines, abhor being off-balance. A dog dislikes being carried in such a way that she can't see where she's going. Also, consider that an animal who wilts under such pressure is not manstopper material.

Q. What if the dog tries to bite during the correction?

A. Not many will make the attempt if preceding obedience lessons have laid a solid foundation. Should hostilities ensue, take the dog to the mat, so to speak, using the aggression-thwarting methods you prefer. Belligerence toward the owner is never acceptable. As a friend remarked, "That's when the dog and I have a come-to-Jesus meeting."

| Step one: Turn toward the dog's posterior and encircle her neck with one arm. . . | Step two: . . . as you put the other under her gut. | Step three: Lift her off her feet, hoisting her butt a tad higher than her head. |

Gradually build to 15 seconds the time your pet will maintain a stand-stay. You should never need more. Then add people your dog knows. Have them pet the animal while she remains motionless. A few days later, add friendly strangers. Keep the training at that level until progressing to the phase outlined in Chapter 14, "Back!", when we will use the stand-stay with strange strangers.

Q. Did Tim use the stand-stay when meeting the children?

A. No. There was no need, as they projected no stress.

Reflection

The dog has seldom been successful in pulling man up to its level of sagacity, but man has frequently dragged the dog down to his.

James Thurber

CHAPTER 6

INSTINCTS AND DRIVES

One way of understanding dogs vis-à-vis training is through a working awareness of instincts and drives—genetic instructions from canine forebears. Books on the subject abound, but we'll touch on just the high points, the essentials of instinct and drive behavior.

Instincts and drives are related yet separate innate motivating forces. Differentiating between them can kindle heated debate among animal trainers. For our purposes, drives trigger behaviors that satisfy instinctual demands.

Regarding cause and effect, instincts are general inborn urges to satisfy basic needs (food, shelter, procreation, and so on). Drives are specific behaviors effectuated to sate such urges (tracking and mating, for instance). Dogs don't think about their responses; they just do them. As a friend once generalized, "Drive is what makes the dog chase the rabbit."

For example, animals have a survival instinct. Dogs attempt to satisfy this instinct through drives to track, hunt, subdue prey, retrieve, defend themselves, flee, fight, cooperate with pack members and return home.

While it's hardly my purpose to reduce the essence of *Canis familiaris* to a tidy array of physiological and psychological nuts and bolts, dogs are born with instincts and drives to varying degrees, and canine actions undeniably derive from inborn behaviors modified by learning. Learned behavior results from experience gained during expressions of these genetically programmed actions or while expressing other learned behaviors.

A Behavior by Any Other Name . . .

No matter what you call a genetic behavior motivator—instinct, drive, need, internal stimulus or some other term—the resulting behavior is the same. For instance, I label canine knowledge about tracking (following a scent trail) a drive. Others say it is an instinct. Whether it is an instinct or a drive can be argued until the cows come home. The salient point is that dogs are born with tracking capability; it is not a learned behavior. When someone teaches a canine to track, in truth the animal is learning to perform on cue. Effective practice improves proficiency, yes, but the dog is born knowing how to track.

Real World

To understand the interaction between instincts, drives and learned behaviors, consider how a young, inexperienced country dog might deal with hunger. After the body communicates to the brain through biochemical signals the need for energy, the brain interprets these signals and causes the dog to feel the discomfort of hunger. This sensation is a biological response that triggers another sequence of physiological and psychological events that lead the animal to resolve the unpleasant feeling through drive behavior.

The dog begins to *hunt* (a drive) and is soon *tracking* (a drive) a scent trail he has discovered. But the critter being tracked in our scenario is a porcupine. Assuming the dog finds and tries to overcome the beast, he learns that this type of creature is more than he can handle. The dog's *fight drive* may flare, but soon his *self-defense drive* kicks in. Then his *drive to flee* erupts as the need to satisfy hunger, a transient condition, is overridden by the longer-term *survival instinct*.

The pup doesn't quit trying to satisfy his hunger, however. He cannot. His survival instinct is too pervasive for that. Moments ago it triggered his *flight drive* and now it reactivates his *hunt* and *prey* drives.

Soon he encounters a small fowl or rodent and transforms the critter into a canine repast *du jour*. He learns from these experiences that, while four-footed pincushions are best avoided, small feathered or furry creatures safely satiate hunger.

All this constitutes instinctual demands being satisfied by drive behaviors modified by learning. In a nutshell, that's the basis of canine motivation. For us, it's a pathway toward comprehension and appreciation of various training approaches.

The syllogism—all drives are inborn; drives guide canine behavior—also suggests an answer to a question often asked of trainers: Do dogs think? Indeed, but mostly they feel. Like drives, emotions guide canine behaviors. Unlike humans, though, dogs don't think about thinking or feeling. No one could accuse them of analysis paralysis. Dogs accept, then react. "The dog's intellect differs from man's because the dog cannot accomplish the following: Plan for the present and future, tell right from wrong, logically follow cause and effect through several stages of development."[1] The dog can, however, distinguish good from evil.

Instincts

Trainers need to understand the survival instinct, which is the primary force underlying all others, and the pack and freedom instincts. Studying other inherited canine tendencies, such as circling in place before lying down (to nest, flatten snow or grass, to look for snakes and establish territory) is interesting, but does not provide crucial information.

Survival

The primary message of this self-evident genetic knowledge is "I must endure!" It is why an injured dog, such as one hit by a car, may blindly strike at the hand of his owner who is just trying to help. Tied to the canine sense of territory, the survival instinct's power can motivate a dog to accept abuse as a condition of survival (see *Learned-helplessness syndrome* in the Glossary). Many training programs, obedience as well as protection, wrongly—inhumanely—key on continual stimulation of this instinct.

Pack

This inner force leads dogs toward a family-like lifestyle, as compared to a hermit-like existence. Appealing to the pack instinct provides a reasonable, effective basis for training. Dogs having low levels of this instinct are called *independent*.

Freedom

While dogs are social animals who prefer companionship over solitude, by nature they are neither clingers nor slaves. Each is his own animal. People unaware or unappreciative of this instinct confuse its behavioral manifestations with rebellion. Understanding the freedom instinct's influence and behavioral effects is essential for shaping the dog's attitude toward training. Rather than

[1]*Deutsche Schutzhundschule—Schutzhund Training The German Way*, Johannes Grewe, page 29.

thwarting this instinct, thereby knocking down spirit, appeal to the pack instinct. Show your pet that submission to human leadership derives from the human's desire for pack contact; that it represents human attraction to the animal's essence, not a diminution of the dog's self.

Drives

Most dog trainers agree that drives can be grouped under three headings—self-preservation, species preservation, and self-preservation and species preservation—although some might argue that a given drive belongs in column B instead of column C.

Self-Preservation

Hunting drive motivates dogs to search. *Air scenting* encourages discernment of airborne scents. *Tracking* is similar to *air scenting* drive, and leads dogs to follow ground scent disturbances.

Prey drive underlies the motivation to attack and kill prey. Like hunting drive, prey drive is rooted in the need to satisfy hunger. A dog with a low prey drive is not a manstopper prospect.

Interrelated with hunting and prey drives is *retrieve*. This motivator leads dogs to move conquered prey. The growth-oriented *play* drive motivates dogs to explore and test their abilities to contend with others.

Self-defense is the willingness to fight in one's own defense. When taken to extremes, self-defense against imagined threats motivates fear biters—dogs who reach fight-or-flight state in normal contact situations.

The drive to *flee* leads dogs to depart from overpowering threats, real or imagined. Like the self-defense drive, it is rooted in fear. Knowledgeable guard dog trainers avoid animals having high levels of flee drive.

Species Preservation

Dominance provides motivation to lead the pack. When present to extremes, this drive places the bold, strong-willed and often hard-to-train dog at one end of the continuum and the super-submissive, impossible-to-train animal at the other. The former resists attempts at control while the latter displays inordinate flat-on-his-back submissive posturing. Some trainers believe there is such a thing as a *submission* drive, but I see that as a lack of dominance drive.

Guard provides the motivation to inform the pack that intruders are violating the territory. *Protection*, which is linked to the drive to guard (some trainers say they are the same thing), motivates dogs to protect pack members. Dogs lacking dominance, guard and protection drives are not sound manstopper candidates.

Sex drive forms the basis for canine mating activities. *Maternal* drive leads dams to support their pups through nursing, cleaning, teaching and general care.

Self-Preservation and Species Preservation

Cooperation motivates dogs to get along with pack members generally and the pack leader specifically. Like cooperation, *fighting* is an essential trait for a protector, as dogs with high fight levels often enjoy a good scrap. Both drives are necessary in a guardian.

Homing drive leads dogs to return to the den. Much of the basis for teaching dogs to come when called lies in this drive.

Trainers tap many drives to build teaching and reinforcement foundations. Rather than correlate every lesson with this or that instinct or drive, which would make this chapter among the book's longer ones, consider this: If canines lacked drives for prey, play, self-defense, dominance, guard, protection, cooperation, fighting and homing, guard training would be impossible.

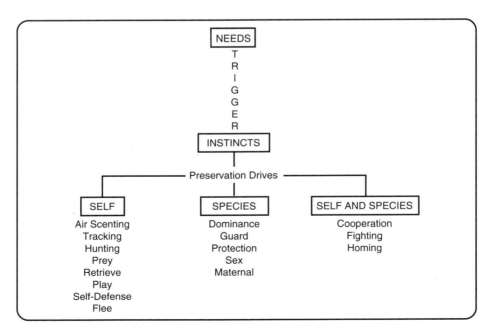

One Other Factor

Although *Manstopper* is not an obedience text, one obedience principle needs mention, as violations of it can stunt a guard dog candidate's drives.

A female wolf left her pups alone in a rendezvous area in the Brooks Range one morning and set off down a trail away from them. When she was well out of sight, she turned around and lay flat in the path, watching her back trail. After a few moments, a pup who had left the rendezvous area trotted briskly over a rise in the trail and came face to face with her. She gave a low bark. He stopped short, looked about as though preoccupied with something else, then, with a dissembling air, began to edge back the way he had come. His mother escorted him to the rendezvous site and departed again. This time she didn't bother watching her back trail. Apparently the lesson had taken, for all the pups stayed put until she returned that evening.[2]

Message: Don't bore and insult your dog by repetitive teaching and practice. That can dull a swift learner. It can also place a barrier between you and your pet, because it says to him that you don't see him for who he is. He might even conclude that you aren't too bright. When your partner gets it right, move on. Many dogs are first-time learners. The notion that lessons must be presented umpteen times is projection: It's often true of humans, but not of dogs. A common approach, it links boredom with training and working.

In the wild, the dog's natural setting, an animal might have but one chance to learn any given lesson. If he fails to get the point, he may lose food, offspring, parts of himself or may become another animal's dinner. As part of the survival instinct, Nature programs dogs to learn quickly and reliably. Hence, learning is difficult if not impossible to eradicate. What the dog learns, he learns for life.

Reflection

With eye upraised his master's look to scan,
The joy, the solace, and the aid of man:
The rich man's guardian and the poor man's friend,
The only creature faithful to the end.

George Crabbe

[2]*Of Wolves and Men*, Barry Holstun Lopez, page 33.

PART II

TRAINING

CHAPTER 7

AGITATORS AND AGITATION

Some statements, at first blush, can boggle the mind. Consider: In a very real sense, no one has ever protection trained any dog.

Q. Say what?

A. Trainers just help the right animal get better at what she already knows.

Only the right dogs should be trained for protection. Those not right for the work won't be dependable. They'll fold, or ignite at the wrong time. Neither course will be taken consciously, but will simply be an expression of the dog's self. Since the right dog is an inherent protector, the phrase *protection training* is something of a misnomer.

Q. So why teach a dog what she already knows?

A. To harness and direct inborn knowledge, to refine the dog's proficiency, and to teach the animal about humans.

What the right dog knows is the appropriateness of combat and when an inferno is needed to halt a blaze. What the animal may not know about is us. What are *Homo sapiens'* offensive and defensive capabilities? How are humans vulnerable to a dog's fighting attributes? Where is the dog's advantage? A skilled agitator can both raise and answer those and similar questions for a canine guardian, and can help her become an accomplished manstopper.

Team Concept

Just as you and your canine protector are a team, you and your agitators must function as a unit. That premise comprises much of this chapter's focus.

You were introduced to the agitator concept in Chapter 1 via the "well-tailored gentleman" who co-starred in the Tim-and-Greta show. While the scene suggested certain realities about agitators and the work they do, we need to expand your understanding of these bad guys, also known as helpers, and the integral parts they play in manstopper training.

Agitators are dog-knowledgeable good guys playing the role of dog-ignorant bad guys. They allow dogs to bite them in order to further the animals' training. Of course, the dogs do not pierce flesh, except by accident; they nail protective sleeves the agitators wear.

To agitate is to tease and excite a dog within her psychological limits. By insulting her pride, agitation entices her to manifest aggression. When I say "within her psychological limits," that means the trainer and agitator must be able to read, without conscious thought, an animal's mental and emotional states to intuit the precise moment when a bite, which is the dog's reward, must be allowed and when it must be offered but denied to maximize the lesson at hand.

In agitation there is one unchanging principle: The dog always wins (that is, the bad guy always loses). Someday your pet may fail in the real world, but to allow that to happen during training can teach hesitancy and doubt, and that could lead to a dog's undoing in a fight she might have won.

Q. But you say we're training for real events. Isn't losing a real event?

A. Look at it this way: Do you remember how the dog in the previous chapter confronted a porcupine and learned from one encounter to avoid them? Well, if a canine loses a battle to a human . . . .

Agitator Selection

In picking agitators (and you will need more than one), seek people who can read dogs, have good balance and coordination, are quick of foot, hand and mind and can withstand in body and spirit the rush of a large, ignited canine. Dog-illiterate folks or those who fear the species are not sound prospects. Neither are people whose personalities prohibit their playing subordinate roles to a canine, or people who are emotionally unstable or mentally unhinged.

Q. Wait a minute! Wouldn't a person have to be half-cracked in the first place to accept and even encourage dog bites?

A. I wish I had a dollar for every time someone has asked me that. The question often indicates anxiety (the asker sees himself in the agitator's role). But sometimes the question is valid, as it presupposes agitation to be dangerous to the agitator. And it is. Letting a large, powerful dog with biting on her mind rush at you is not what I would call a carefree pastime.

Every agitator should know this: You may be injured. Severely. That thought should always hover at the rim of consciousness, to keep you alert and focused. However, my agitation experience spans more than two decades and I have not been hurt. Knocked flat a few times, yes; compression bruises from too much ego and too light a sleeve, yes; scratched when I was too lazy to don protective apparel, yes; but injured, as in broken bones or bleeding like a sieve, no.

Know this, too: Anyone who agitates a dog only once will never be safe around that animal again. Dogs don't forget, and someone who has fired up your pet just a single time could wind up hospitalized from slapping your back in friendship.

Q. Dogs remember people that well?

A. Yes, though as much or more by scent than visually.

Q. Couldn't a dog react just as defensively to a similar action by a stranger?

A. Sure, but it's less likely to happen with a stranger than with a back-slapper who is a known bad guy.

Therefore, three groups from which *not* to select agitators are children, family members and close friends. Never. Ever.

Avoid using people undergoing emotional trauma—divorce or death of a loved one, for instance; they have chosen the wrong time to learn agitation. Anger, a natural byproduct, could flare and cause injury. Also, as obsession is a stepchild of addiction, danger and violence can be narcotics on which some people get hooked. Like all users they endlessly seek higher highs, and thus have no place in agitation.

An ideal pool of agitators includes men and women of various sizes, races and ages, excluding children, of course. People have different scents according to gender and race, and exhibit particular mannerisms as functions of size, age and sex. Thorough conditioning requires your guardian to discover these disparities during training, rather than in a real situation. Otherwise, your protector could hesitate at a moment when the clock is ticking.

Kinder verboten. Though mentioned earlier, this point needs to be hammered: Never use children as agitators! While not always true in the real world, teach your dog by omission that little people are never a threat. This reduces the chances that your pet might ignite at a child.

Q. What about people in their mid to late teens?

A. As a general rule, no. I say "general rule" because the age of majority can vary regionally. Only legal adults may make binding contracts, such as agreeing to help you protection train while absolving you of liability related

What's wrong with this picture? Don't even think about letting children agitate.

to any injuries the agitator may sustain. Were a teener wounded, you could find yourself looking down the barrel of a lawsuit.

Regarding contracts between you and your helpers, have a local attorney draft one. Liability laws vary by locale, and any generic pact I might offer could cause you more trouble than it might prevent.

Safety

Agitation's first three rules are: Protect the agitator, protect the agitator and protect the agitator. Rule number four: Never violate any of the first three rules.

Work only one dog at a time. Leave techniques like line and circle agitation (see the Glossary) to those with self-destructive urges.

Conduct all agitation on-leash. Although the lead should be attached to a harness, your dog should also wear a pinch collar with a tab—a short length of stout cord tied where you would normally attach the leash—to provide emergency control. If the collar fits snugly, add an extra link to lessen its pressure, which can distract.

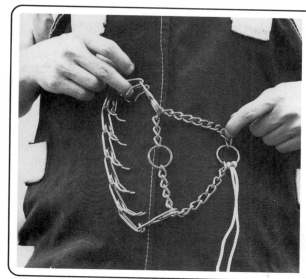

A tabbed, medium-size pinch collar.

Use leads strong enough to restrain your dog and three more like her, but avoid nylon. While nylon is a strong material, the stitching is often inadequate and the snaps frail. Besides, a nylon leash zipping through your hands can inflict memorable friction blisters.

Limit sessions to 20 minutes. Agitation can tire all concerned, and weary humans make mistakes. A fatigued dog can lose interest, decide it isn't worth the effort, or learn to associate tiredness with protection work.

After feeding, let a couple of hours pass (along with anything else) before working your dog. Not only does a hungry dog work better, the combination of strenuous exercise and a full stomach can cause cramping. Though she should have access to water, don't feed your pet right after agitation. That can only distract her after the fact. She should be alone for a time, to let the lessons percolate.

Train in secluded outdoor areas free of spectators and away from pedestrian and vehicular traffic. You, your dog and the agitators do not need the distractions of people not involved in training, and you do not need the liability should your dog nail an onlooker. The site you choose should be roomy and open. Don't train in confined areas that might make your dog feel trapped. We want confident, not paranoid.

For now, train just at this site. In time, it will become an environmental trigger that stimulates a defensive mindset. Trees or buildings should grace the setting, to provide hiding places for the agitator.

Work your dog once a day five days a week. If a given session is unusually brief, a second short training period later that same day is permissible.

Before each session, verify that the area is free of debris that could injure your dog or could cause you or the agitator to stumble. Likewise, don't train on slippery surfaces or in bad lighting, which would increase the risks to all concerned, including your pet.

Work with the sun at a right angle to the agitator and the dog, to keep it out of their eyes.

Establish a code word or phrase for the agitator's use should she really be in trouble. The trainer must know that an agitator is acting when yelling "Get it off me," but is not acting when she yells "Real bite!" During protection training, though a helper may feel pressure but not pain through a sleeve, she should bellow and carry on as though in agony, like someone being bitten would if the confrontation were genuine.

Q. Why?

A. So during a real situation the bad guy's howls don't cause the dog anxiety and disrupt her certitude.

Always have extra equipment on hand, such as leashes, collars, sleeves and sleeve covers (cylindrical cuffs made of jute that slide onto the sleeves).

Sleeve cuffs provide a better biting surface and prolong sleeve life. The cuff is the outer layer.

Bring cool, fresh water for your dog, keep a first-aid kit handy and know how to use its contents. Memorize the quickest route to a doctor's office or emergency room, and to a veterinarian's clinic.

Forbid smoking during training. It's too distracting to user and dog. Also, permit no booze, including beer, before or during a session. Should a helper claim, "I need a wee drop o' the creature to steady my nerves," get another agitator.

Helpers should not, at first, wear dark glasses. People without eyes intimidate at a visceral level, and we seek to build canine confidence.

Don't try to blueprint sessions down to the inch. Just as Nature abhors a vacuum, perfection seldom attends human endeavors. It's equally true that sometimes the best plans make themselves, and because events often veer from those anticipated, build tolerances into your training periods. Working within acceptable ranges is safer than walking a tightrope, especially when you don't have a net.

Never proceed to a next step until the dog is rock solid on the one before it. While that's true in obedience, it's crucial in protection. In guard dog training, to build on a shaky foundation is to facilitate tragedy.

Just as an agitator must handle the work's physical demands, a trainer must be able to control the dog. A seminar student once said, "My dog is powerful enough to pull a leash from my hands. Should I attach a second leash for insurance?" I answered, "You shouldn't be handling that dog." One of the student's agitators hollered, "Hear! Hear!" Litmus test: Can you control your dog using only your bare hands? If not, you yourself should not train the animal.

Q. Every trainer and agitator should approximate a giant redwood?

A. I myself am four inches short of six feet, weigh about 150 and possess moderate strength. Over the years I have never declined to agitate a dog based on size, but I have refused to handle a few. They were of sufficient capacity and power that I doubted I could control them if things went wrong.

Q. But won't obedience training prior to bitework establish sufficient authority to prevent an accident?

A. A trainer might ask that, but an agitator never would. I mean, would you, as an agitator, care to bet your body against the odds that a dog who is learning to dislike you might not follow all the obedience commands? Reread agitation's first three rules.

Two last quick points: One, all agitators and trainers must have current tetanus vaccinations. Two, trainers and agitators: Never turn your back on a dog during bitework, even for a few seconds.

Q. Have you ever seen anyone do that?

A. Yes, twice. It didn't work out.

Sermonette

As people grow familiar with a task, they become comfortable with it. That's okay in protection work, even desirable, because an opposite attitude—perpetual anxiety about personal injury—can lead to a self-fulfilling prophecy: Worrying too much about a possibility can cause it. Then imagination becomes an enemy. Trust your experience and instincts. If things don't feel right, they probably aren't, but don't confuse that with fear. It's no good to be afraid of being afraid. An inner voice might ask when your talents might fail you. The answer I respect is, *Someday, perhaps, but not today.*

At the same time, comfortable should not mean complacent. Don't drift into a false sense of security. Don't get sloppy. Remember, sometimes the game, not the players, makes the rules, and regardless of your knowledge and skill, you are not invincible. I've known agitators who thought they were. I've known them to be hurt, too. Wherever your body goes, your mind should have already gone. Concentrate. Anticipate. Ask, *What can go wrong?* Then be ready. When you err, always do so on the side of safety, because hindsight always comes too late, and it's never retroactive.

Armor

Agitators should wear protective apparel. I've seen helpers work while wearing T-shirts and cutoffs. *Amateurish* and *irresponsible* are the kindest terms I can manage.

Steve SeRine demonstrating why an agitator dressed like this is an accident looking for a place to happen.

During initial sessions, bad guys should wear scratch pants and sturdy, protective footwear. Weather too warm for safe clothing is likely too hot for the dog. Later, once the animal is solid on the sleeve (not attracted to parts of agitator anatomy other than the arm), jeans may be sufficient. Still, remember that cloth provides scant protection against bites and can prove to be just one more thing a doctor has to dig out of a wound. Male helpers should wear an athletic supporter and a cup, and agitators of either gender should wear a groin protector.

Q. What are scratch pants?

A. Intended to protect against injury from nails, they look like leather bib overalls and afford some protection against low-intensity bites.

Scratch pants.

Q. And a groin protector?

A. Similar in appearance to a diaper, but made of leather. (Don't let your vanity get in the way of your good sense!)

Q. Where can I find such equipment?

A. Look through the training supplies ads in canine periodicals. If Schutzhund or ring-sport clubs meet in your area (local veterinarians, groomers or kennel operators should know), ask members where they get their equipment. If a local law-enforcement agency operates K-9 units, ask their trainers for equipment suppliers' names and addresses.

Comparison shop. Don't assume all companies charge similar prices. They don't. Also, be seated when requesting prices. Protection training equipment can be very expensive. You can max out a credit card in seconds.

You will need more than one type of protective sleeve. Sleeves come in two basic styles, exterior and hidden, and the difference is just as the names imply. We will explore hidden sleeves in Chapter 17.

Exterior sleeves are classified as soft or hard. Both cover the arm from shoulder to hand, but many models of soft sleeves are open at both ends, while hard sleeves are sealed at the hand end. With dogs who have faint bites, use soft sleeves.

Soft sleeves can be compressed. . .   . . . while most hard sleeves cannot.

The type of hard sleeve I prefer includes a *bite bar*, an insert of stiff material three inches wide by a foot or so long attached along the sleeve's cylinder and angled toward the direction of a dog's rush. The purpose of a bite bar is to make the animal use her entire mouth, not just the front teeth.

A hard sleeve (shown without a sleeve cover) with a bite bar. This type of sleeve comes in either left-arm or right-arm models. This one is for the left arm.

A hard sleeve (shown without a sleeve cover) without a bite bar. This type of sleeve can be worn on either arm.

These sleeves contain an inner handle at the hand end. Clutch it in a death grip during agitation. When you do release, let the dog pull the sleeve from your arm rather than yanking your arm from the sleeve. Motion could attract the animal toward your unprotected limb.

Don't skip this one: Agitators who wear glasses should affix a retaining strap to the frames. The jolt from a charging dog can knock glasses off, and in this business, a sudden loss of vision could be more than inconvenient.

Breed Tendencies

Related to the safety concept, know that breed tendencies can affect how a dog bites a human. For instance, German Shepherds tend to launch high and hard toward a target, as though intending to go through it.

However, most leg-biter problems originate with German Shepherds as well. I've encountered few Dobermans or Rottweilers who ignored a proffered sleeve in favor of a leg, but I have met a disproportionate number of German Shepherds so inclined. Though uncommon, you should know about the predisposition.

While German Shepherds tend to try to knock a helper off balance, Dobermans often prefer to pull one down. Many Dobes bite and then shift their balance to the rear, trying to yank the mark onto the ground where the animal can do better work.

Dobermans and Rottweilers tend to hit stiff-legged, their front paws driving into the bad guy like spears, while German Shepherds often bend their front feet under them at the carpus (the canine equivalent of the wrist) just before impact.

If a Doberman keeps her mouth closed while coming at you, don't presume she isn't going to bite. Dobies often keep their jaws shut, or very nearly so, until the last instant. The breed also tends not to growl or bark during an advance, and many run on silent paws, as quietly as a dog of that size can. In a friend's words, "You seldom hear a Dobe coming."

Though a raised hand can trigger any dog, Dobermans often react violently to the gesture. Also know that Dobies tend to smile, so to speak, and when seeing this exposed-fangs phenomenon, you have to decide in an instant whether the animal is serious. More often than not, if the dog's head is down and the mouth is closed, you're seeing playfulness. If her head is up and the jaws are open, look out!

Rottweilers often charge low, as though targeting a knee, then explode upward at the last instant, going right up the agitator's front. I've also seen more than one try to go under a sleeve to hit the agitator's midsection. Like Dobermans, few Rottys snarl, bark or open their mouth during an advance, but they often growl just before or right after striking, as do many German Shepherds.

Breeds other than those I prefer have their quirks, too. Bouviers des Flandres often try to hop and face bite. Rhodesian Ridgebacks prefer the legs or—more specifically—the hamstrings. Belgian Malinois tend to show teeth and clack them together more than many breeds. More than one Great Dane I've agitated seemed disposed to drag me off, perhaps intending to bury me like a bone.

But understand, the foregoing are some tendencies I have observed (others appear in subsequent chapters); but in context, *tendency* does not mean, "Every dog of this breed does it this way every time." Not at all. I've seen Dobermans strike like German Shepherds and German Shepherds who applied Rottweiler tactics. There are no absolutes, no rules about canine behavior that a trainer or agitator should ever depend upon. No rule, in any endeavor, can anticipate all situations. Each dog is an individual who does what she does, regardless of how others of her breed tend to work. If you forget this, or if you try to live by breed tendency canons, I make you one promise: Someone, perhaps the dog, probably the agitator, will be injured. The only variables are when and how severely.

Q. What about agitating my own dog? I live in a sparsely populated area and helpers are hard to come by.

A. I know the problem. I lived in a Wyoming hamlet with a population of 317. Still, you can never be your pet's bad guy. That could send as bassackwards a message as possible about the relationship that should exist between you and your pet. Definitely, no.

Take Pen in Hand

Record training objectives, techniques, results, problems, their resolutions and so on. Human recall can be selective, and written records can contribute invaluable information when training other dogs or duking it out in court, as well as provide a scrapbook of memories.

Reflection

A dog is like an eternal Peter Pan, a child who never grows old and who therefore is always available to love and be loved.

Aaron Alexander

CHAPTER 8

AGITATION METHODOLOGIES

This chapter's title might seem to lend a scholarly cast to agitation, making the activity appear somewhat scientific. Lab jackets, theoretical pursuits, fold tab A into slot B. Nice, precise, safe.

Sure.

Every bit as safe as walking into an airplane propeller.

I've seen people ripped before they knew they were bitten. Faster than you might believe, a chunk of yourself can be torn away. And swallowed.

Q. Hype?

A. Fact. Agitation is neither nice nor precise. It's never safe. The dog is faster than we and, in his way, smarter. He is naturally skilled in the use of teeth and jaws. His choices are primal and hardwired, not civilized or reasoned. Virtuous concepts like right and wrong don't clutter his decision making, and he would view the concept of a fair fight as oxymoronic, or simply moronic.

While some of our animal instincts may have gone dormant beneath layers of intellect and education, canine contact with the sphere of explosive, all-out ferocity is as close as your next thought. The dog seldom fights to a draw and knows nothing of mercy.

Know, too, that the dog's world is sharply binary: On or off, go or stop, obey or disregard. Very few grays litter canine options.

Read this section more than once. Then, *sans* dog, practice its methods until they become reflexive. During a catch, there's no time for conscious thought.

Q. "Catch" means. . . ?

A. An agitator's method of accepting a bite. The term derives from similarities to catching an object, like a ball. Somebody throws one to you, you catch it in your hands, if only to prevent it from hitting you. A dog flies at you, you "catch" him on a sleeve, for much the same reason. To a human, the sleeve may seem the target. This perception can make the helper feel protected, secure. Remember, though, a dog may see a sleeve and its wearer as one.

Every catch's objective is multifaceted: To protect helper and dog; to build canine fire and habituate the location of the bite; to induce accurate, powerful hits; and to teach not just "Bite!" but "Hang on!"

This chapter lays a foundation. It details many but not all aspects of agitation. Subsequent sections outline additional techniques . . . excuse me—methodologies.

Agitation is tiring work. David Dodd is doing a perfect run-by to build desire in my Doberman, Chattan, shown a millisecond after the dog snapped his jaws shut inches from the sleeve.

Success, at least for Chattan. Note the bite is full-mouth. David soon opted to switch to a hard sleeve.

Jenny

Every helper who ever watched Jenny agitate agreed she was tops. Hummingbird quick and an equally fast study, Jenny personified a natural blend of talent and desire. She also harbored an offbeat wit. A sense of humor is an underrated asset, unless it actually serves to cloak ego, the foremost human weakness.

Without a dog present, I began Jenny's education with burlap sack work, a sometimes underestimated agitation element. We used sacks that were 21 inches wide by 36 inches long. We washed and rinsed them to remove herbicide/insecticide residue, as they had been acquired from a feed store.

"Let me understand this," Jenny said, *"I'm supposed to greatly displease a large, powerful dog."*

I nodded, deadpan.

"Then, once he's thoroughly teed off, at me, you're going to send the frothing beast, at me."

"Uh-huh." Smile suppression was getting harder.

"And there I stand, good old Jenny, with nothing to hide behind but a by-God burlap sack!"

"Damn well told!"

"Wonderful," was her word choice, but her inflection said, *"I must be out of my mind."*

Jenny knew she'd wear scratch pants and that the dog would be on-leash. But dog training wasn't new to her. She had a strong obedience background and had seen leashes pop.

Don't have dogs nearby when teaching new agitators. Play the canine role yourself.

"Here," I said, handing Jenny a sack. *"Bunch up one end in your right hand. You're the bad guy, I'm the dog."*

"Does that make you a son of a—?"

"Steady, Jenny. Now let your right arm hang at your side. Let the sack droop to the ground. Turn your left side toward me. Feet comfortably apart, knees bent, balanced, fluid."

"Why left side toward you? For that matter, why sideways? Why not frontal?"

"You're right-handed, so the sack's in your accurate hand. You'll see why that's important in a minute," I said. *"Left side facing me—the dog—to hide the sack*

until we're ready to use it. We want the animal reacting to you, not to what you're carrying. Sideways, not frontal, to make you seem less imposing. We need to build canine confidence. We start by making you appear smaller, and fearful of the dog."

"I'll bring my worry beads."

People say much through their aspect. Jenny's didn't evince fear—frightened folk have no place in agitation—but she knew that a little paranoia can be healthy. It can keep you sharp.

I walked 30 feet away. "Okay, Jenny, here's the script. You're a mean-spirited so and so, a coward who likes to tease and torment dogs, a human fear-biter. You've left your hiding place and are out for a skulk. You haven't noticed the dog—me. Go ahead. Slink on."

Jenny edged toward me, radiating a creepiness that would do a grave robber proud.

"Watch the dog—me—out of the corner of your eye, Jenny. Okay, he jerked his head toward you. He just saw you. Freeze. That's when you'll first 'see' him.

"Act scared. Back off. Then, after a few seconds, move toward him hesitantly. If the dog barks or steps toward you, back away. He's frightened you. Rabbit if he really sets off. Then return. You've realized he can't reach you, that the leash stops him. Ease in close, to about four feet."

It can take several approaches to get that close to a dog, because every time the animal shows fire the agitator must retreat, to reward the animal's reactions. The trick is to come a little nearer each time while not stressing out the animal.

Jenny added a cayenne touch most new agitators need to be taught: She kept her gaze darting about, never fixing on me—the dog—as a cold, hard focus could intimidate an inexperienced canine.

Bunch up one end in your accurate hand.

"Gradually turn more frontal, Jenny, for better balance. If that spooks the dog, switch back to sideways. Snap the sack to one side of him—me—about knee high. I'll try to—"

Whisk.

"—grab it." I missed. I'm quick, but Jenny was sudden. Two muffs later I asked how she was anticipating me so well.

"Your eyes. They say where you expect the sack. I put it a few inches elsewhere."

As I said, Jenny was a natural.

Then I got lucky. I snagged the sack.

"Okay," I said, steadily pulling the burlap, *"Shift your. . ."*

She shifted her right side toward me, to improve her balance and leverage. *"Like so?"* she asked through an impish smile, feigned innocence sparkling in her eyes.

Just then, grinning, I yanked the sack, hard, nearly jerking Her Smugness off her feet. My hand a blur, I released the burlap and tapped her face. Her head snapped back as her arm flew up, but—too late. Way too late. *"Your ego just got you disfigured, Jenny! You don't have a left cheek anymore!"*

Agitation is not a game.

Jenny was stunned as from a fall, though the true hit was psychological, not physical. Jenny's eyes became a couple of watery poached eggs as a month's worth of realization dawned in a heartbeat.

"Damn." She touched her cheek, a tremor in her hand. She looked at her fingers, a distant part of her expecting to see blood. Jenny shut her eyes, shook her head and shivered, in July. Deep breath. *"I may not be right for this."*

Never argue that point with a student agitator. If the nerve goes, the person should go as well.

Several seconds trudged by. Then, "I should have let go of the sack, right?"

"The instant you felt your balance start to go," I said.

Jenny studied the ground.

"Devil-may-care is fine, Jenny, so long as you acknowledge that Satan got the job because he's good at what he does. It's a false shield, a beacon that shows calamity where to find you."

She squinted at me. *"You're talking attitude, not aptitude."*

I nodded. *"Aptitude you've got, in spades."*

"But my attitude needs work." Acceptance, not self-abuse.

"New agitators often need to look at attitude. Some of them rethink. Others go the hard road. It takes a major harming to wake them up."

Knowledge and mechanical techniques contribute to helper safety. Attitude plays a bigger part. Many agitator injuries result from nothing more than cockiness. Some folks go through humility's motions, but just to wave a passing greeting.

"I can't walk away from this," she said.

"Hey, pride's for lions, Jenny, and for losers."

She shook her head. "It isn't that, it's determination. I want to learn guard dog training!"

"So do."

"Yeah, but now I'm spooked. Dogs're quicker than you, and . . . damn!" She touched her cheek again, looked away.

Anxiety makes bad decisions, especially when anger is added in.

"Dial it back some, Jenny. Learn agitation now, decide whether to do it later."

She focused within for a moment, then nodded once, twice, more emphatically the second time.

"Here," I said, handing Jenny a sack. "Bunch up one end in your right hand. You're the bad guy, I'm the dog."

Jenny turned sideways. Beneath cold eyes, her jaw set, her mouth was a hyphen.

"Judgment comes from experience, most often a frightening experience."[1]

The next day, I toed an arc in the dirt, then stood eight feet behind it. Still without a dog present, I said, "That's how far the jaws can reach, Jenny. Don't breach it. When we're working for real, gauge your limit at eight feet from where I'll be standing, behind the dog, restraining him."

I use 15-foot leashes. Six feet from the clasp of each, I wrap several layers of tape to alert me by touch when the dog reaches the proper distance from me.

Q. Six feet? You told Jenny eight feet.

A. The distance from where the lead attaches, to the dog's muzzle is another two feet.

Still playing the dog's part, I stood just behind the line. "Okay, Jenny, the dog is firing strong, snarling and carrying on. Snap the sack at my feet. They're the dog's paws. Don't hit 'em. Just raise dust close by."

[1]*Clear and Present Danger*, Tom Clancy.

I grabbed at the sack each time, and missed equally often.

"If the dog shows courage, twist your upper body from side to side as you snap the sack. Dip your shoulder. Put fire in your movements. That challenges the animal, makes him madder."

Jenny did agitation's version of the macarena.

"Act like you're going to snap the sack to your left, Jenny, but go to your right instead. Fake the dog out. Nothing irritates him like being fooled."

An agitator can heighten canine hostility by scorning and deriding the dog's attempts. The words mean nothing, of course, but the tones communicate that the animal's misses are raising the bad guy's confidence. This gives the dog something more to tear down.

"Stamp your feet, Jenny. Faster, faster. That enrages. Now stop and snap the sack from side to side, to pull attention off your legs and onto the burlap. A bite's coming." I pointed at Jenny. "That was the signal that here comes the dog. Quick now—stretch the sack between your hands, a couple of feet apart, to frame a stable target, a little above waist high and almost as far out in front of yourself as you can reach." I jumped forward and grabbed the sack.

"Good job," I said. "Next time, step back as I lunge and release one end just as I grab. That lets the sack give with the dog's strike. It'll teach him to hit faster and harder."

"How so?"

"Moving the sack backward at the last moment encourages the creature to hit faster. Your releasing eliminates resistance and teaches the dog to slam through a target, so he doesn't involuntarily soften a blow at the instant of impact."

"So in a real situation, the dog'll hit hard enough to flatten the no-good?"

"That's the idea."

"Then as Lassie strikes, shouldn't I turn away as well?"

"Uh-huh. As part of the same move. Get out of that dog's path. Spin away from whichever end of the sack you release."

"If I let go with my right hand, I should step backward with my right foot, pivoting on the left one?"

"There you go."

"Which hand should I let go with?"

I tilted my head to one side. "The one nearest the dog's mouth might be best."

Jenny grinned, relaxing a bit. "Well, yes. Eight ball, side pocket."

Like I said, Jenny had a way of putting things.

As the dog bites, keep the leash taut to protect the agitator while making the animal strain for what he wants. To do this you'll have to move. Quick.

Imagine a compass. The agitator is at north, the dog south. Both are facing each other, and you're two steps behind your pet. Suppose the animal lunges nearer the helper's right (west) hand. With that hand she releases the sack and pivots clockwise a quarter turn on her left foot, stepping back and to her left with her right foot. She winds up facing west, the dog looking east. Ergo, you must simultaneously move left (westward) to keep the lead tight.

Q. Why the need for a constantly tight lead?

A. To keep the dog on the sack—that is, off the agitator. A loose lead at this stage can drive a dog to go after the helper.

We tried again. As I grabbed the sack, Jenny released with her right hand and spun clockwise a quarter turn on her left foot. Her technique was almost perfect, but almost counts only in horseshoes and nuclear weapons.

"No!" Quick as a snake I released the sack and grabbed Jenny's other hand. "Protect yourself. Whip your free hand behind your back the instant you let go, or use it for more pull on the sack, but don't hang it out there like a target. One more time."

A trainer never ends a session just after the dog has goofed. He makes sure the animal gets it right first. The same principle applies to teaching agitators, because in either case, ending high—or low—can carry into the next training period.

"Okay, Jenny, now we're fighting. I'm the dog and I've grabbed the sack. I'm pulling it. Now I'm jerking it, like a dog will. Release and fall backward to one side, away from the animal, to get out of range while letting the critter think he knocked you down. Roll. Howl. Scramble up. Run away. Stumble, but keep running. Show the dog you're afraid, Jenny. You've lost your sack. It's your power and you've lost it. You're terrified. Run, Jenny! Run!"

Jenny developed into the best agitator I ever saw.

"Joel, what if a dog goes for my legs during sack work?"

"Toss the sack at him; he may settle for it. But back off fast and don't bend forward. That would put your face in target range."

"What if a leash breaks? Skedaddle?"

"No. You can't outrun a dog. Trying to just draws him more. Freeze. Forearms against your chest, elbows in, hands fisted. If you're knocked down, tuck your knees under you, keep your face down and cover your head and the back of your neck with your hands. I'll get there as fast as I can."

Jenny demonstrates the cover-up position, standing.

The cover-up position if you're knocked down.

Q. Has it ever happened, a broken leash?

A. Once. See Chapter 22, Lessons From the Best Teacher, for more on that.

Q. Do you ever attach two leashes to one dog, for safety?

A. Often.

Mike

If Jenny was the best agitator I ever saw, Mike was the most intense. Compact and powerful, I never saw anyone immerse himself in a learning program like Mike did. His motivation—a deep affection for dogs—overrode his lack of formal training experience.

I began Mike's education by having him watch Jenny and me for several sessions as we agitated various breeds. Then, with Mike as the bad guy, Jenny and I took turns playing the dog.

"Mike," Jenny said, *"with a novice dog take short steps as you approach, not grand leaps."*

"How come that?"

"Imitating the St. Louis Arch could spook a beginner."

Let your experienced agitators train new ones. This teaches the latter while giving the former many opportunities to reinforce in their own minds what they know.

"Besides," Jenny said, "you're defenseless during hang-time. Jumping about puts you in the air too long. A dog could hit you in the legs and bring you down the hard way. Got it?"

"Sho'nuff." Mike grew up in Alabama.

"Awhile ago you watched me sack agitate Tank, that two-ton Rottweiler," Jenny said. "Did you see I kept the sack below his head? Today was his first session, and you can hold a sack above nose level, but don't wave it at him above his head."

"How come?"

"New things above a dog can inhibit him," I said.

"Nothing short of artillery would inhibit that dog," Jenny muttered. "Mount St. Helens with an attitude."

"We show a manstopper he can handle anything," I said. "A way to teach that mindset is by not even risking"—I glanced at Jenny—"giving a dog more than he can deal with during training. Get the idea, Mike?"

"Sho'nuff."

Mike would say that a lot during the next few sessions as he watched Jenny and me agitate various dogs. Soon we began teaching him sleeve work.

"Mike, the sleeve techniques you have to learn are the ones Jenny used today with Chattan and Smokey, my Dobe and my German Shepherd. I trust you remember them."

"Gawd, yes!" Mike chuckled.

"We sent Chattan at Jenny from a short distance, six feet or so. What did Jenny do?"

"I guess I was watching the dog."

"Watch the agitator," Jenny said. "That's what you should be studying. Chattan took one bound and bit the sleeve. Just as he started moving, I took a short step toward him with my left foot, timing it to touch the ground just before he hit the sleeve."

"Why step at the dog?"

"To build his confidence that he can handle someone coming at him, and to get my rhythm going to get in sync with the dog's speed. If you're flat-footed or backing away when he comes in, you'll get knocked down or he'll learn to hit soft, because there's no give."

"But y'all go backwards when using a sack."

Jenny shook her head. "When a dog nails burlap, none of the impact transfers to you because you aren't wearing the thing, unless you've fallen on hard times. When the dog hits a sleeve, you have to absorb some of the shock. So stepping backward *wearing a sleeve can get you knocked down. Or you could stumble over something you didn't see."*

This marks an important difference in method between sack and sleeve agitation. Step back as the dog strikes a sack; but when using a sleeve, step at the animal just before he hits. Then, in either case, move in concert with the dog's momentum.

Mike asked, "Why do y'all step at the dog with the left foot? Why not the right?"

"Because the sleeve was on my left arm," Jenny said. "Step with the same foot as the arm the sleeve is on."

Mike pondered this. "What for?"

Having read this young dog's angle of flight, I've already started to step backward with my right foot . . .

. . . and an instant later the hand nearest the animal's mouth is on its way to safety behind my back.

"As the dog strikes, you pivot on that same foot, the one you stepped at him with, to disperse his momentum. If you don't spin, the dog could jam his neck because there'd be no give when he hits."

"So just as the dog leaves the ground," Mike said, concentrating, "you step at him"—he closed his eyes—*"with the same foot as the arm wearing the sleeve."*

"Right," Jenny said, grinning, remembering her own first catches.

"So if y'all are wearing a right-arm sleeve, step forward on your right foot."

"Bingo!"

"And as the dog hits," Mike said, "you pivot on the same foot."

Jenny gave a thumbs-up sign.

"To teach hard hits and to scatter that there energy."

"You bet. Which way do you spin?" Jenny said.

Mike thought. "Don't that matter which arm the sleeve's on? Clockwise with a left-arm sleeve, counterclockwise with a right-arm one?" He made circling motions with his hands.

"You're getting it, Alabam," Jenny said.

Think this through. It's crucial. Fact one: An agitator should keep his elbow bent to hold the sleeve close to his body. That's because of fact two: If the elbow is not bent and the sleeve is extended from the body, it's easier to lose your balance when the dog hits and he can rip the sleeve from your arm. Or he can slip under the cylinder and nail you.

Don't hold the sleeve against yourself, like this . . . **. . . or out from yourself, like this . . .** **. . . hold it with just enough space from you to absorb the shock, like this.**

Now, this clockwise-counterclockwise business—which way to turn as the dog connects—depends on personal preference and whether you are right- or left-handed. Let's say you are right-handed and wearing a left-arm sleeve. If you spin counterclockwise as the dog hits, his momentum could pull your arm away from your body and yank you down. But if you turn clockwise, the dog's force tends to push your arm toward your body and keep you upright.

"Same way with Smokey, the German Shepherd?" Mike asked me. "Even though he had a whole lot longer run there at Jenny?"

"Same," I said, "except everything happens faster. Smokey came in a lot harder than Chattan. Then you spin quicker and farther. Jenny took Chattan a little over a quarter turn. With Smokey, she spun more than 180 degrees."

"*Because Smokey was running so much harder, coming from farther off and all,*" *Mike said.*

"*Sure,*" *Jenny said.* "*More momentum to spread around.*"

"*This don't sound so all-fired hard,*" *Mike said, smirking.*

Jenny glanced at me and fingered her cheek.

"*Good. I'll get Smokey.*" *I stood.* "*He loves new helpers.*"

"*Does he ever!*" *Jenny said.* "*I'll call 911 now. It'll give us more time later for consoling next of kin and all.*"

Mike's glibness fled. "*Well, uh, I don't know, that is, I mean, uh, now y'all looka heah. . . .*"

Jenny lost it, cackling so hard she had to sit down.

"*Sho'nuff,*" *Mike said through a boyish grin,* "*Y'all was afunnin' me.*"

Then I had to sit.

"*Look, Mike,*" *I said, catching my breath,* "*that was just to get your attention. A savvy hitter like Smokey would eat your lunch. Put a sleeve on and practice footwork by yourself awhile. Tomorrow Jenny and I'll take turns running at you, to help you get your timing going.*"

"*'Kay.*" *Mike looked relieved, and not a little sheepish.*

Later, Jenny told him, "*Stance and timing are everything. Get them right, you'll be okay. Get one wrong. . . .*"

"*And the dog could be hurt,*" *Mike said.*

"*Or you could be,*" *Jenny said.* "*See here, Dixie—*"

"*Say whut?*"

"*—that's the other reason for pivoting, to keep you on your feet. Forget to spin, or do it wrong, and you could wind up on your tail feather, fighting to keep teeth from your face, or other parts of your anatomy.*"

Silence. Then, "*Sho'nuff.*"

Jenny and I worked with Mike, she and I playing the part of the dog. We took turns rushing at him, occasionally changing angles at the last second, as dogs sometimes do.

Jenny grabbed the sleeve, twirled Mike like a top—"*Go with it, Mike, go with it! Don't fight a wave, go with it!*"—*and hammered her point by driving the cylinder hard into his ribs when he spun too slow. Then, one afternoon, Jenny tore the sleeve from Mike's arm.*

"*You just let a dog rip your sleeve off!*" *Jenny screamed, inches from Mike's nose.* "*He's spit it out and is eyeing you like a Sunday ham!*" *Suddenly Jenny was a drill sergeant, moving forward, and Mike was a green recruit, walking backward.*

Jenny demonstrates the catch stance.

"But that ain't love in his eyes, Appomattox. Now just what the hell are you going to do?" Jenny stamped away in utter disgust—and shot a conspiratorial wink at me.

Mike, blinking and blushing like a schoolboy, scratched his head and contemplated his shoes. "Damn."

Never slip (release) a sleeve until you are ready. Never! Never! Never!

A few days later I had a word with Mike. "That German Shepherd bitch you watched me work in obedience this morning—her protection training gets going tomorrow afternoon. I think you're ready to sack agitate a dog. Want to start with her?"

He hesitated a moment, caution glaring at eagerness. Then, "Guess so."

Mike and I had one more matter to discuss. I told him about a scene from the movie *The Karate Kid*:

Reflection

Mr. Miyagi told his student, "Daniel-san, when you walk on road, walk right side, safe. Walk left side, safe. Walk middle, sooner or later, get squished, skkkt, just like grape. Karate same thing. Either your karate do 'yes,' or your karate do 'no.' Your karate do 'guess so,' squish, just like grape. Understand?"

B.B. Hiller

CHAPTER 9

LISTEN!

British cabbies speak of "the Knowledge," mental databases they access to thread their way through London's bewildering rabbit warren of avenues and side streets. Trainers and agitators need a similar cache of insights; similar in that if followed, they lead to the journey's end—a trained dog. We've studied travel brochures and topographic maps. Now we're en route to training a manstopper.

The familiar scent of leather triggered memories of other dogs, other first sessions, as I buckled the aged harness onto the young German Shepherd. Its feel no longer distracted her, since she had worn it many times before.

During her one year on the planet the dog had met only nice people. That was as it should be. This afternoon she would discover that human nature has a dark side. We walked across patchy dry grass fighting for survival between a forgotten factory west of us and a stand of aspens 30 feet to the east.

Each training period is a potential breakpoint. A dog who shows pronounced fear must be expelled, but "pronounced fear" is not mild uncertainty. A pet who has learned not to jump on visitors may hesitate when first encountering an agitator.

A long-ago Rottweiler epitomized fearfulness by racing behind my legs during a helper's approach and peeking around them, trembling. He was like a horse I once fell off, a mare so gentle she nearly died of fright. The Rotty was a great pet but unsuited to guard work. Trainers can help build canine confidence but not courage. Like instinct and drive levels, that's a genetic variable born into each animal.

Southwest winds were kicking up, hinting at a coming storm, as I clipped a 15-foot lead to the harness's rear ring. I removed and pocketed the six-foot leash from the dog's pinch collar, donned gloves, gripped the lead two-handed, stood behind the

Shepherd and adjusted my cap. Mike, wearing a floppy hat and ragged overcoat that might have been through the Calgary Stampede, emerged from the grove.

The dog's head snapped up from a leaf she was sniffing. Standing as still as porcelain, she took in the curious sight edging toward us. Barely louder than the breeze, I whispered a new command. Two seconds later I repeated it. "Listen!"

Recall that "Listen" means "Focus on the person." It cues your pet that she should become alert, that you sense trouble.

As light draws the human eye, canine focus is attracted by motion.

Mike scurried toward us like an arthritic crab on speed, crouched and sideways, in fits and starts. Dragging a burlap sack, he peered more downward than ahead and seemed not to notice us. The dog, her curiosity lit, stared at him.

Dogs exist at a primitive level. "To understand the dog's mind we have to enter a different sensory world—the world of canine sensation—and imagine how the dog perceives and responds to life around him"[1]

The Shepherd stands motionless, a graceful contour silhouetted against a pewter sky, deep primal wisdom in her features. Her tail stirs, then stops. Slowly her head cranes forward as her peripheral vision constricts to a narrow tunnel shrouded in gray light. Scraggly lawn, swirling dust, leafless trees all fade out. Tiny spiders dance along her spine as the shape at telescope's end takes on razor clarity. **Intruder.**

The place becomes as quiet as shadows.

Nostrils twitch. **Man scent.**

Eyes widen, then narrow. **Furtive movements.**

Neurons fire. **Threat.**

Adrenaline floods tensed muscles. Heart rate and blood pressure quicken. Shallow breathing replaces rhythmic panting and the mind clicks to an earlier age, a crueler plain.

Defense drive stiffens the dog's hackles. Her mouth slowly parts, then closes. Icy concentration. Guard drive sparks a low, dirty rumble. Saliva runs inside feral jaws as protection drive ignites. The animal steps forward.

"The dog is motivated to act or not to act solely by emotions, instincts and drives, not by some special intellectual capabilities or logical thought processes."[2]

---

[1]The Dog's Mind, Bruce Fogle.
[2]The Police Service Dog, Johannes Grewe.

Mike was 15 feet from the animal when he felt the dog's eyes on him. Badly startled, he crossed his arms over his chest. "Gawd a'mighty!" Wide-eyed, mouth agape, leaning away and frozen in place, he was a man afraid.

Mike's a particularly good actor. Effective agitators are born to the stage. Sometimes the helper hesitates and reacts fearfully, but in a blink he can switch to a foot-stomping, arm-waving, screaming madman.

Ignoring my presence, Mike shuffled backward a few paces, staring at the dog. As though joining him in a macabre dance, the Shepherd strode forward on stiffened legs. Staying well behind, I moved with her, keeping the leash taut.

Mike froze. So did the dog. Now, unbeknownst to her, he was playing the animal, beautifully.

Allow a bite too soon and the dog may learn she need not generate fire to receive satisfaction. Deny a bite too long and her frustrated anger may turn inward and become depression. Grant relief at the proper instant and she finds that her advantage lies in igniting to a fever pitch because that brings fulfillment, a bite.

Mike's stare battled the dog's. Still crouched and angled sideways, he curled his upper lip and hissed as he maneuvered toward her, stalking her.

The German Shepherd held her ground and matched Mike glare for glare. I tightened the leash. Again she stepped forward. Mike stopped dead in his tracks.

Trainer and agitator must watch for "what if?" Both must see all that can occur and be alert to protect the helper while not allowing the dog to lose a confrontation.

The dog halted in mid-stride. Seconds later, Mike again eased toward her.

Suddenly he snapped the sack downward at his side and scraped a foot against the harsh ground. The Shepherd snarled and lunged against her restraints as fight drive accelerated. I paid out another two feet of leash. Mike stamped his feet, his legs churning like pistons. Rising onto her back legs, the dog roared and pawed the air.

Mike raced away, terrified and shrieking. He looked back just before ducking behind a tree. The dog was riveted on his hiding place.

Q. If the trainer handles the dog and the agitator plays the bad guy, who does the training?

A. Both, but the agitator teaches more actively. For folks grounded in obedience, this paradigm shift—like protection training's no-force aspect—marks another conceptual departure for those accustomed to being their pet's sole teacher.

Mike soon returned, still crouched, still sideways. He stared wide-eyed at the dog's mouth as he slunk to within four feet of her. She bared her teeth. Mike ducked lower. As the animal growled and pulled forward, Mike flicked the sack right at her face.

She snapped at the burlap but Mike flipped it just out of reach and taunted her. "Y'all just a wuthless damn Yankee!" He whipped the sack behind his leg and stamped his feet again. Now fully aroused, the dog roared as only a German Shepherd can.

Skilled agitators cannot only read a dog at a glance and respond reflexively, they can also handle the work's physical and mental burdens. Possessing exceptional quickness and timing, seasoned helpers respect canine abilities but do not fear them.

Mike popped the sack near the dog's forepaws. She bit at it but he made her miss, again by millimeters. He ridiculed the animal as she tore turf, raging in frustration. I eased toward her, gathering the leash as I went.

My gesture unseen by the dog, I pointed at Mike. He jumped back and extended the burlap just as I slackened several feet of leash. "Action!"

Communication, coordination and timing between trainer and agitator are crucial. Both must know when the dog will be sent.

A roaring black-and-red blur flew at the assailant. For a suspended moment man and dog locked in combat, each pulling against the sack. I tightened the leash to prevent further advance.

Just then the snarling animal bucked backward and jerked her head. Mike instantly let go, falling away and rolling clear. He scrambled to his feet and bellowed defeat as he ran to the trees.

Breathing hard, the Shepherd stood in place and watched him go, the sack hanging from her jaws like freshly killed prey. She shook it ferociously, then stared at Mike's hiding place. I eased to her side. Softly, "You did good, babe." She thrashed her prize once more. I patted my leg. "C'mon, let's go home."

The dog exhaled a burst of heat through the burlap, then looked at me, the glaze leaving her eyes. She was decelerating, passing from one reality to another.

We walked away, my hand gently rubbing her neck, Greta proudly clutching her trophy.

This was an initial agitation session. In the next chapter we'll dissect it.

Reflection

The poor dog, in life the firmest friend,
The first to welcome, foremost to defend.

Lord Byron

BACKTRACK

Although every training period is critical, initial sessions are especially so because they set the foundation, and you know about building on weak foundations. Pressuring a novice dog too much can sow seeds of self-doubt or even a belief that humans cannot be defeated. Ruffle canine feathers too little and the gravity of confrontational situations may not be clear. Read, handle and agitate the animal correctly—that is, in keeping with her physical and psychological states—and a solid base develops, one that can support increasingly stressful lessons.

Any first session is also a double exposure: of the dog to life's harsher realities, and of his essence to the trainer. You should sense beforehand how your pet will respond, but only afterward can you be certain what lives at the leash's end.

Should a dog remain in place and appear fearful or try to back away during the agitator's approach, abandon that animal's guard training. It's likely you are seeing the dog's genes in action. And just as all the training in the world cannot cause an animal born with three legs to grow a fourth, neither will it stabilize a genetically unsteady or fearful dog.

Remember, training creates nothing; it can only enhance what is already there. Yes, some spooky dogs can be taught cosmetic protection, but in a real situation you want the genuine article, not a facsimile who may back down. Does this mean that such a dog is a lesser animal? No. It only means that, as some things are not right for you and me, protection work is not right for him.

In the preceding chapter you read about a typical first agitation. Now let's go through that session with a rake.

Greta's First Session

"I buckled the aged harness onto the young German Shepherd." For now, harness your pet for all training periods. Harnesses cost more than collars but are safer. A dog can more easily pull out of a collar, and a harness is easier grabbed should a sudden need arise. Also, when a collared dog hits the leash's end, it can dampen the fire or, much worse, cause neck or spinal injuries.

Avoid nylon harnesses à la discount houses and pet supply shops. You want heavy-duty leather. Nylon itself may seldom tear, but the stitching can prove inadequate.

Because I had harnessed Greta previously, "Its feel no longer distracted her." Distractions of any kind are the last things we want during initial agitation. Starting weeks before the first session, occasionally harness your pet so the rigging won't be new and unfamiliar during training. When adorning your partner in her new duds, psych her up as well, communicating your pleasure at how pretty she looks in the equipment.

"We walked across patchy dry grass." Greta wasn't heeled to the training site. Initially, don't use obedience commands before, during or just after a session, lest your dog perceive overtones of control or suppress urges at the training area or during the activities.

"I clipped a 15-foot lead to the harness's rear ring. I removed and pocketed the six-foot leash from the dog's pinch collar." Don't reverse this sequence, lest you momentarily have an unleashed dog. Mistakes like that cause accidents. Don't toss your shorter leash aside, either. Keep it handy should the longer one break.

The long lead is to let your pet operate away from you. She should have no doubt that it is she who is scaring the bad guy away, that the helper's fear is of her, not you. That's one reason I stood *behind* Greta, not next to her, so she was between me and the agitator. Nor did I want to risk distracting the dog. Obedience has taught her to key on me; now I wanted to say that during a hot situation, she should focus on the bad guy, not me.

Using the long leash also facilitates safety. Should a dog pull a short lead from your grasp, she's loose. But a longer leash provides length you can grab to maintain control.

I "donned gloves" for a better grip and protection against friction burns, and "gripped the lead two-handed." Never hold a leash one-handed. Your agitator can tell you why. I "adjusted my cap" to signal my readiness to Mike. Change your sign before each session so as not to teach your Greta an unintended cue. And to anticipate a question, yes, some dogs are that observant.

Because "southwest winds were kicking up," Mike hid eastward to keep his scent from drifting to the dog before he appeared. We wanted the animal's

A dog may have some misgivings when first being harnessed . . .

. . . but if you use calm words and a gentle touch while first slipping the new equipment on . . .

. . . he will have forgotten about the harness's newness by the time you are buckling the back strap . . .

. . . and will be more interested in a passing field mouse moments after you're done.

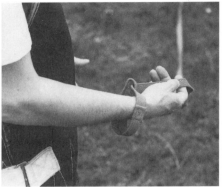

Security-wrapping the leash as shown can prevent accidents. The loop is shown loose here, so you can see it clearly, but cinch it tight before working your dog.

If you prefer not to security-wrap your leash, try holding it like this.

first impression to be visual, for learning impact. Also, Mike arrived well before us and approached from a direction other than the one Greta and I took, so as not to scent the training area.

When you and your pet arrive, allow her a few moments to sniff and otherwise check out the new area. That's what Greta was doing when her "head snapped up from a leaf she was sniffing."

"She took in the curious sight edging toward us." Teach the "Listen" cue using the *verbal-bridge* technique, timing the word so you use it the instant the dog spots the agitator. "Barely louder than the breeze, I whispered a new command." Speak the new word softly, to entice but not distract or dominate. "Two seconds later I repeated it," to let Greta hear the new command again.

Don't repeat the "Listen" cue more than once. That could suggest to the dog that she missed the point, that she should do something other than what she is doing. Also, say nothing except "Listen." Extra words, including the dog's name, could confuse at this stage.

Q. Shouldn't I praise my dog when she reacts to the agitator's approach?

A. Not yet. Don't risk splitting your pet's attention. Not censuring her actions is praise enough. Your silence sanctions.

For heaven's sake don't pet the animal during agitation! Not only might that distract, but you could wind up being known as Lefty. An agitated dog can flash toward an unexpected touch.

As part of their survival instinct, Nature programs dogs to key on the out-of-place, the extraordinary. Thus, at a first session the agitator should appear odd—"a floppy hat and ragged overcoat"—and act strangely to catch the dog's attention and tell her something unusual is afoot.

Notice, though, I did not tell you Mike wore a sleeve. That's because he didn't. A sleeve at a first session equals too much too soon, because some novice dogs initially hesitate to bite a sleeve, since they see it as part of a human and have learned non-aggression toward people. Let sack work stoke the canine fires before advancing to sleeve agitation.

Mike "peered more downward than ahead and seemed not to notice us." Had he responded to Greta's presence from afar, she might have doubted that he was indeed reacting to her. If your pet barks before the helper "sees" her, the agitator should do what Mike did when he "discovered" Greta's presence. "Badly startled . . . frozen in place, he was a man afraid." That's the first reaction an agitator should send: The human fears the dog, not because of anything she is doing but just because she exists. This empowers the animal. A canine's sensing of human fear can catapult her responses to the boil-over point; then she not only has the edge, she knows it. The fact that sensing fear can kindle canine bravery is a cornerstone of agitation.

"Mike shuffled backward a few paces." In a tense situation, backing away from a dog attracts her. Mike knew this. Now you do. It elicits the response you want—your pet moving toward the helper—while making the animal think it was her idea.

"Staying well behind" (so as not to distract), "I moved with her, keeping the leash taut." Though I could have just let out more leash, I followed Greta to protect Mike: Had he fallen and had she tried to bite him, I could more easily have reined her in using less leash length. For reasons of physics, controlling a wired canine is easier using a shorter length of leash.

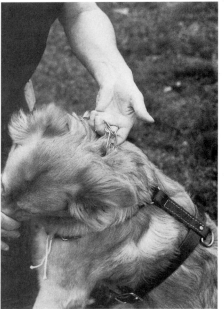

Whatever your grip preference, avoid this one. A large, powerful dog's lunge can injure your hand.

Another no-no. A dog's movement as you grab his pinch collar's links this way can snap or dislocate your fingers.

Mike "was playing the animal, beautifully." In drawing Greta out, he was training her.

Mike "curled his upper lip." He displayed his teeth to rile Greta further, knowing that the act signifies challenge among canines. Then, Mike "maneuvered toward her, stalking her." At this point some dogs fall apart. Their genes won't allow them to fight when flight is possible. Although there are ways to try to overcome hesitancy, it's better to train the right dog, one whose first reaction is not to run away.

"I tightened the leash. Again [the dog] stepped forward." Too much restraint would have halted Greta; too little could have had the same effect. When you pull a curious canine one way, she reacts by pulling in the opposite direction. Take an untrained dog for an on-leash walk and you'll discover the truth of this. Use the principle to drive a protector forward.

"Mike stopped dead in his tracks." He wanted to let Greta build herself up more before using his sack. Had he been unsure whether to stop or swing

Some trainers pass a length behind the back near waist height, but they still hold the leash with two hands.

I prefer to keep the lead in front of me. Suit yourself as to style, but never use only one hand.

the sack, he would have stopped. When in doubt, don't escalate. Don't risk defeating a primary objective: letting your pet build self-confidence. Greta believed Mike stopped because he feared the mightiness of her dog self. Her self-assurance was expanding second by second.

"Mike again eased toward her." Had he detected hesitancy in Greta, he would have backed off so as not to lose what we had achieved so far.

"Suddenly he snapped his sack downward at his side." He wanted to draw attention to the object; but notice he didn't snap the burlap *at* Greta. That could have been premature. It might have driven her backward. First get the animal's attention, then madden that focus.

"I paid out another two feet of leash," because "the Shepherd snarled and lunged against her restraints." She was trying to reach Mike, so I abetted her. The lead's tension provides the dog with a sense of security—you, her friend and pack leader, are at its other end. That's why I slackened the lead slowly, rather than all at once, to avoid the possibility of spooking Greta by making her feel cut adrift. As mentioned, leash pressure can drive a curious dog forward; gradual slack in a confident animal's lead can have the same effect.

"Mike stamped his feet." In the animal world, from ants to elephants, tapping or scraping a foot on the ground communicates danger (ants whack their heads against stones in their tunnels). The act can also signify a challenge. Mike gave this signal to arouse Greta further. As you see, it worked: "Rising onto her back legs, the dog roared and pawed the air." This from an animal who had never shown hostility toward any human.

"Mike raced away, terrified and shrieking." Another victory for Greta, her biggest so far. "He looked back just before ducking behind a tree," accenting that she had triggered his flight.

Mike allowed Greta a few moments for processing, then returned for more *in-out, back-out*: The agitator moves *in* (toward the dog), drawing the animal *out*, then reacts by moving *back*, thus luring her *out* farther.

"He stared wide-eyed at the dog's mouth." Riveting on an angry dog's jaws can provoke a flash of fangs. Though some dogs never get around to displaying their enamel, preferring instead just to growl and bark, "She bared her teeth." That's why "Mike ducked lower," to show fear of Greta's response.

"Mike flicked the sack right at her face." We had reached another critical juncture. With a hesitant animal, delay the sack attack until she can handle it. Settle for the dog running the bad guy off. Mike's reading of Greta coincided with mine, however: She could handle fight work now.

Greta "snapped at the burlap but Mike flipped it just out of reach." Try not to let the dog grab the sack on the first try; make her fight to reach it. "He whipped the sack behind his leg," to shift Greta's attention from the burlap onto himself, as focusing on the bad guy is an overall goal. I mean, we're training a manstopper, not a sackstopper. One purpose of sack work is to present an easy first target in a manner relatively safe for the agitator.

Allow a few seconds between each sack attack, to let the dog's craving and frustration grow. Mike "stamped his feet again" to keep Greta focused on him during these interludes.

Besides, we didn't want to hand her too easy a victory. Greta saw Mike's challenge as outright taunting. We wanted her to scream at him for what she wanted. She did. "Now fully aroused, the dog roared as only a German Shepherd can."

Mike changed his aim for his next assault. He "popped the sack near the dog's forepaws." After her second try and miss, "she tore turf, raging in frustration." It was time to let Greta win. Another near miss could have caused her interest to fade. If you aren't sure, let your dog nail the sack. That's safer than risking flameout born of too much failure.

"I eased toward her" unobtrusively, so as not to distract, "gathering the leash as I went"—to give Greta lunging room when I released the excess. We want to teach the dog from day one that she should hit as hard as she can. Thus, provide space for your pet to build momentum.

"My gesture unseen by the dog" (it wouldn't do for her to conclude that Mike and I were in cahoots), "I pointed at Mike. He jumped back"—one last enticement—"and extended the burlap just as I slackened several feet of leash." I let go of enough leash so that Greta could nail the sack, but not so much that she could reach Mike himself. "Action!" Like the "Listen" cue, teach "Action" by verbal-bridging: Link the command with the animal's response.

"A roaring black-and-red blur flew at the assailant." This raises an often overlooked yet important point. Mike had frustrated Greta to such an extent that he and I sensed that, when released, she would charge with everything she had. She did, and thereby further discovered her own strength and power—which increased her escalating confidence and led to more strength and power.

An instant after Greta reached the sack, "I tightened the leash to prevent further advance," to drive the dog forward and to protect Mike, should he stumble or should the animal spit out the sack and go for him.

Q. What if a dog gets lucky and bites the sack before you intended?

A. The helper should do what Mike did when Greta grabbed the burlap: Fight with the animal, then let go and get gone. Don't try to take the sack from the dog with the idea of starting over. Don't negate her conquest.

"For a suspended moment man and dog locked in combat." To have merely thrust the sack at Greta would have cheapened her victory. After grabbing the burlap, Mike's reaction said he wanted it back. Greta won. Mike heightened her achievement by timing his release: "Just then the snarling animal bucked backward and jerked her head." Mike knew that the dog would do this, so when she did, he "instantly let go," rather than disengaging while the dog pulled steadily. We wanted Greta to feel that her jerking action had won the battle.

Mike's method of release, "falling away and rolling clear," was to protect himself by getting out of range as part of the same movement. Also, by falling away from Greta, Mike created the illusion she had knocked him down, which further raised her confidence.

Mike "scrambled to his feet and bellowed defeat as he ran to the trees." Greta had won the sack, scared the bad guy and run him off, all in one action.

"I eased to her side." Be careful how and when you do this. Allow the dog to settle for a few seconds. Let her come back to Earth, lest ye be gnawed.

"I patted my leg"; this is a testimony to Greta's stability and a reminder to work only with sound dogs. A schizophrenic animal might have reacted by nailing the patted area, sensing that the gesture signified she should continue her aggression toward the new target.

"My hand gently rubbing her neck" is a seemingly minor point, but get in the habit of petting your dog only on the head, neck, chest or withers (shoulders). When we discuss "Out!" (in Chapter 13), the reason will be easy to see.

Another soft point: Beginning with your pet's first nailing of a sack, never deprive her of a bite when visiting the training location. Don't let her come away empty. Ever. Remember, the dog always wins.

Back at our car, Greta dropped the sack as I unbuckled her harness and reattached my short leash to her collar. I drew no attention to the decimated burlap, but just left it where it fell. Mike knew to pick it up after our departure. At this stage, it matters little whether the dog drops the sack two seconds after the agitator flees or continues to hold it until her next meal. Once you've left the training area, though, remove the sack from your pet's sight and scent when she does release it.

Q. Why not leave it around for her to chew?

A. She'd get bored with it, a mindset we surely don't want when it comes to her protection training. Besides, if it disappears, a subtle lesson is conveyed: Hang on!

Next

During the following day, do no agitation and don't visit the training site. Take your dog to familiar, peaceful places, have friends pet her, and let the session's lessons simmer while you provide situations offering marked contrast to bitework. Show your pet that all humans have not suddenly changed into Darth Vader.

Watch for an onset of improper aggression toward strangers. I've never seen such a spillover, but I know it's possible. However, don't get on your pet's case should she woof at someone during a stroll. Instead, command her to heel and alter your route. Should the animal continue to rage, correct her for her failure

The next six photographs are of a sequence. First the agitator entices the dog to bite the sack.

Sensing mild uncertainty in the dog, the helper feeds him the sack.

The dog, having bitten the sack, struggles to pull it from the helper.

To prolong the battle, the helper drops to one knee to operate at the dog's level and from a less-dominating position.

Once the dog secures the sack, the helper moves away.

A transition step can be to entice the dog with a sleeve, having first loosened the sleeve cover so the dog can pull it free (instead of suddenly winding up with a surprisingly heavy object). Notice the helper is bending so as not to tower over and inhibit this young animal.

to heel. Don't "reassure" your pet if she fires by patting her and telling her, "Everything's okay." That sends the wrong signal as, in her eyes, it constitutes praise.

If she continues to storm at every new face, terminate her protection training forthwith. She's unstable. One session as described won't carry over like that with a psychologically sound, properly socialized dog who has a history of friendliness toward strangers.

Whew!

That's what an obedience-knowledgeable friend who knew nothing about protection training said after reviewing this chapter. "I never realized how much was involved." Lest you feel similarly overwhelmed, know that while this first segment is extensive, you will use many of its principles and techniques again and again. We have a good deal yet to cover, yes, but far less than when you opened this book.

Reflection

Acquiring a dog may be the only opportunity a human ever has to choose a relative.

Mordecai Siegal

ACTION!

Tank was a Rottweiler of daunting proportions and scant reticence. His strike was an avalanche and his thunderous roar could make you jump off your bones. As a toothpick-chewing friend once mused, "A steamroller, with teeth."

Tank's first session paralleled Greta's in structure and result, except for one detail: After grabbing the sack, Tank spat it out and went for Jenny.

"Before he went for the sack he charged and looked past it. At me!" she said, describing the typical action of a dog who would rather take the person. "That beast understudied at Jurassic Park. He's outside the margins, I tell you!"

Agitator anger right after a near miss is not uncommon.

Most protectors, after wresting a sack from a bad guy, look away from the agitator, if just for a second. To the mind of an inexperienced dog, the sack, not the human, is the momentary attraction, and it's as though the animal wants to see what he has taken hold of. A dog who stares unabated at the helper sends a clear message: He wants something—or, more specifically, some-one—else.

Given Tank's poundage and power, I made one subtle adjustment: I attached my leash to the front ring of his harness, the one near the withers (shoulder blades), not the rear one. A lead on the front ring gives the handler more leverage than one attached to the back ring.

Now, amid all this, Jenny made an error. I want to tell you about it before detailing Tank's second training period.

Recall from Chapter 9 that during Greta's first session, "I pointed at Mike. He jumped back and extended the burlap just as I slackened several feet of leash," and you know the rest. Focus on the sequencing: he jumped back and then extended. It's crucial because that's what I anticipated Jenny would do with Tank; it's a pattern my agitators follow when we're ready for the dog to nail the

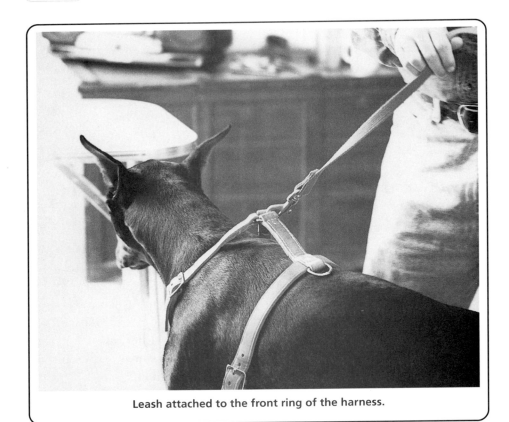

Leash attached to the front ring of the harness.

sack—they jump back *before* extending the burlap. It's also where Jenny blundered; she forgot to move back first. She was three feet from Tank when she raised the burlap. I had expected her to be five feet back and had freed that much leash. She began her move backward *as*, not before, she offered the target.

As Jenny stretched the cloth barrier between her hands, I recovered what slack I could. Even so, the dog strung me out like a kite tail as he slammed against Jenny with a lung-emptying blow, and she hit the ground with all the elegance of a sack of grain.

"Thank God the burlap was between me and the Grand Canyon of teeth there," she said later. "I think he bit the thing only to get it out of his way."

By the time Tank bit, Jenny was rolling clear and I was leaning backward against the lead. Final score: Jenny had a new-found appreciation of the adage "Keep your head in the game," my back needed liniment from restraining the raging 800-pound Rottweiler, and Tank was clearly ready for sleeve work.

I relate this incident to remind you that protection work can be most unforgiving of mistakes. The action is viper quick. Jenny's skill and mine, along with each of us having fast access to the reptile part of the brain where the instincts and reflexes lie in wait, combined to save her from injury.

But good luck played a part, too, and in protection work you don't ever want to count on luck, because "good" isn't the only shade it comes in. That, and luck always changes.

Tank's Second Session

The mammoth dog stood as still as the morning air as Jenny appeared from behind the deserted factory. When Tank spotted her I whispered "Listen," as I had at his first session. Aside from a twitch of his scalp muscles, the dog seemed not to hear me.

He was tracking Jenny, but just by moving his eyes. He closed his mouth in concentration and held his massive head still. John Dryden's caveat, "Beware the fury of a patient man," applies to dogs as well. At least to this one. Tank seemed to have decided that Jenny may have thwarted him yesterday, but today he would prevail. He'd bide his time. He'd wait.

Q. Dogs think?

A. Dogs think.

Some canines sense from day one that this is no lark. Tank was one such dog. He saw Jenny as an adversary, someone he must defeat. Few dogs reach this level right away—Greta didn't—but when one does, you should recognize and foster the behavior. To do less is to dumb the animal down.

Jenny skittered toward us in a cone pattern that tapered toward Tank. Moving in quick go-and-stop fashion, right to left to right to left, she crouched less than the day before.

I hauled back on the lead to drive Tank forward. It was wasted effort. He stood stock still, unaffected, tracking Jenny's zigzag movements, waiting for her to come within range. An image came to mind: an alligator, motionless as a log, with only the beast's ancient eyes glinting above a swamp's murky surface as a small, unsuspecting creature swims toward it.

Dogs who remain immobile while eyeing a target often swing for the fences when the agitator nicks the strike zone. They seldom bark, growl or even bare

Tank, double-leashed and ready to work.

their teeth in warning, lest they alert the prey. Though most dogs vent accumulating tensions by intermittent barking and movement, the Tanks of the world let the pressure build, second by second, until they reach critical mass and the moment is at hand—at mouth.

Session two often matches the first. Igniting the dog's aggression drives remains the focal point, since more than one exposure is often needed to kindle enough fire to get the animal ready for sleeve work. Given Tank's reaction to the sack, however, Jenny and I were moving on.

Jenny wore a heavily padded soft sleeve on her left arm. In her right hand she carried an agitation whip. She scurried to a halt six feet in front of Tank and to his right. Facing the dog sideways, she swiftly stamped her feet and screeched, "C'mon you sparrow brain!" Tank didn't flinch. Spearing her with his gaze, he ignored her dance. Jenny jabbed the sleeve at him several times, but Tank remained a statue. Then Jenny cocked her head, said, "What the hell?" and charged.

Did the term "agitation whip" leap out at you? Upon first hearing about one, many people react with, "My God! They're going to beat the dog!" Rest easy. Canines aren't beaten at my kennels, during guard training or for any other reason. The agitator cracks the whip to her side, behind her leg, or hits the ground in front of a dog, but not the animal himself. A whip's high-pitched sound, which a dog can hear but you and I cannot, excites.

Jenny snapped her whip and screamed a thought-provoking expletive as she darted at the Rottweiler. Watching his eyes, she kept the sleeve level and inches from her side as she dashed within two feet of Tank's muzzle, attempting to feed him the cylinder. I put pressure on the leash to drive the dog forward, but he remained rooted. An instant later Jenny shrieked "Gotcha!" and popped Tank's nose with her sleeve as she flew past him. That was when Tank came to life, much like dynamite comes to life.

Do you know why Jenny watched Tank's eyes as she ran toward him? She knew that where the gaze goes, the dog follows. Eyes presage direction. Jenny would be very close to Tank, so she wanted to see him tracking her sleeve or upper body, not her legs.

Now, consider another point: Tank was being mule stubborn. Clearly, he had drive, but when Jenny "darted at the Rottweiler" and "I put pressure on the leash to drive the dog forward," he refused to react. He wanted Jenny, but on his terms. Just as resistance to sit on command results in a collar yank, failure to fire at someone threatening him got his beak bopped. Result?

Enraged does not do justice to Tank's reaction. Jenny's after-session comment, "A seething wolverine on PCP," comes closer, though I would call it a seething, indignant, HUGE wolverine on PCP—one who looked a lot like a Rottweiler.

I yelled "Action!" an instant before the black-and-rust powerhouse nearly jerked me out of my shoes. As it was, I ended up skiing across the dried lawn. I turned my feet sideways to dig in as Jenny circled back to her initial run-by starting point, six feet in front of Tank and to his right.

Facing him, Jenny jerked her sleeved arm from side to side: to the left, freeze a beat, to the right, freeze a beat. Tank roared like a winter wind. Jenny hummed "Black Diamond" and teased the animal by blowing kisses as he repositioned himself in rhythm with her every move. She saw she was running the dog. Even so, Tank was primed, straining violently against the lead and snarling like an NFL linebacker. Jenny knew she'd have to make her next move just so. She scraped a foot along a patch of bare ground.

Jenny's return "to her initial run-by starting point" demonstrates an important agitation technique related to working a new dog: Repeat successful patterns. In agitation's early stages, the helper should give the dog a sequence and, if it works, stick with it so the animal knows what's coming. Then the dog has a better shot at success, which is the whole idea.

Of equal importance, ineffective techniques, ones that don't produce instant positive results, should be dropped for that particular animal. I've heard trainers holler, "Try it again! He'll get it!" and more often than not the result has been a defeated dog. The idea is not to make the creature fit into the trainer's scheme of what *should* work, but for the trainer to discern what will speak to the dog.

Jenny cracked her whip. I tightened the leash, ostensibly to hold Tank back. This time it had the desired effect—he pulled forward.

Jenny froze, staring at Tank. He imitated her. His eyes cast a muddy light, like a match shimmering behind dark glass. Jenny snapped her whip and raced toward him. I slackened the leash. Tank felt the sudden freedom and became a runaway freight train. "Action!"

Jenny yelled, "Great God!" as the dog crashed against her. He engulfed the sleeve and Jenny released it as she allowed his momentum to knock her out of range. She hit the ground rolling and leaped up screaming as she ran toward the factory. Tank gave the sleeve a murderous shake, then dropped it and tried to persuade me to let him chase Jenny.

I led the dog from the area, patting his neck and telling him what a good job he'd done. He heard me but had other things on his mind, for as we walked from the training site he kept looking back at the factory, where he'd last seen Jenny.

Q. Why quit when the dog is doing so well?

A. That's the best time to stop, when an animal has just won a tremendous victory yet is still hungry. A dog's mindset at the finish of one session becomes his psychological starting point at the next.

Scrutiny

I told you Tank's first session paralleled Greta's. What changes did you spot in his second agitation?

Start with "as still as the morning air." Since wind direction wasn't a factor, "Jenny appeared from behind the deserted factory," not the trees, where she had hidden before. As mentioned, for now we use the same location for each session, but the agitator should use different blinds to heighten alertness.

Note, too, this was not an afternoon session. Do enough agitation every day at noon, for instance, and in time your pet will become antsy around lunch time. Worse, he could learn that aggression is proper only then. Vary your training times.

"Jenny skittered toward us" to make it clear to Tank that she was suspect, "in a cone pattern that tapered toward Tank" to emphasize the fact that she was zeroing in on him. She moved "in quick go-and-stop fashion" to attract and excite him. Also, Jenny "crouched less than the day before" to seem more confident and more challenging, which is also why she faced Tank not sideways but frontally when "she swiftly stamped her feet."

"Jenny jabbed the sleeve at him several times" to get a rise out of Tank. When he didn't react, why do you suppose I didn't pull his leash forward, toward Jenny? For three reasons. One, the essential fire has to come from the dog's natural reservoir of defense drives; the trainer should not induce it.

Q. Why not?

A. If the dog is right for the work, such priming won't be necessary. If he isn't right, he shouldn't be there.

Two, pulling the dog forward could make him move backward. Remember, pull an inquisitive dog in one direction and he reacts by moving in the opposite direction.

Three, push the wrong dog forward, one you have misread, and anxiety may cause the animal to go for you.

That last point needs a bit of expansion. I perceived Tank as a manstopper candidate of the first order. I also knew that no trainer is perfect, not just in handling but also in reading man's best buddy. A dog who reacts like Tank, with smoldering patience, often goes off like a string of firecrackers when he does respond. But a small percentage remains frozen out of fright. Such a dog, if pushed toward the fear stimulus, may try to nail the pusher. I sensed Tank had never met fear, didn't even know its name, that when he was born he probably hit the ground running. But he was not *my* dog. Like Greta, I was training him for his owner. I knew the animal, but only up to a point. Thus springs a trainer's corollary to agitation's first three rules: Protect yourself, protect yourself, protect yourself.

"Jenny jerked her sleeved arm from side to side" to draw Tank's focus to the sleeve while not wearing herself out by hopping about. Agitation tires all concerned, but especially the helper. Quick, side-to-side sleeve movements fatigue the bad guy less but excite a dog every bit as much as sudden dashes left and right.

"Jenny froze" to further empower Tank while threatening him—sudden cessation of movement is a challenge—and to allow him a final moment of concentration before she made her move.

"I yelled 'Action!'" Like "Listen," teach "Action" by timing the word with the dog's act. Has Tank learned the verbal trigger at this point? No. We've suggested it has meaning, but that's all we've done. He will learn over the next few sessions that it's a command, similar in one respect to one that calls a dog to his owner: It says, "Okay, you can do it now."

Tank "engulfed the sleeve and Jenny released it," to ensure the dog instant success. Soon he would have to wrench the sleeve from the helper, but you should enable victory during startup sessions. Jenny "leaped up screaming as she ran toward the factory" to accent Tank's triumph, that he had overpowered her and captured her sleeve, that he had made her afraid of him.

Greta's Second Session

Though Tank was clearly ready for sleeve work, Greta contented herself with cloth, a fact she evinced by hanging on to the burlap and by not trying to pursue the helper. With Tank we poked a stick into a hornets' nest; we got the dog mad, stuck a sleeve in his face and let him vent his rage, knowing dogs generally do so against the nearest available moving object. Because Greta's innate aggression levels were lower than Tank's, as most dogs' are, we got her onto a sleeve with a different approach.

Crouched less than before, Mike approached in cone fashion. He harassed Greta with his sack, twice swinging it at her, both times causing her to miss. As her rage hit its flashpoint, he ran in panic to his sanctuary behind the factory. Moments later he sneaked toward us, but in addition to dragging a sack, he wore a medium-strength sleeve on his left arm.

Using his right hand, he swung the burlap once more at Greta. Again she missed, but this time her teeth cracked together like the snap of a large branch. She was ready for better things. Mike quickly wrapped the sack around the sleeve, staring at the objects to focus Greta's attention on them.

Then Mike stamped his feet, snapped his whip and raced past the German Shepherd, extending his sleeved arm toward her. As she jumped at the sleeve-sack, I let out slack and said "Action!" A second after she bit, Mike allowed her to pull the combination from his arm and fled, screeching as though pursued by the Furies. Greta strode to the car carrying her prizes, her pride radiating like a rainbow after a spring shower.

For the same reason that obedience people don't switch trainers daily with new dogs, during initial agitation don't change helpers often.

Q. Why not?

A. It's easier for a canine to learn from one person than from a committee. Remember, the agitator teaches more actively. Also, as mentioned a few pages ago when discussing run-by techniques, "Repeat successful patterns."

Point two: Just as you have to show a puppy the stick before you throw it, we married the sack to the sleeve while Greta observed. Of course, when she bit the former she got the latter.

At the next session I said "Listen" as Mike crept toward us wearing a sack-enshrouded sleeve. From six feet away he popped his whip and stamped his feet. I slackened the lead and said "Action!" As Greta grabbed the sack-sleeve, Mike released the combination and ran.

Within seconds he reappeared. On his left arm he wore a sleeve, but this one was sans sack. As Greta dropped her prize and watched him approach, I said "Listen!" A moment later she held the second sleeve as she stared at Mike's disappearing form. If the new sleeve's lack of sack troubled her, she hid her feelings well.

Mike is demonstrating a vital safety tenet of the helper's credo: Even when running from a dog, don't take your eyes off him.

Sheathing the sleeve with the sack made a bridge that led Greta to the sleeve. Then, once she was with the program, Mike switched to a sleeve alone.

Q. Why not just show Greta a sleeve in the first place and see what happens?

A. Such an abrupt change could produce hesitation, which, once induced, is difficult to eradicate. It could have also led Greta to go over or under the sleeve, at Mike. When first seeing a sleeve, some dogs perceive not a target but a barrier. I didn't read Greta as having that tendency, but remember: When in doubt—that is, when you are not sure—play it safe.

Reflection

Why is it that my heart is so touched whenever I meet a dog lost in our noisy streets? Why do I feel such anguished pity when I see one of these creatures coming and going, sniffing everyone, frightened, despairing of ever finding its master?

Emile Zola

CHAPTER 12

THE NEXT THREE HOURS

As no training period should exceed 20 minutes, this chapter outlines the next nine sessions. Approximately. Repressing a quick learner serves no good purpose, yet no dog should be pushed faster than he can develop. Some need several sack experiences, for instance, before they're ready for sleeves. I'm not suggesting these animals are stupid; unintelligent dogs should not be guard trained. But some dogs, like some people, need longer to grasp certain concepts and build confidence. This makes them no better or worse than others—such terms don't even apply—it's just part of who they are.

But understand: A fast learner does not just pick up an idea's hints and whispers, he quickly locks in entire concepts. Remember, too, never proceed to a next step until the dog is rock solid on the one before it. You're training for the future, not the immediate moment. Ignoring that counsel cannot only stress out a willing animal and impede his training, it can get someone hurt.

The training periods described in *Manstopper* follow a session one, session two format for chronology purposes, but think of them as stages or phases, not days or sessions. Stage one entices hostility, the next stage induces biting a sack. Both levels are often reached during the first session. Phase three inaugurates sleeve work.

Agitators: As you progress through these stages, beware *acceleration*, whereby a hesitant dog erupts as though suddenly making up for lost time. The phenomenon often occurs in initially reticent dogs.

Alike, Yet Different

Greta and Tank represented the behavioral tolerances acceptable in a guardian. As you see, it's a narrow spectrum. Both favored fight over flight, but Greta settled for objects while Tank keyed on warm-blooded prey. These tendencies bespeak a breed disparity but not an absolute—I've known more than one German Shepherd to react toward agitators as the Rottweiler did, and vice versa. It's safer to presume that every new dog will respond like Tank.

Both dogs' inclinations needed slight adjustments. This is typical, as no canine hits a zenith during Act One. My approach is to elicit innate reactions, then polish the responses over time.

I'm feeding a sleeve to a novice protector whose owner had forcefully taught him never to jump on a human. In time the animal will have to take the sleeve very near the bad guy's body, but before we can expect such confident acts, we have to build his desire for biting to a point where it will override his hesitancy.

Possession of fabric so satisfied Greta that I felt she might quit a real fight after ripping an assailant's clothing. On the street, that could prove embarrassingly bad form.

Tank targeted the person, which is as it should be, but a dog can be too eager to drop a slipped sleeve and go after the helper. A proclivity for the quick release and rebite can produce a rip-and-slash artist who inflicts unwarranted damage by biting again and again along an arm. Also, it could further heighten the danger attendant to teaching "Out" (meaning "Let go"). To teach that command the dog first must be holding on, and for reasons you will discover

Attaching a leash to the retaining strap on a sleeve-cover.

in Chapter 13, it's safer to begin "Out" lessons by making a dog drop a sleeve the helper has shed, rather than one being worn.

Tank's Third Session

Tank furrowed the ground in rage as Jenny shouted abuse at the Rottweiler and stamped her feet while jerking her sleeve from side to side and cracking her whip. Just before the dog topped out, I slackened the leash and said "Action!"

As Tank struck, I pulled against his lead just hard enough to stimulate him to hang on. Jenny leaned away, trying to pull the sleeve from him. Tank clamped down with awesome force.

We wanted to teach Tank to hold on. You see how we did it. We triggered his inherent tenacity by trying to pull him from the sleeve and it from him. I hauled the dog one way while Jenny, still wearing the sleeve, pulled the other. It's a balancing act: not enough force to make Tank actually let go, but enough that he had to struggle to hang on. He soon became a devotee of the hit-hard-and-bite-harder school of protection work.

As Tank gave a mighty yank, Jenny slipped the sleeve and tightened the six-foot lead she had earlier clipped to its outer cover. I maintained enough leash pressure so that Tank couldn't jump toward her, to protect Jenny while driving him to maintain his hold. To yield to the force Jenny and I exerted, Tank would have had to release the sleeve, which he was not about to do.

We wanted Tank to maintain his bite even after Jenny slipped the sleeve. Again, this was to make teaching "Out" safer. It's also a proofing scheme. A dog who won't release a dropped sleeve tends to hang on to one being worn. Ergo, in a real setting, the animal knows not to quit before he's commanded. This lesson, that the dog should tear the sleeve from the bad guy and continue to hold on, transfers to real-world settings by teaching the animal to bite, yank and hang on, slamming an assailant to the ground and keeping him there.

Insight

To make a dog crave something, suggest that he is about to lose it. It's as though the following exchange occurs between human and dog:

Owner: "Do you want this new thing?"

Dog: "Not particularly." Yawn. Scratch.

Owner: "Then—you can't have it!"

Dog: "Oh! In that case, let me at it!"

The pull on the leash Jenny had attached to the sleeve cover made Tank feel he had not subdued the sleeve, that it still lived and was fighting him.

Q. Whoa! How could a bright dog like Tank think a sleeve was alive, capable of combat?

A. The sight of wounded prey fires a harsh sequence in a canine brain, enough so that the reactive process loosens torrents of saliva. Remember, we are educating a *dog*, an animal whose perceptions and frontal lobes are not the same as ours. Were the sleeve not an opponent in Tank's mind, he would have held on after Jenny's release only from play drive; and as Jenny and I can attest, this dog wasn't playing.

Ten seconds later Jenny dropped her leash and stood stock still several steps from Tank while he slammed the sleeve from side to side, slaying it. I reduced my pull but kept enough tension to protect Jenny and maintain Tank's interest on the object.

The sleeve slaughtered, Tank released it. Unlike his first session, however, he didn't go for Jenny next. He didn't have time. As the sleeve hit the ground I kicked it to her and she jammed her arm into it and cracked her whip.

"Action!"

For Tank, the sleeve had been resurrected.

Jenny and I repeated the sequence: I pulled one way, she the other, and after a brief but heartfelt skirmish she slipped the sleeve and pulled against her leash attached to it. Tank decimated the prey, Jenny dropped her lead and, seconds later, Tank released the sleeve. Once more I booted it to Jenny and we commenced the day's final fight. At its conclusion we added an embellishment.

"My dog's put up with you long enough. Get the hell gone!" I said, pointing in the direction Jenny should go.

"Okay, I'm going. You just keep that miserable beast back."

The words meant nothing to Tank, of course, but the tones and gestures confirmed that Jenny was still not a nice person. She and I had engaged in some obvious teamwork (obvious to a human, anyway), and an intelligent dog like Tank could have gotten a glimmer that Jenny was no longer an enemy. Our parting shots dispelled any such notions.

Greta's Fourth Session

Mike edged our way, his sleeved left arm toward us, his right arm hidden behind him. Hissing at Greta, he stamped his feet. As I restrained the raging German Shepherd, Mike flipped the sleeve from his arm, causing it to land at the dog's feet.

Greta dove at the lifeless object and took it in her jaws. Just then Mike rapped her neck with the sleeve she hadn't noticed on his right arm.

Even during double-sleeve agitation, close-in work is very dangerous. Greta might have nailed a leg before Mike could jump away, which he did just as he bopped the dog. That is, he didn't strike the animal and wait to see how she would react—he struck and jumped away in one motion. He was betting that Greta would retaliate against his sleeve, since it had struck her and was moving. He won. This time.

Greta dropped the first sleeve and tore the second one from Mike. As she turned away to demolish her new prize, Mike yanked out the whip he had concealed in a hip pocket, swatted its handle against the dog's butt and leaped back. It was good

that he did—leap back, that is—as Greta missed him by an eyelash. Mike let out a
whoop and made tracks for elsewhere.

Greta learned much during those busy seconds: Snatching a sleeve doesn't mean the fight is over, never turn your back on an assailant and the problem is the person, not his armor.

Now remember, we never beat dogs. The swats with sleeve and whip handle were just that: swats, not whacks. Their purpose is to refocus the dog's attention, not wallop her.

Chaska's Fifth Session

The red-and-rust Doberman bitch was stunning in many ways. Chaska was gorgeous, as tough as an old boot, didn't know the word *bluff* and led one agitator to consider taking up another line of work: "Something calmer, like defusing ticking bombs."

My immediate goals for Chaska were increased focus when hearing "Listen," an instantaneous bite-and-hold response to "Action" and incorporating her obedience knowledge with guard work.

Many dogs grasp the "Listen" concept at once. They hear the cue timed with the appearance of a curiously garbed person rambling toward them, and understand. Each canine sees things in her own special light, however, and Chaska's perceptions needed some fine-tuning.

"Listen" isn't vague, but it can be subtle. While "Listen" means "be alert and focus on the person," it also implies, " . . . because I sense trouble." For a dog who enjoys confrontation, as any manstopper should, the command's second element provides motivation for the first and heightens communication—and thus teamwork—between handler and dog.

When we arrived at the training site Chaska became antsy, hopping about and
looking toward the trees where she last saw Mitch, the agitator, the day before. I
peered at the grove, shrugged and sat on the ground.

Chaska looked at me as though I'd lost my mind.

At one point I thought she might stand on her rear legs and frantically gesture
with a front paw toward the trees. I just bowed my head as though dozing.

The dog trotted to me, licked my face and whined in consternation. I raised my
head, gazed at the grove, shrugged my shoulders and nodded off once more. Chaska
looked at the trees, paced, said "Wurf" and sprawled next to me.

A minute passed. Chaska rested her chin on her forepaws. Soon her eyelids were flickering. A few more seconds crept by.

My head jerked up. Chaska caught the movement and imitated it. I craned my head forward, then leaped up while staring at the grove. Chaska did the same. Still focused on the trees, I leaned toward the Doberman and extended my arm. I pointed at the aspens and whispered "Listen." Tingling with excitement, Chaska stared at where I was pointing.

Two seconds later Mitch emerged from behind a tree. As he sneaked toward us I repeated the cue softly: "Listen."

Chaska glanced at me, made eye contact, then looked again at Mitch and leaned forward and closed her mouth, concentrating. "Bingo," I thought, "she's getting the idea." I'd seen a light in her eyes, a learning phenomenon I call the moment of recognition.

Mitch scurried close and enticed Chaska to bite. She obliged him. Cursing admirably, Mitch scuffled with her, then slipped the sleeve and ran to the grove, leaving the Doberman delighted with her prize. She shook the sleeve violently, then dropped it and stared with longing at the trees.

Chaska enjoyed protection's bite and fight aspects more than she did mere possession. Dogs with this tendency will sometimes come off a slipped sleeve before an agitator can get out of range. Moral: Always release and retreat in the same motion.

Guiding her with my leash and nudging her with my legs, I aimed the Doberman toward the factory. I pointed at it. "Listen." Chaska spun toward the grove. Not quite, I thought, once more maneuvering the animal toward the building. Again I pointed at it and stage-whispered "Listen." Before Chaska could turn away, Mike leaped from behind the structure and began slinking toward us. "Listen," I repeated. Chaska glanced up at me. Her eyes said "Aha!" Leaning forward, she glared at Mike as he edged toward us.

You see what Chaska thought "Listen" meant: locations, not people. She believed she should focus on either the trees or wherever she last saw the bad guy. Notice "she spun toward the grove" after I aimed her toward the factory and said "Listen." During her first three sessions Mitch had hidden among the aspens, owing to wind direction. Thus, whatever conclusion Chaska had reached was understandable from her point of view. The first clue that she had learned the wrong lesson was her excitement toward the trees when we arrived. When I steered her toward the factory and Mike appeared just after I said "Listen," she started to get the idea to zero in on a person rather than a place. But the Dobie still could have thought "Listen" referred to a location, just a different one. Clarification was on the way.

After Chaska blasted Mike's sleeve, he retreated to the factory. She dropped the cylinder and I petted her and told her what a neat dog she was. Then I turned her toward the trees, aligned myself in the heel position and commanded "Sit." She sat. Just then another helper, Bud, appeared from the grove and walked toward us.

Chaska had learned obedience months before, but this marked the first time I tapped that knowledge during agitation. I began with "Sit" because it was the first command she learned. It was an old and comfortable friend.

The agitators' persona and appearance had changed during this time, too, from less crouching and fewer raggedy coats to more normal and everyday behaviors.

Chaska glanced at me as Bud approached. Dressed in normal street clothes, he walked casually and paid us no particular mind. I said nothing but watched the man. Chaska stood as he neared us. I repeated "Sit." Momentarily embarrassed, Chaska sat. (My dogs know that "Sit" or "Lie down" includes "Stay.") Bud greeted us as he passed within 10 feet. I returned his salutation and returned my attention to the trees. Chaska followed my gaze.

A few seconds later Jenny appeared. Like Bud, she didn't act odd in any way. "Hi" she beamed in passing, adding, "nice Doberperson." Jenny held scathing views about political correctness. I thanked her and patted Chaska.

Chaska had never met Bud or Jenny. Travis was new, too.

Travis ambled toward us from the trees. Like Bud and Jenny, he seemed just another person taking in the air. Chaska saw him but didn't seem interested. The effect of routine events was settling in, as I knew it would. When Travis was 15 feet away I pointed at him. "Listen."

The Doberman riveted on Travis. Softly, to reinforce but not distract, I said "Good listen. Good listen."

I praise with "Good," followed by whatever command the dog has just obeyed. Chaska had this format in obedience training—"Good sit," "Good stay" and so on. When she heard "Good listen" after riveting on Travis, she knew she was doing the right thing.

Travis grabbed the sleeve he had stashed behind a shrub. He jammed his arm into the cylinder and ran toward us, yelling threats.

"Action!"

Chaska took it from there.

Bud and Jenny had played harmless folks out for a walk. They provided contrast, to demonstrate that not just anyone who stepped from the grove was a problem. They appeared from the tree line, but the place from which they emerged proved incidental to Chaska, which was part of what we were trying to teach her.

Travis seemed to be just another person taking a constitutional, until I said "Listen." Then, in Chaska's view, he changed. "Listen" said Travis was trouble. When he "ran toward us, yelling threats," he validated her act of locking in on him. From this experience, Chaska learned that "Listen" refers to people, not places.

Chaska's Sixth Session

The Doberman's next session was a continuation of her fifth one: People appeared from different locations and walked past us; I said "Listen" when I wanted Chaska to home in on one of them. This day, however, everyone wore sleeves, a new twist that led Chaska to break her sit-stay twice. Both times I got her back into position with her collar using minimal pressure—not an ounce more than needed. Chaska was not disobeying as in challenging my authority. She was just enthusiastic, hence the minimal pressure, which more approximated a reminder than a true correction. I didn't want to douse her fire, which untoward force can do. Essentially I was saying to her, "I see these people are wearing sleeves—maybe it's a new fashion—but when I've said 'Sit' you must sit until you hear from me."

Q. Does it matter if your dog stands rather than sits, so long as she doesn't move from you?

A. Later it won't, but during initial training the problem can extend. The dog who stands in response to strangers will soon move forward. Later she'll take the next step of lunging. As it's easier to keep a dog sitting than standing in place, reinforce obedience concepts with the sit. Modify this to the stand later, if you wish.

Near session's end, Mike rushed us and Chaska got her bite. That, as you know, was her reward. Mine was watching her as we left the training site, the dog carrying the sleeve and trotting next to me in the regal way that only a Doberman can.

Chaska's Seventh Session

You must confirm for your pet that you play no part in bad-guy bashing, that her victories are hers alone.

Standing on my tiptoes, I attached the woven-steel cable running from Chaska's harness to a chainlink backstop at a deserted Little League diamond. I patted her neck, said "I won't be long" and left her sight.

Notice that I didn't say "Stay" or give any other command. I just wandered off for a bit.

Moments later Mike hopped from a dugout. Methodically slapping his whip handle against his sleeve, he stalked the Doberman.
When I returned moments later I said, "You must have done good, Chaska." Lying comfortably with a paw on the whip, she tore another strand of jute from the sleeve's cover. Mike was nowhere to be seen.

During tie-out agitation, run a stout, non-chewable line to something secure yet flexible to reduce shock when the animal lunges. Attach the cord to it well above the level of the dog's head, so she can't wrap the line around her legs.

This is once-in-the-dog's-life training. Repeated practice can produce an animal you can't leave at a vet's office or a boarding kennel.

Not parenthetically, dogs pick out from sentences words they know, like "good, Chaska." Such approval means a lot to them.

Chaska's Eighth Session

Earlier I timed "Action!" with Chaska's lunge at the sleeve, to link the word with her response. Now I wanted to firm up the lesson that "Action!" was a command, like "Sit," which she must respond to but not anticipate.

"Sit."
Chaska sat at heel. I slackened my leash. Seconds later Mike approached from behind the aged factory. He wore a medium-strength sleeve—Chaska's bite still lacked enough firmness for a hard one—and carried an agitation whip. He halted in a

normal, erect posture six feet from us, his sleeve horizontal at waist height, his whip pointed downward along his leg. Chaska continued sitting.

I nodded. Mike jerked his sleeve upward an inch or so. Chaska stood. I snatched the tab on her pinch collar and sat her. Seconds later Mike flicked his sleeve again. Chaska started but remained sitting. To myself I counted off three seconds. Then, "Action!"

Mike jumped into his catch stance. It was well that he did.

"Good action! Good action!"

After a brief struggle Mike slipped the sleeve, ran to a shrub and jammed his arm into another sleeve he had stowed there. As he moved toward us, Chaska dropped the prize she had just won.

"Sit." *Chaska obeyed.* "You want more trouble?" *I demanded of Mike, now six feet from us. He looked at Chaska. Growling, the dog eyed him like an interrupted meal.*

"Naw" *he said, shaking his head, staring at the Doberman, nervous hesitancy creeping into his voice.* "I be goin'."

He stepped away from us. Then he stopped and turned toward us. "Aw, hell. That dawg ain't so all-fired much." *He spat to one side and raised his whip.* "The South shall rise again!" *He leaped at us.*

"Action!"

A red-and-rust missile hit Mike. He slipped the sleeve and ran like someone in fear for his life, screaming unintelligibly, in Southern. The Dobe, holding the sleeve, watched him go.

"Good action. Hits those high notes right well, doesn't he, Chaska?"

That evening, Mike called me and asked to switch to a hard sleeve.

Stinger's Ninth Session

The year-old Doberman male was well named. Ask any agitator who ever caught him. "A four-legged buzz saw" is not a stretch. "Action!" transformed the curious, affectionate sidekick into an airborne streak. However, "howdy," "Celtics" or a sneeze had the same effect.

Stinger stood next to me as Mitch, be-sleeved, walked toward us. He stopped six feet away, his arms at his sides.

"Get gone," *I ordered him.*

Stinger flew at Mitch. I stopped the handsome animal in mid-leap. I didn't say "No," *because to my dogs* "No" *means* "never." *Pulling him to my side, I shook my head.* "That wasn't the magic word, Stinger."

"It was close," *the dog seemed to protest.*

Stinger next to me once more, I growled at Mitch, "Get lost!"

Stinger flinched forward but halted himself. I glanced at the dog and said "Good."
Then, looking at Mitch, I said "Go on!"

Again, a one-inch forward movement that Stinger himself squelched. I was
watching the animal peripherally, not directly, lest he infer that I expected defense.

Then, "Action!"

Bang!

Stinger's Tenth Session

Jenny swore passionately during her drunken stagger toward us. I'm constrained from
quoting her, but the invectives were colorful, imaginative and offered solid mental
images. For effect, she had sloshed beer on the old coat she was wearing.

I said "Listen," then switched my attention to Jenny. "Keep back! Don't scare
my dog!"

"@*%★!!"

Every session with Jenny was at least a two-cushion shot. I always knew what
she'd do but not how she'd do it.

Stinger growled but made no move to leave my side. Jenny thrashed her arms
out from her sides, then above her head. Stinger snarled, staring at her.

"Now you're fixing to get hurt," I told her. "Get lost!"

"¡œßø~!"

I hadn't known Jenny was bilingual.

"Let's go, Stinger." I told him to heel.

Stinger needed to learn that some confrontations are better deflected. We walked
several yards away, I petted him and told him how well he'd done. Then, as we
neared the decrepit factory, Mike rushed us and Stinger got his daily bite.

Tank's Eleventh Session

Jenny wore a sleeve on each arm. Standing right side toward us, she spun and of-
fered the left-arm sleeve just as I said "Action!" Tank hesitated, but only for an in-
stant. Later, Jenny showed me the sleeve cover. "We're going to need a new one."

This is a subtle yet vital technique, the agitator switching the target at
the last moment. Though I've never seen the move stop a dog cold, I know it
could. And if an animal is going to hesitate, better he so do in practice than
on the street, so we can get him past it.

Footnote

This one is from the school of hard knocks, so to speak. Many hard sleeves are crowned with steel-like plastic to protect the upper arm and shoulder area. A trainer standing near the dog must beware of the sleeve after a helper slips it. The animal, holding it, thrashing it, can whack the plastic against your leg hard enough to make you clutch your shin and leap about, perhaps shouting unprintable oaths.

Reflection

Properly trained, a man can be a dog's best friend.

Corey Ford

CHAPTER 13

OUT!

"Out" means "cease aggression but remain alert." Teach it after your pet is biting with such desire that forcing her to release won't dampen enthusiasm. Teaching "Out" too soon makes a dog anxious in anticipation of the command and causes her to become handler sensitive, which describes a dog who is so extremely attentive to the handler that she will shift her attention from a bad guy to the handler when the handler comes near.

Keep in mind that "Out" demands your pet override some very powerful drives. It is not the dog's way to release prey while it's still kicking.

Don't get me wrong: When the dog should release, she should release. Otherwise the trainer has insufficient control of the animal's behavior. But if a dog is preoccupied—"I have to listen for 'Out'"—or if she diverts her focus whenever the handler approaches, her training is being undermined. In extreme cases she could learn she is better off not biting in the first place.

Tank collided against Jenny and jerked his head sideways to wrest the sleeve from her. She released it, stepped back and stood immobile. Over the next few seconds, things would get pretty dicey.

Flip to the Warning in the front of this book. Read it again. Take notes. The following technique can be very dangerous.

Jenny stood dead still, less than six feet from the well-named Rottweiler. The dog thrashed the sleeve, slamming it about. Standing next to Tank's right shoulder, I said "Out" and counted to three. I could have counted to infinity; Tank wasn't going to release.

Allow the dog three seconds to disengage his teeth from the sleeve's mesh material.

Tank's owner had taught him "Out" for toys. Had this not been so, I would have shown him the command using toys before starting his protection work. In this way it is easier and safer during bitework to command or reinforce "Out," because the dog already knows the word.

Q. What if an animal shows no interest in playing with toys?

A. It signals he may not be right for guard work. Low play drive often goes hand in hand with low prey drive, and a guardian's drive to subdue prey should be high. However, for reasons I've never quite understood, some owners seldom play with their pets, and a dog who has been denied this outlet may hold back at first when shown toys.[1]

Jenny and I had hoped Tank's familiarity with "Out" for play objects would transfer to sleeve work, as it often does. Tank, however, could not make the mental jump, or so he would have had us believe. Remember, the animal had an obstinate streak, a trait not unknown in the breed.

Tank peeked at me from the corner of his eye and continued holding the sleeve. I shook my head, muttered "Rotty stubborn," and glanced at Jenny. She raised an eyebrow and grinned. "Better thee than me." She knew the dangers ahead.

Facing the same direction as Tank, I grabbed both chains of his pinch collar with my right hand, having made sure the chain portion was at the back of his neck, not under his jaw. In the same motion, I shot my left hand over the dog's back and grabbed his left flank, the one farthest from me. As one movement, I squeezed the flank, released it and whipped my left hand behind my back.

The flank is the small patch of loose skin between the floating rib (the 13th) and the upper front part of the rear leg. Flanks are very touch-sensitive. Compressing one as I described causes pain, but I've never known it to injure a dog. I targeted Tank's left flank, the one away from me, as I knew he might spin toward the pressure. Using the right flank could have had him turning not away but toward me, which I preferred he not do.

Q. Why did you grab the collar?

A. To keep Tank in one place or, more to the point, off me.

Q. Has a dog ever gone for you while you were doing this?

A. No.

Q. Then why characterize the technique as "very dangerous?"

---

[1]Techniques for interesting a dog in play toys appear in *Dog Logic—Companion Obedience*, page 27.

Use your right hand to grab both chains of the pinch collar . . .

. . . like so.

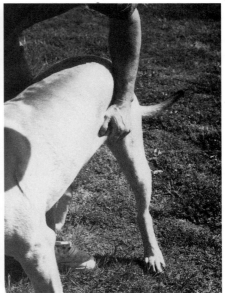

Be sure to target the flank away from you, not the one nearer you. Grab the flank in a quick motion . . .

. . . and squeeze, then immediately release, getting your hand out of harm's way.

A. Potential. The trainer uses pressure on the dog's body to take a sleeve from an animal who has fought for it, wants it, whose mind is churning in bite mode and whose teeth are inches away.

The Rotty yelped, which caused him to drop the sleeve. I released his collar and said "Good out! Good out!" As the sleeve fell from his jaws, Jenny stamped her feet and struck her whip against the ground. Tank threw his attention at Jenny. All this took maybe two seconds.

Don't underestimate the value of praise in teaching "Out."

In agitation, the dog bites and thus gets the satisfaction he craves. When he Outs, he should hear your emphatic approval, which he also wants.

A point about technique: I held the collar to afford me some control of Tank's head, but "I grabbed both chains" so the device could not close. Pinch-collar pressure could get the trainer bitten. More about this in a moment.

I kicked the sleeve across the ground to Jenny. Its movement captured Tank's attention as he watched it zip across the lawn and onto Jenny's arm.

"Action!"

Tank flew at Jenny like the wrath of God. The enraged animal wanted his sleeve back.

In time the dog comes to see the sleeve as his and believes the bad guy has taken it from him. Wanting it back develops the fire we want.

After a quick tussle, Jenny slipped the sleeve. Tank shook it several times, I said "Out!" and ticked off three seconds. The dog held on, breathing hard, staring at Jenny, raw challenge in his eyes.

Once more I grasped his flank, then booted the dropped sleeve to Jenny, who had gone into the same flurry of activity as before. As she plunged her arm into the cylinder, I commanded "Action!" Seconds later Jenny slipped the sleeve. I said "Out!" As my mental count reached two, Tank pitched the sleeve to one side.

You see how the method works. If the animal has no intention of releasing, the trainer flanks him. The dog opens his mouth in response, causing the sleeve to fall away. Straightaway the trainer boots it toward the helper, who dons it posthaste and entices the dog. The trainer sends the animal at once. After a quick skirmish the agitator slips the sleeve and the process is repeated.

"Good out! Good out!"

I released Tank's collar and booted the sleeve to Jenny. She shot her arm into it, cracked her whip and I commanded "Action!" Tank flew at her, white-hot fury on four driving legs.

Just after praising, "Good out! Good out!", I switched my gaze to Jenny. This way, if the dog turned his eyes toward me he would not see mine staring at his, which he could interpret as confrontational. Had the animal glanced at me, my focus on Jenny would have caused him to imitate me, looking at her.

I also adjusted my balance so if Tank came up on me, my right knee would already be loaded and cocked to drive him back.

Have you wondered why "Jenny stamped her feet and struck her whip against the ground" as Tank released the sleeve? Notice the timing. She went into her dance "as the sleeve fell from his jaws." Not before, not after—*as*. That's the instant when the trainer is most vulnerable. The dog had the sleeve. He abruptly lost it. He wanted it back. I, the trainer, was handy. Jenny's actions served to capture Tank's attention and to keep him off me.

Jenny's performance had one other subtle effect. By agitating the dog the instant he lost the sleeve, and with it his feelings of power, control and fulfillment, the bad guy became the reason, in the dog's mind, for the loss.

When booting a sleeve to your helper, use your instep to lift and toss the article, rather than kicking it with—and perhaps injuring—your toes.

Notice how this technique of kicking the sleeve reignites the dog and focuses his attention on the object.

Send the dog again the instant the helper is ready. Notice the handler's pointed signal to the agitator. It says, "A bite is coming."

Q. How can that be? You, not Jenny, flanked the dog. That caused the sleeve to fall away. Then you kicked it to Jenny. She didn't reach for it.

A. Recall Johannes Grewe's observation, "The dog cannot . . . logically follow cause and effect through several stages of development." Jenny's sudden animation was critical, because dogs react to the nearest cause; the one that occurs right after an event. Eventually the dog will see that the trainer's command causes loss of the sleeve, but by then the animal should have accepted that "Out" is just another command and that it does not call for rebellion.

Jenny prolonged the battle several seconds, making Tank fight harder and longer to win the prize. As the dog gave a mighty yank, Jenny slipped the sleeve and ran away. I did not command "Out" but stood next to the massive animal as he held his trophy and watched Jenny melt into the trees.

During the initial teaching of "Out," don't repeat the lesson right after the first time the dog responds correctly. Let him keep his souvenir; allow his victory to end the session. Repeated Outs at this point could suggest to the dog that he should automatically let go every time he gets the sleeve. While we want him to release on cue, we do not want him to even ponder the notion of releasing before the command.

Understand, teaching "Out" relies on a *quid pro quo.* Dogs always want enjoyment they don't have. Feed two puppies the same amount of the same food from identical bowls and you'll see them switch dishes repeatedly during the meal. When a dog has the sleeve, he will release for the joy of nailing it again; and, of course, when he has released it, he wants it once more.

We suspended Tank's training for two days, to allow him some time for what he'd learned to simmer. Then Jenny and I worked him to see if the lesson had taken. She fired up the animal until he raged at her. Screaming at Tank and leaping from side to side, Jenny snapped her whip and darted in and out twice, causing Tank to bite and miss by millimeters each time. Then I told the frenzied dog "Action!"

Tank hit like a wrecking ball, driving Jenny backward several steps. She fought hard to retain the sleeve, then suddenly released it. Tank thrashed the cylinder for several seconds.

"Out!"

Tank spat out the sleeve.

"Good out!"—I kicked the cylinder toward Jenny—"Good out! Action!"

We allowed Tank a lengthy tussle and ended the session. I still did not command "Out" after Jenny slipped the sleeve the final time, however, but allowed the proud Rotty to carry it off. Had the dog not released, I would have had to flank him and repeat the sequence (so as not to end on a low note), and all concerned were already tired.

Q. What if flanking doesn't cause the dog to let go? Some animals are pretty rugged.

A. Squeeze harder. It's true, some dogs are tougher than a 50-cent steak. I recall more than one canine so determined I had to lift the flank to effect a release.

Q. You mean you took the dog off the ground, via his flank?

A. Indeed.

Thinking Time

Trainers: Do the flanking technique incorrectly—or with the wrong dog—and you may find yourself perforated. Study and mentally rehearse the method over and over before ever trying it.

Q. Why not compel the release via pinch-collar pressure?

A. With a tough dog, as a manstopper should be, it's unlikely to work. Seldom can a pinch collar generate enough force to deter a hard dog who is locked in fight mode. Worse, it could confuse. The animal has learned through obedience training that collar corrections relate to positioning: sit, lie down, heel at my side, and so forth. Obviously, "Out" does not command a position. Collar pressure could effect a release, but for the wrong reason—so the dog can nail the trainer.

Q. Why not try to get the dog off the sleeve while the agitator still wears it? That's more real world.

A. True, it is, and that's where we're heading, but it's safer for all concerned to start by teaching a dog to release a slipped sleeve.

Q. Why?

A. Consider, with a dog standing on his hind legs against the helper and biting the sleeve, flanking is more dangerous because the jaws are nearer the trainer's face. If the dog has all four feet on the ground and is biting the sleeve, the helper is bending forward and is somewhat off balance. In either instance, a rebite could target an unprotected area of someone's anatomy. If errors are compounded, such as trying to yank a dog by the collar from an unslipped sleeve, damage to the animal's teeth or neck could result.

Kicking the sleeve to the agitator is an important technique. Otherwise the helper has to reach forward to pick it up, or the trainer must toss it to her. I imagine you can see why the agitator shouldn't reach for the sleeve—that would bring an unprotected helper close to the angry possessor of 40-plus teeth. Leashes have been known to break.

As for having the trainer pick up the sleeve and throw it to the bad guy, don't do it, for three reasons. One, it takes too long. After the dog Outs we want him back on the sleeve ASAP, to maintain his fire. Two, bending to retrieve a sleeve has the trainer off balance, and should the dog lunge at the helper, the trainer might be powerless to restrain the animal. Three, the handler should never touch the sleeve, thereby putting his scent on it, because the dog should never associate this object of aggression with his human partner, not even for a few seconds. That's a line no trainer should cross. Ever.

Remember, we are dealing with a canine mind. Should the animal ever misunderstand why you—his buddy—are grabbing an object he is learning to fight, especially while you are bending over and are vulnerable . . . need I draw a picture?

Petting and Flanking

I told you three chapters ago, "Get in the habit of petting your dog only on the head, neck, chest or withers (shoulders)." I said I'd tell you why in a subsequent chapter. We've arrived. The flanks are so sensitive that even a gentle touch in the region can make a dog anxious, regardless of whether the animal has ever been flanked. Once a dog has been flanked, putting your hand near that area can not just stress your pet, it can get you bitten.

A flanking rule: The dog always gets a bite afterward and, therefore, another chance to respond correctly to "Out." Never quit a training period right after a flank correction. That would constitute finishing on a negative note, which just isn't done in any form of training. Always end high, to maintain a positive working attitude.

Q. I tried the flank method. It worked well. A few days later, while my dog held a sleeve, I commanded "Out" and he didn't release; he just turned his head away. As I reached for his flank he let go. Should I have flanked him anyway?

A. At once, to the accompaniment of "I said OUT!" The dog must respond to command, not to gesture. Allow the critter three seconds to disengage—we don't want him to become handler sensitive—but if he continues to hold on, even if he drops the sleeve as you reach for the flank, complete the correction.

Release the Agitator

Once your dog knows he must drop a slipped sleeve on command, the next step is to teach him that, when cued, he must also release a sleeve being worn by a bad guy.

After resting Tank a day so he had time to absorb what he'd learned, Jenny and I picked up where we had left off. She agitated Tank, I commanded "Action!" and after Jenny slipped the sleeve, I said "Out!" The dog dropped the article. I kicked it to Jenny and sent Tank once more. After a few seconds, with Jenny still wearing the sleeve, I said "Out!" Jenny froze and Tank, after a moment's hesitation, released his bite. He didn't like the idea, but he did let go.

"Good out! Action!"

Jenny struggled with Tank, then slipped the sleeve and raced away. The moose-size Rotty watched her fade into the distance, then walked with me to the car, toting his sleeve.

The session took less than two minutes. We repeated it later that day. The next afternoon, I required Tank to "Out" twice. I allowed him another bite after each release, and Jenny slipped the sleeve and fled after the third hit, so the dog wound up with his prize.

We rested Tank a day, then made two slight changes. Mike and Jenny played switch: He agitated Tank, she worked Greta.

Q. Why?

A. Variety. We didn't want either dog to think bad guys came only in one size or gender.

Q. What was the other change?

A. You'll see.

"Hot damn! I see what Jenny's been yappin' about." Tank had nearly blasted Mike out of his sneakers. I chuckled and said "Out!" Mike froze. Tank released and stood inches from Mike. Nobody breathed. Seconds later, "Action!"

Kee-rash!

Then, "Out!", but this time Mike continued to move the sleeve slightly while pulling away from Tank. The dog started to release, then hesitated, enticed because

Mike had not become still as before. Since I saw confusion in the dog, I did not flank him but repeated the command. Tank released.

Once more I sent him at Mike and, once more, after a quick struggle, I said "Out!" from the back of my throat with lots of spit. Mike continued pulling away, Tank didn't release. This time, bewilderment was not the issue. "Tank," I thought, "you're making a bad choice." I nodded to Mike. He slipped the sleeve and I instantly flanked the gargantuan animal, admonishing "OUT! OUT! OUT!" I never had to flank Tank again.

Don't be surprised if your pet does not release the first time the bad guy doesn't freeze after you command "Out!" Confusion is the probable culprit. The dog has associated his act of letting go with the helper's act of freezing. Handle the situation the way I did with Tank.

Q. Why have the agitator freeze in the first place?

A. Because it's easier—and, more important, safer—to get a wired dog off a stationary helper. Note, though, that phase went by pretty quickly; we didn't condition Tank with weeks of having the agitator stop. More than unfair, permanent faulty learning could have resulted. Just as soon as we felt Tank was ready for the next step, we progressed to having the bad guy continue to move.

Q. Why not just always have the agitator be still when he hears "Out!"?

A. Because a real assailant would probably continue struggling.

Over the ensuing week, Tank responded to "Out" despite the helper's escalating struggles. Then Jenny and I threw the dog a curve.

"Action!"

Jenny fought Tank several seconds, then screamed "Out" right in his face. As the confused Rotty started to let go, I yelled, "No! No! Action! Action!" But Tank had already disengaged enough that Jenny was able to pull away. As she did, she popped his shoulder with her whip handle. This was not to Tank's liking.

"Ac—"

Wham!

"—tion!"

Jenny seemed like a rag doll in Tank's jaws.

"Out!" she screamed. Tank didn't buy it. She yelled "Out!" again. The Mount Everest of Rottweilers jerked her sideways so hard that she almost pinwheeled.

"Out!" I said. Tank released. Seconds later I sent him against Jenny once more. She caught him, fought him, slipped the sleeve and ran.

That evening on the phone, Jenny said, "I was faking it."

"Uh-huh."

"Really. I just let Tank think he almost took me down. For his male ego and all, you know."

"Yeah, right." It was the best laugh either of us had in a couple of days.

Lying next to my chair, his chin resting between his paws, Tank continued his whistling snore.

Reflection

God sat down for a moment when the dog was finished in order to watch it . . . and to know that it was good, that nothing was lacking, that it could not have been made better.

Rainer Maria Rilke

CHAPTER 14

BACK!

"Action" sends a guardian at a target. "Out" commands him to release what's left of it. "Back" says "Hurry to the handler's left side while focusing on the bad guy." The idea is that you don't need to be distracted by attempts to control your pet during a fiery situation. Having him move to your left side, the customary heel position, establishes control while leaving your hands free.

The move also serves a subtler purpose: To get the animal away from the assailant.

A dog who quits his bite in response to "Out" remains highly stimulated for several moments. The notion of a canine protector calming on command is pure Hollywood. A dog who stays near an attacker could rebite in response to innocent movements.

Understand, I'm concerned only partly for a wrongdoer's welfare, and then only slightly. The continued good health of some moral meltdown who has threatened my well-being (or my dog's) doesn't top my priority list. But, were a rebite needed, the fact that the animal would start from very close range would decrease his momentum. That would lessen the "Wham!" effect, which comprises much of the dog's physical and psychological weaponry. Lacking this advantage, a bad guy could injure my pet.

Q. C'mon! How could someone a guard dog has just flattened harm him?

A. Ramming a stiffened finger through his eye might work.

"Back" also provides a bit of insurance. Protection dogs like their work but seldom adore "Out" They would rather not quit. That's fact one. Fact two: A reliable obedience worker seldom resists two sequential commands, especially when he has to do the first to accomplish the second. Thus, following "Out" with "Back" increases the likelihood the dog will indeed release, because to "Back" he must first "Out."

Q. Shouldn't a dog reliably "Out" in a real situation?

A. He should, yes, but the only events you can rehearse are ones you have contrived. A real bad guy causing your pet genuine pain could drive him to fight beyond "Out." The smell and taste of human blood, or of the dog's own, and perhaps the sound and feel of cracking bone, can shoot canine urges to a higher level—urges a single cue may not interrupt.

Now let me ask you a question. When you obedience trained your pet, did you teach the inside finish? I hope so, because "Back" commands a modified inside finish and is easier taught to a dog who knows the concept.

To make sure we're in sync here, a finish requires pooch to move from a position in front of and facing the trainer to the heel position. The dog does this in one of two ways: by going past the handler's right side and circling behind him to arrive at the heel position on the left—that's the outside, or military or go-around finish; or by swinging his butt or jumping to the handler's left and aligning in the heel position, which is the inside finish. Once there, the dog must sit, facing forward.

If your dog knows the outside finish, or hasn't been taught the finish at all, it isn't the end of the world. He should learn "Back" without great difficulty, but it may take him a little longer to catch on.

"Back" calls for a response similar to an inside finish, except the dog should keep an eye on the bad guy while moving to heel and need not sit upon arrival (actually, I prefer my dog remain standing) but must stay near you without needing a leash correction to do so.

Teach "Back" in stages. Begin with no agitators present and only after your pet is reliable to "Out." Initially work the animal in a pinch collar, later in harness, your leash attached to its front ring.

Begin by saying, "Sit, stay" (or, if you prefer, "Stand, stay") and moving to a point six feet in front of and in line with your dog. Keep your back to him. Hold the leash in your right hand, turn your head to the left, glance at your pet and command "Back" while patting your left leg. (If your dog heels on the right side, reverse the left-right instructions.) Slight leash pressure to guide your pet to you is okay, but avoid it if possible. Better to use the animal's attraction to you to support this new lesson.

As the dog arrives at your side, pet him and tell him, "Good back," then, "Stand, stay." (Substitute "Sit" if that's what you want your pet to do upon future arrivals.)

I prefer my dog to stand when he arrives at my side, but tell yours "Sit" if that's what you'd rather he do.

Gradually lengthen the distance over the next few days. We want your pet reliable (i.e., responsive to a single "Back" command) from 20 feet behind you. Eliminate patting your leg once you no longer need the additional cue, so the dog does not learn that it takes both word and gesture to call him.

This is the first step, and it will facilitate learning the second one, which is for your dog to "Back" from a distance to your left. After commanding "Sit, stay," take a long step to your dog's right and face the same direction as the animal. That is, after leaving your dog he should be parallel to you and five feet to your left. Command "Back," patting your left leg as needed. Pet your dog and praise "Good back" when he arrives. Over the next several days, steadily increase the working distance to 20 feet.

Q. Let me guess. The next step is to "Back" the dog from a position in front of me, right?

A. Wrong. At this stage, were you to "Back" your pet from in front of you, he would face you while moving. We want to habituate him to look forward, where the bad guy would be, and to check where he's going using his peripheral vision and his sense of awareness as to where you are. Hence, at this juncture, add an agitator to the equation to keep the dog's focus away from you.

Once your pet reliably comes to you from 20 feet behind you, start teaching him to "Back" from your left.

Summoning your dog from behind you easily transfers to coming to you from the side.

With your dog at heel, signal the bad guy to appear. The helper should wear a sleeve and carry a whip but should walk normally—no threatening or enticing moves—to a point 10 feet in front of and facing you and your dog. Once there, the agitator should not move.

Command "Sit, stay," and step five feet to your dog's right, as you did during the preceding stage. After a few seconds, command "Back." One of four events, listed in order of probability, will occur:

1.   The dog moves to your side.
2.   The dog lunges at the agitator.
3.   The dog remains in place.
4.   The dog sits or lies down.

If your pet moves to your side, respond with quick praise, "Good back, good back." Then command "Action!" Give the animal a rewarding bite. The agitator should slip the sleeve after a short skirmish, and you should then take the dog from the area, allowing him to carry the sleeve if he wishes.

Should the dog lunge at the agitator, restrain him and give a collar correction pulling toward yourself while admonishing "No! Back!" This correction is appropriate—the dog is exercising his will, because in no way does "Back" sound like "Action." Then set up the situation a second time. Tell the dog "Sit, stay," step to his right five feet and command "Back!" If your pet responds correctly this time, praise him, then command "Action!" But if the animal lunges at the agitator when you say "Back," signal your helper to depart and continue "Back" lessons for several days before adding the bad guy to the program again.

Should your dog remain in place, or if he sits or lies down, the problem is inattention. Tell him "No! Back!" and give a smart tug on the lead running to the pinch collar. If he then responds correctly, repeat the setup once more. Command "Sit, stay," step five feet to the dog's right and command "Back." If he performs as ordered, praise the animal and reward him with a bite, as though he had gotten it right the first time.

In time the dog will accede. In point of fact, training is at a standstill until he does. Do no further agitation until your pet will "Back" to your side from five feet to your left in the presence of a motionless agitator. Once you've accomplished this, incrementally lengthen the "Back" distance to 10 feet. I know: We took the dog to 20 feet earlier, but 10 feet is adequate with the agitator present because that would likely be the maximum working range on the street.

The final step elicits the correct response when your dog's back is to you. This goal is easier to attain than you might suppose, but it can take a few sessions to polish.

Have the agitator wear a left-arm sleeve. Harness your dog and attach a 15- to 20-foot lead to the front ring. Cue the bad guy to appear and entice your dog. Restrain your pet for a few seconds to allow the animal's furnace to heat. Then command "Action!" During the scuffle, move to a point five feet to your dog's right, so he can see you from the corner of his eye. Command "Out!" The agitator must not slip the sleeve. As the dog's teeth leave the cylinder, command "Back!" This new demand, releasing the sleeve *and* leaving it, can stress a dog, so repeat "Back" if need be. We're after long-term results here, not near-term cosmetics, which untoward corrections can create. You may have to give a light tug on the lead running to the harness, however, to interrupt the dog's concentration without impeding it.

One of two responses is probable: The dog will move to your side or will rebite. Moving to your side earns quick praise followed by "Action!" This time the bad guy should slip the sleeve soon after the hit. You should neither "Out" nor "Back" your pet but should take him from the training site. A rebite, not to be confused with a nose-tap against the sleeve (which is not cause for concern), means you have brought the dog through the "Back" teaching stages too fast.

Q. You tend to fault the trainer when things don't go right.

A. Is someone else teaching the dog?

If your pet has shown solid responses thus far, rebites are unlikely. Should one occur, go back to summoning him over five-foot distances from your left side without an agitator present.

Presuming your pet does well in the above test, gradually decrease the number of steps you take to get near him before commanding "Out." Within a week, your dog should be able to "Back" to where you were when you commanded "Action!" Also, the agitator should begin to keep moving the sleeve after the "Out" and "Back" commands, as was done during "Out" training. Should the dog turn toward you—away from the helper—the agitator should stamp his feet to redirect the animal's focus. If that doesn't work, a tap from the helper's whip on the dog's butt will.

Anticipation

In time, your dog may "Back" in response to "Out." Though a purist might say this constitutes anticipation, as the animal would be returning to your side before commanded, fret not. "Out" and "Back" spoken in tandem constitute not a reference to Australia, but linked commands with a related objective, and a trainer should appreciate, not censure, a dog showing such initiative.

If your dog anticipates "Back" when hearing "Out," the "Out!–Watchim!" variation, useful for its own sake, may alleviate the situation without requiring force. (In Chapter 1 you learned "Watchim" means "Threaten by barking, growling, snapping jaws and/or showing teeth.") Show your pet you will sometimes direct "Watchim" (covered in the next chapter) right after "Out." Then, of course, the dog releases his bite and barks at the helper without first returning to you.

Teach "Out!–Watchim!" to a dog who knows the commands singly just by following "Out" with "Watchim" the instant the animal clears the sleeve. Reward your pet with another bite for getting both commands right as soon as he has barked a few times. Should your dog display hesitancy born of confusion when he first hears "Watchim" right after "Out," position yourself a few feet to his right before giving the cues. Your nearby presence should remove any mental static regarding the two commands. Then practice the sequence at increasing distances.

Teaching your dog that "Out" may lead to either "Back" or "Watchim" defeats anticipation, of course, because it breaks the pattern. Your pet learns he cannot anticipate your next command. This is proper, because in a real situation he can't predict your cues.

The Stand-Stay, Revisited

Nine chapters ago I told you we would later extend the stand-stay to use with strange strangers. We're there.

Chaska and I were strolling through a city park when Jenny approached us. The dog had seen Jenny before but had never met her. More germane, Jenny had never agitated the young Doberman.

Jenny stopped six feet from us. Acting somewhat inebriated, she spoke.

"Hazsen-flatt quintus bork!"

Jenny was wound up like the Energizer bunny.

"That may be," I said, struggling to keep a stern demeanor, "but leave us alone."

Catching my tone, Chaska's tail stilled. Her stare pinned Jenny like a laser. Jenny stepped toward us.

"Watchim!"

Bark! Bark! Bark! Bark! Bark!

Jenny jumped back, then sat on the ground.

"*Out!*"

Chaska hushed. Seconds later Jenny stood.

"*Watchim!*"

Bark! Bark! Bark! Bark! Bark!

Jenny sat once more.

"*Out!*"

Silence.

"*You'd best leave us be. The operative word is leave.*"

"*I should go?*"

"*And sin no more.*"

"*Can I pet your dog first?*"

"*What do you think, Chaska?*" *The Doberman caught my lightened tone. Her tail fluttered.* "*Stand, stay.*" *Chaska struck a show stance as if she'd been posing in the ring most of her life (which, in fact, she had, being out of a very nice bloodline protected by a polished conformation exhibitor).*

"*You may pet her now, if you wish.*"

Jenny, magically normal, stood, approached Chaska, said "*Hi pupper*" *and stroked the animal's neck and shoulders. I kept the leash an inch from tight to protect Jenny while not driving Chaska forward, which a tight lead could do.* "*She's sure easy on the eyes,*" *Jenny said.*

I agreed.

Chaska's reward for barking on command was her power in making Jenny sit. Then we showed the dog that someone she has barked at is no threat if the trainer says the person is safe.

You read the line, "You may pet her now, if you wish," in Chapter 1. It's what I say to strangers who ask to pet my dog. I leave the choice up to them, so that on the off chance someone gets bitten, I can testify I did not ask the person to approach my dog.

Reflection

The best thing about man is the dog.

Voltaire

CHAPTER 15

WATCHIM!

How effective is this command? I've cropped this photograph to show just the dog, not the trainer or the helper, to make it easier for you to ask yourself, "How would I like to have to face this?"

Recall "Watchim" means "Threaten by barking, growling, snapping jaws and/or showing teeth." Teach the cue only after your dog has become ravenous for the sleeve and reliable to "Action!" and "Out!"

I said "Listen" as Mike walked toward us. Holding a whip in his left hand, his sleeved right arm hung loosely at his side. He stopped six feet away and stood as still as a fence post. He stared at Greta. Standing next to me, her gaze bored a hole in him.

I nodded at Mike and said "Action!" The German Shepherd flew at him.

So far, so good. Greta had turned on to sleeves weeks ago and was responding to "Action!" Notice that Mike made no move to attract her; she reacted to my verbal cue alone.

Mike slipped the sleeve and stepped from Greta's range, which my leash limited. She trounced her jute-covered prize, whacking it from side to side.

Always allow the dog a moment to subdue the prey before commanding her to release.

"Out!"

Greta dropped the cylinder. I kicked it to Mike. He pulled it onto his arm and stood still, both arms at his sides. I took up all but an inch of slack and said "Watchim!" Greta made no sound but tried to charge Mike.

Lunging was predictable. Greta knew to bite in response to a two-syllable sound, and—to a dog—"Watchim" is not phonetically unlike "Action." This is why "I took up all but an inch of slack." Excess would have found the dog hitting the leash's end with a considerable jolt, which could have confused the animal and dampened her drive.

Mike remained stationary while I restrained Greta. Gently I told her "No, no," then with heat in my voice, "Watchim!" The dog shot me a questioning look, then looked at Mike and whined in confusion.

"Good watchim! Action!"

Wham!

That's how to introduce the "Watchim" command. Once you've said it, any sound by the dog—including a clacking of teeth or a fast open-close of the mouth—earns her an immediate bite, which is the reward.

As mentioned in Chapter 12, the dogs I train know from previous work that I praise by linking the word *good* with whatever command the animal just obeyed, as in "Good sit," Good stay," and so on. Thus accustomed, "Good watchim" meant more to Greta and she soon learned the command.

Two other benefits accrue from following "Watchim!" with "Action!" First, the dog learns that they are indeed two separate words calling for similar yet different responses. Second, "Action!" becomes a possible reward for a proper reaction to "Watchim," thereby developing a quicker and more enjoyable response to both commands.

After a quick fight, Mike released the sleeve. Greta mauled it, savoring the juices of victory.

"Out!"

I booted the sleeve to Mike. He donned it and stood stone still. "Watchim!"

At first the agitator must not entice during this phase. His previous movements were to encourage a bite. For the trainer to restrain the dog now, in the face of helper inducement, would risk subverting what was learned in "Action" lessons to date.

Once more I said "Watchim!" As Greta had yet to discern the cue's meaning, she snorted in frustration.

"Good watchim! Action!"

Mike and I repeated the cycle twice more. I said "Watchim!" and Greta finally made a noise. The instant she did, "Good watchim! Action!" After the fourth joust, Mike slipped the sleeve and scurried away. Greta and I walked to the car, the dog carrying her plunder.

During the next session we struck pay dirt.

"Watchim!"

Nothing.

"Watchim!"

Greta pulled against the leash. Mike, sleeved, stood motionless, his arms at his sides.

"Watchim!"

Straining harder, Greta made a noise somewhere between a moan of frustration and a groan of effort.

"Good watchim! Action!"

Again, "Good watchim! Action!" occurred the instant Greta made a sound. We had picked up where we'd left off. My message to her remained, "Make some noise and get a bite."

After a brief bout, Mike slipped the sleeve.

"Out! Back!"

As Greta moved to my side, I booted the cylinder to Mike and adjusted my cap.

"Watchim!"

Mike had caught my signal. He didn't move, but his stare pounded menace at Greta as he began flick-of-the-wrist slapping of the whip handle against his leg, a slow, hypnotic, sinister rhythm. He hissed, catlike.

"Watchim!"

Mike could do it. His affection for and appreciation of Greta equaled mine, and this allowed him to radiate white-hot hate at the dog on demand.

The tame part of Greta watched in amazement as cunning born of countless generations of Gretas pushed the gentle part of her aside and stepped forward. Her eyes widened, her breath caught. Rage became a long-lost ally as the Shepherd bared her teeth and snarled in chilling fury.

Afterward, Mike said, "Something went click in her eyes. I never knew what it felt like to be afraid of a dog. Now I do." Time and experience would see him past that primal reaction, but for now Greta had sensed his fear, and her mind pounced on it like a starved jackal.

"Good Watchim! Action!"

Greta struck in demonic rage. Seconds later Mike released the sleeve, with relief it seemed, and stepped back. "Shazam," *he muttered, shaking his head.*

"Out!"

The Shepherd ground the sleeve in her jaws, in her mind the prey not yet undone.

"OUT! BACK!"

Greta dropped the object and, by rote, hopped to my side. She blinked as though awakening. Bingo, I thought, *knowing she'd experience less culture shock in days to come when sliding from one emotional zone to another.*

As stated in the Preface, "Our focus is combat. Successful combat." Manstopper is not just an image, it's a destination. If your welfare is ever on the line and you have a dog trained for the real world, you'll know the value of genuine canine reactions.

Q. When Greta didn't release on your first "Out!" command, why didn't you correct her?

A. She couldn't hear me, in the true sense of the word. Her head had jumped to another level. Force could not only have gotten me bitten, I could have damaged an alliance based on respect and trust, training's foundation. Also, correcting Greta while she was in the spirit could have lost "Watchim" for all time.

Greta kept growling at Mike. She had dropped the sleeve and returned to me, but she persisted in saturating the atmosphere with portent. That's not all bad, I thought. A manstopper's continued threats after a release can discourage an assailant's further hostilities.

Q. Then it could take two "Out"s to shut down a dog? One to make her release and then a second one to quiet her?

A. Correct.

I booted the sleeve to Mike and made a snapping motion with my hand, as if it held a whip. He didn't pick up the sleeve but bent over it and locked eyes with Greta as he struck the object with his whip handle, twice, hard. To Greta this challenge said, "I fight you." As the dog quivered in rage, I said "Watchim!"

Greta barked. Mike grabbed the sleeve.

"Good watchim!"

Bark!

"Good watchim!"

Bark! Bark!

"Good watchim! Action!"

Greta hit harder than she ever had—and continued growling! I raised a fist, cueing Mike not to slip the sleeve.

"Out!"

Greta released.

"Watchim!"

Bark!

"Good watchim!"

Bark!

"Good watchim!"

Bark! Bark!

"Action!"

Wham!

Again I raised my fist.

"Out! Back!"

Greta stood next to me. I said nothing. Neither did she.

"Watchim, Greta! Watchim!"

Bark! Bark!

Mike crouched and snapped the sleeve to chest level.

"Watchim! Watchim!"

Bark! Bark! Bark! Bark! Bark! Bar—

"Action!"

Greta spun Mike like a top. He slipped the sleeve and departed at a heretofore unseen pace.

"Out! Back!"

Greta spit out the sleeve and moved to my side. Still growling furiously, she stared at Mike's retreating form.

"Out!"

The dog snapped her attention to the discarded sleeve, then focused on Mike's hiding place.

Grrr!

We needed to smooth out an edge, because now Greta wouldn't shut up. Clearly, she didn't know she had to. Some dogs, upon learning "Out," see right away that it means stop all mouth activities. Given her inherent intensity, Greta had not made that connection. We would deal with this later, once she had internalized "Watchim." To push the issue now could hamper her training.

"Get his arm, Greta," I said, bumping my foot against the sleeve. Greta and I walked to the car, she with a soft grrr every few steps, carrying her sleeve, I with an occasional chuckle.

A few days later we slapped the lid on.

"Watchim!"

Bark! Bark! Bark! Bark! Bark!

"Action!"

Boom!

Mike slipped the sleeve and raced toward the tree line.

"Out! Back!"

Greta dropped the sleeve and hopped to my side. She stared at Mike's sanctuary. Grrr.

I let the animal growl for several seconds. Then, curtly, "Out!" Surprised, Greta the growler hushed in mid-grrr, an exclamation point rather than an ellipsis. "Good out." I stroked the back of her neck. "Good out." Before she could start up again, I told her to heel and led her directly away from Mike's hiding place. The dog walked with me, but continued to growl softly while glancing back toward the trees.

No, Greta did not switch from enraged growls and flashing teeth to peace and love in a blink, but I didn't expect her to. So long as the animal does not resist the command to heel, let her wind down at her own rate.

After heeling Greta a few minutes, we returned to the working area and I signaled Mike to return. As he approached, Greta began growling.

"Out!"

Smerf.

I allowed the German Shepherd her tiny assertion, following my philosophy of letting the small stuff slide. There is such a thing as pushing too hard.

Greta stared at Mike, who stood motionless a few feet away. I bent toward her.
"Watchim!"
Bark! Bark! Bark! Bark! Bark!
"Out!"
Silence. A mental two-count.
"Watchim!"
Bark! Bark! Bar—
"Action!"

As Mike later commented, "Now I know what it feels like to get hit by an 18-wheeler." Truly, he looked like Beetle Bailey after one of the Sarge's thumpings.

"Out! Back!"
Standing at my side, Greta stared at Mike and bounced on her front paws but made no sound.
"Watchim!"
Bark! Bark! Grrr.
"Out!"
Grrp—
Silence. Three seconds.
"Watch—"
Bark! Bark! Bark! Bark!
"Out!"
Quiet. Two seconds.
"Action!"
Crash!
Sho'nuff, I thought.

"Watchim" Technique, Revisited

Understand, there's no mystery to teaching "Watchim." The method corresponds to training a dog to speak for a biscuit.
"Speak!"
The dog looks wide-eyed at the food in the owner's hand.
"Speak!"
The animal fidgets, licks her chops, perhaps drools.

"Speak!"

Maybe the dog sits up, her forepaws dangling near her chest.

"Speak!"

Eventually, out of sheer frustration or confusion, the animal whines, yips, groans or barks. Any such response instantly earns her the biscuit. Over time the dog learns through trial and error that "Speak!" means "Bark and you'll get the tidbit." By a very similar process, Greta learned "Watchim" meant barking at the bad guy earned her a bite.

Q. The dog wants a bite as much as she wants a food bit?

A. Exactly. To a dog, both represent victory.

The first time your pet barks, you have to make a quick call, whether to give her a bite or try for a second bark. If the response is tentative, say "Good watchim!" and send your dog. A canine who barks hesitantly seldom repeats herself, and we don't want to let the animal's correct response go unrewarded. Moreover, at this juncture we can't afford to let that happen.

But if the bark is forceful, as Greta's was, say "Good watchim!" and wait a millisecond before commanding "Action!" See if the dog responds to the "watchim!" part of "Good watchim!" with a second bark. If not, immediately launch her at the bad guy. If she does bark a second time, repeat the praise and see if it elicits a quick third. An instant later, whether the animal barks or not, send her. A dog new to commanded barking will need a bite at this point to sustain her behavior.

During the next stage your dog learns she must bark twice after one "Watchim" command before you'll say "Action!" You institute this policy simply by not sending the dog following a single bark. Be patient. The animal will give you the second bark if you wait. Soon it will take three barks, then four, the goal being for your pet to bark, roar, growl or clack teeth nonstop when she hears "Watchim!" Clacking the teeth, incidentally, is a breed tendency among Belgian Malinois, German Shepherds and Doberman Pinschers, principally among bitches. The mannerism scares the whatever out of real targets.

Variation Number One

Although Greta and Tank—and most dogs I train—learned "Out" and "Back" before "Watchim," in some cases it is advantageous to reverse the sequence. Then, however, getting the sleeve from the dog to return it to the agitator can be a problem. Solution: Have a second sleeve handy.

"Action!"

Timba, a male Tibetan Mastiff, blasted the sleeve. Jenny slipped it and grabbed another that she had hidden behind a bush. Timba, holding his trophy, watched her ease the second sleeve onto her arm. As Jenny later put it, "You could see Fur Mountain doing the math." Realizing he couldn't bite Jenny's new sleeve while holding the one he had, he released it. I kicked the dropped cylinder out of his reach and readied to teach him "Watchim!"

Remember, a dog wants what he doesn't have, as much or more than what he does have. When biting, he wants possession of the sleeve. When he has the sleeve, he wants to bite, and if he sees a second sleeve, he wants that one because he doesn't have it. That's just how dogs are.

Variation Number Two

I told you in Chapter 10 that if your pet barks at the bad guy before the helper "sees" the animal, your agitator should immediately stop for a moment, then advance slowly and hesitantly toward the dog. And if your dog barks sporadically, that's exactly what the helper should do.

However, if the dog commences non-stop barking every time the bad guy takes a step, the first agitation needs to go a little differently. Chaska, the red-and-rust Doberman bitch you met in Chapter 12, barked like a tape-loop. Most dogs bark or growl as they exhale, but Chaska growled while she inhaled as well. (She also tended to drool when fired, a trait that would stupefy a real assailant.)

Because Chaska barked extensively at Mike's initial approach, we shifted to a different plan, one we had discussed beforehand because we both sensed Chaska might be a noisemaker. First I'll show you what we did. Then I'll tell you why.

Mike hadn't moved more than five feet from his hiding place when Chaska spotted him and lit up the training area with repeated barking. I repeated "Good watchim!" several times as Mike scurried back behind his tree.

Once Chaska settled, Mike reappeared. After taking a few tentative steps, he suddenly scuttled sideways toward us, skidding to a stop some 10 feet away. Then he took one more slow step toward Chaska and she again launched into serious barking, which again caused Mike to run for his life.

Mike's sudden rush surprised Chaska—remember, this was her first experience with a bad guy—and she didn't have time to set off. Thus, Mike was able to get close before the Doberman ignited. We wanted to show her that someone acting strange at a great distance is not cause for alarm, that she need not threaten anyone from afar.

Also, Mike and I needed to get a reading on another matter: Was Chaska's barking a fright response? Sometimes when a dog sets off on a distant person, especially during an initial session, it says that the animal fears the individual and wants to keep him far away. If Chaska had folded from Mike's rush, he would have slammed on the brakes and reversed course the instant she began to wither, so as not to sow permanent seeds of doubt and to leave her with as much of a victory as possible. Of course, the Doberman's protection training would have been halted right then and there for all time.

This notion of stopping the training of dogs who are not right for the work may seem arbitrary and harsh, but one purpose is to maintain these dogs as pets, rather than ruin them by continued exposure to stressors they cannot handle. If a dog shows fear during a bad guy's approach while you are saying "Listen," in time the "Listen" cue will trigger not the animal's alertness but her anxiety. "Listen" sets off not an active response but a mindset. Continually subjecting the wrong dog to overpowering situations could develop a fear-biter who might respond to "Listen" by taking on the owner, as it is he who is keeping the animal in the feared environment and the dog might see no other way of escape.

As we suspected she would, however, Chaska came to life when Mike took that one sneaky step too close. We then knew that her barking did not signify fear, but was a manifestation of high guard drive.

As Mike made his third approach, this time slow and wary, I stood next to Chaska and repeated "Good listen" as she observed him. The dog growled in low tones but didn't bark. When Mike was within six feet, I backed away from Chaska, so as not to distract her, just before Mike stamped his feet.

To this day I maintain I beat Chaska to the punch, saying at least the "Wa" in "Watchim!" before she got her first bark off. Mike, ever the diplomat, grins and says "Sho'nuff." In any case, after the Doberman had barked four times, I said "Action!", slackened the leash, Chaska bit Mike's burlap sack and he vamoosed.

An objective had been to slow Chaska down some. My praise distracted her just enough so that, although she kept an eye on Mike, she didn't bark during his approach.

A Common Problem

Some dogs, when learning "Watchim!", bark readily enough but they also continually lunge at the bad guy. On the street, this would be a distraction you don't need. Though I often prefer to cut problem behaviors off at the pass, addressing this one too soon can cost the barking lessons to date and perhaps permanently silence the dog.

If your pet tends to drive at the agitator while barking, put up with it until the animal's fire for barking is deeply ingrained. Then, just before the bad guy appears, switch your leash to the pinch collar and maintain about one inch of slack in the lead. In this way the leash will tighten the instant your dog surges forward in response to "Watchim!" This not only times the consequence more closely with the undesired action, it greatly lessens the degree of force which, if it were excessive, could undo training to date.

As you pull the dog back, tell her "No!—Stay!—Watchim!" while pointing at the helper. Your pet's knowledge of "Stay!" in this chain of commands should allow her to make the desired mental link. The first time she holds her position while barking at the agitator, instantly grant her a bite: "Good stay-watchim! Action!"

Preschool

I was dulling-out with television when Cricket, my 45-pound crossbreed who carries 60 pounds of oomph, barked at the slam of a car door in the driveway.

"Good watchim."

Cricket knew "Good" from our obedience lessons, but "Watchim" was new. Ears pricked at the foreign word. Then came the sound of walkway gravel scrunching underfoot.

Bark! Bark! Bark!

"Good watchim. Good watchim."

Cricket glanced at me and barked once more. Again I praised him.

Footfalls on the porch elicited a deluge of woofs and I hurled "Good watchim" responses in auctioneer tempo. The ringing doorbell caused Cricket to lower the warnings in timbre, if not in frequency and decibels. After a final "Good watchim," I opened the door.

"That little mutt makes a big-dog sound," the pizza delivery driver said warily.

You get the idea. When a noise causes your pet to bark, respond by linking praise with the "Watchim" cue. Over time the dog learns the command's meaning through the back door, as it were. With Cricket, I added a final touch.

Cricket was still gurgling as I closed the door.

"Good watchim."

Rumble, rumble.

"Good watchim."

I plunked onto the couch, plucked a slice of pepperoni, blew it cool and tossed it to Cricket. The dog's digestive system could handle the treat, so the nibble wouldn't hurt a thing. Besides, ancillary positive reinforcement of a correct response elicited during operant conditioning and all that other scientific mumbo-jumbo, don't you know.

Reflection

Whilst part of what we perceive comes through our senses from the object before us, another part (and it may be the larger part) always comes out of our own mind.

William James

CHAPTER 16

FASTER, HARDER, TOUGHER

From Chapter 2: "A manstopper does not prance up and woof at or daintily nip a target. He overpowers. He becomes a *tsunami* with teeth. He overcomes force through greater force." In the following pages we'll examine how to train a quick, hard hitter to hit faster and harder, and how to make a tough dog tougher. I won't load you up with a raft of techniques—the training thus far should have produced a more-than-adequate defender—but I'll provide enough optional post-graduate work to enhance your pet's prowess.

Q. My dog already bites solid. Why care about how fast and hard he hits?

A. The blast can trigger as much wrongdoer regret as the bite. Pain from the teeth may take a moment to fight through shock and reach the brain, especially if the assailant is in a drug-induced haze, which many are. A running dog's momentum slamming against a human can knock the person off his feet and drive him to the ground. About then, the searing pain from the bite takes hold in full fury. The effect is utter demoralization.

Faster

A byproduct of teaching a dog to hit faster is that his increased momentum makes him hit harder. An easy way to increase speed is for the agitator to spin out of the animal's path at the last possible instant, causing the dog to miss.

Mike faced Greta from 30 feet. He wore a left-arm sleeve, which he held level and close to his side just above belt height. I said "Action" and released my two-foot leash.

As Greta raced toward Mike, I trotted behind her. Mike was moving forward and to his right when the dog launched herself. But the German Shepherd's jaws snapped shut on air as she flew past Mike, for just after she went airborne he spun clockwise on his left foot, taking the sleeve inches from Greta's line of fire. She was turning toward Mike before she landed, but by then I had interposed myself between the dog and her favorite bad guy and said "Out."

I grabbed the leash and led Greta back to the starting point. As we passed Mike, he taunted the dog and stamped his feet and flicked his whip at the ground. Greta didn't take the insults kindly.

Once again I cued "Action," but this time with a pressing edge, as in "Don't let him get away with that kind of crap!" My tone wasn't lost on her.

I wish I could have had a radar gun tracking the German Shepherd during her second rush. She kicked things up a notch. Later Mike said he felt he had spun away with the same speed as before, but this time Greta nailed the sleeve just as it was passing beyond her reach. She generated enough momentum so that, had Mike not known to pivot when the animal connected, Greta's impact would have knocked him off his feet.

Caution: For the agitator, this is risky technique. It's for one-session-only use. Repeat it with a bright dog and she may settle for the bad guy's legs or his momentarily exposed ribs or back.

Use a very short leash if you have solid obedience control, so it can't foul in the dog's legs as she runs. If the animal's obedience work is underdeveloped, use a long lead for helper safety, which must remain paramount.

A variation of spinning from a dog's line of fire to raise her concentration and striking power is simply to lift the sleeve a few inches once the animal has launched herself.

Another technique for heightening the Wham! effect is the runaway: A fleeing agitator extends his sleeved arm, level and at a right angle to his line of flight—if the helper runs north, he points the sleeve west as the dog comes from the south. Send the dog from several feet away.

Q. Hold on! What about that line in the Preface, "Our goals include neither pursuit nor investigation"?

A. Nothing's changed. The purpose of this activity is not to train the dog to chase and apprehend. It just looks that way. We want to say "Faster!" An easy way to do that is to give the dog a reason to increase his speed, and nothing attracts a guard dog quite as well as a bad guy running from him with the sleeve held as a bull's-eye.

Agitators: When doing a runaway, keep your eyes on the dog as he nears you. He may decide to skip the sleeve and go for you.

Don't—repeat, don't—combine the spin technique with this one. That is, during a runaway don't yank the sleeve away just as the dog strikes. A fleeing agitator doing that can teach a canine to slow down during his last few steps to make sure where the target is.

Or he might decide to hit the helper's back or neck.

The runaway catch, sometimes called the airplane.

Preparation for a runaway. Notice that the agitator starts several yards away from the dog before the animal is sent.

Harder

From the get-go, Tank's battle cry was "Lemme at 'im!" Recall from Chapter 11 that during his initial session the Rottweiler grabbed the sack, "spat it out and went for Jenny." Tank was a dog with just one setting—loaded and cocked. I've seen him level more than one stout agitator who knew how to avoid being flattened. Now, does this mean a Tank cannot learn to hit even faster and harder? No. Not by a long shot.

After attaching a 15-foot leash to Tank's harness, I gripped the lead at six feet from its clasp and signaled Travis to appear. Wearing a hard sleeve and carrying an agitation whip, Travis, a nearly unstoppable tailback in high school, stepped from his hiding place and raced toward Tank, skidding to a halt 20 feet away. When Tank first saw him I said "Listen." Now I said "Watchim!" Hearing the animal's deep-chested rumble, I speculated that residents of surrounding counties were surprised not to see storm clouds.

I nodded, and Travis went into his act. Stamping his feet, jumping from side to side, cracking his whip, he yelled all manner of earthy abuse at the dog. Tank's irritation exploded to outrage. My feet dug in, the leash taut, I commanded "Action! Action!" Tank surged against his restraints until the leash hummed like a plucked bowstring.

I wondered which would give out first, the leash, the harness or my back. It wouldn't be Tank. His Ohio-size paws made seed furrows as I let him drag me toward Travis—at a rate of one foot per second. I continued saying "Action!" while Travis harassed and taunted the animal by striking the sleeve with the whip handle, kicking dirt at him and, at one point, spitting at the fuming black-and-rust marauder. Then, when the dog had driven to within four feet of Travis, I released the leash.

Afterward, Travis requested a raise in pay. Tank's hit was of seismographic quality. After man and dog tussled several seconds, I tightened the lead as Travis dropped to one knee. Then, in one flowing motion, he slipped the sleeve, fell back and crawled away on his hands and knees with amazing speed, looking back once with panicked eyes at Tank.

Over the next few days, Travis and I followed the same procedure, save that I released Tank at ever-increasing distances from Travis once the animal was surging full-bore.

As you see, after telling Tank "Action!" I made him work for what he wanted. Then I abruptly freed the dog. Over the next few sessions I lessened the drag-the-trainer distance. By releasing Tank just as he fought to advance, the animal learned to rocket from my side. He heard my message of "Really turn it on and I'll cut you loose."

Travis' act of dropping to one knee was risky. He did so to show enticing submission before slipping the sleeve; but an agitator must have impeccable timing and quick reactions for this move, as the dog could sail over the sleeve and hit the helper's face.

Strategy can also teach a harder hit. Knowing that dogs learn patterns of behavior, allow only a single bite per session for three sessions. Then switch to two bites for three more training periods. Finally, intermingle the pattern, so the dog never knows whether he will get one bite or two. Since the animal likes the work, uncertainty over "One bite or two?" teaches him to hit very hard on every bite, as it may be the only one he gets that day.

Tougher

What do plastic jugs and cardboard tubes have in common? Answer: They can be used to make a tough dog tougher.

The plastic jugs I have in mind are gallon-size containers often used to hold milk. The cardboard tubes are three feet long and come with gift-wrapping paper around them. The agitator throws the (empty) jugs at the dog; he strikes the animal with the cardboard tubes.

Q. Dog bashing? That isn't like you.

A. You're right, it isn't. Canine abuse agitates me. But consider two points. First, throwing empty plastic jugs at a dog and swatting him with lightweight cardboard tubes does not equal bashing. Second, your protector may someday have to fight for his life, and perhaps yours. He may have to contend against some idiot wielding a tire iron. Not to include blows from harmless objects during training would be to neglect the animal's welfare.

After fighting Tank for several seconds, Mike slowed, then froze. Sensing the lack of resistance, Tank started to release. Mike instantly stung the dog's shoulder with his whip handle.

Tank reignited. Soon Mike became a statue once more, his handle ready. Tank growled and bit harder, rage flashing in his eyes. Mike slipped the sleeve and fled in authentic fashion.

Q. Didn't you say something to the effect of, "No member of *Canis familiaris* has been or ever will be whipped at my kennels, during guard training or for any other reason"?

Humble equipment.

A. Smacked twice with a lightweight whip handle is not tantamount to "whipped." We're raising low-level stress, not welts. Besides, harsh lessons make for long memories. Ponder the implications should a dog release because a real bad guy stopped moving. It could get the animal killed.

Consider this: To mother-hen the dog can endanger him. Enter his sphere a moment. Look around, but don't take anything. Canine needs are modest but intense, and his treasures few. His cardinal ones are his own essence and the right to be, which includes not being misled by his best friend. As a defender—which is ultimately the dog's choice, not ours—he has a right to know that among the world's two-legged masters are those who would hurt him—and he can handle them!

Days later we threw the proud Rottweiler a final curve. With Tank biting the sleeve, Mike screamed "Out" at the top of his lungs, right in the dog's face with the confident expectation of a trainer. Mike later noted a sense that, for the next few seconds, time took a break.

I knew what he meant. Among my memories are freeze frames of Tank's jaws slackening, his gaze uncertain, searching for me, me yelling "Action Action Action!" and the whip dropping to the ground as Tank chomped back down with crushing force, the dog's eyes burning into Mike's.

Q. You had Jenny do this with Tank in Chapter 13. Why have Mike repeat the lesson?

A. Gender. Tank knew to take orders from me, a male. That he refused Jenny's command doesn't mean he would ignore Mike's.

My right palm made a quick wiping motion down my left forearm. Mike saw the gesture and slipped the sleeve. Tank thrashed it while staring at Mike.

"Out! Back!"

The dog released and moved to my side. I kicked the sleeve to Mike.

"Action!"

You could never accuse Tank of a dearth of passion.

Seconds into the battle, Mike commanded "Out!" Tank roared and drove him backward.

I signaled Mike to not slip the sleeve and counted to five. Then, "Out! Back! Watchim!"

Standing next to me, Tank gave Mike hell. I nodded to Mike. He threw down the sleeve right in front of Tank. The dog became a vocal Vesuvius. Mike ran, howling like he'd sat in turpentine. As Jenny might have put it: one, 800, boogie.

Tank's final reward of the day was his newfound ability to run the helper off just by barking. Though I wouldn't have thought it possible, the big dog swelled a little bigger as Mike fled. He glanced at me for a second, as if to say, "Did you see what *I* did?" I patted his neck.

Q. Why did Mike throw down the sleeve?

A. To accentuate to Tank that he could earn a victory—the sleeve—just by barking. Of course, that's also why Mike ran when Tank roared at him.

I walked Tank to the sleeve and tapped it with my foot. "Want a souvenir, big dog?" The Rotty nosed the object, sniffed it twice, then marked it.

Q. Marked it? You mean he. . . ?

A. Raised a leg and opened the floodgates.

Q. Victorious contempt or assertion of territory?

A. Knowing Tank, and from his expression at the sleeve's denouement, probably some of each, but only he can really know.

Reflection

All knowledge, the totality of all questions and all answers,
is contained in the dog.

Franz Kafka

CHAPTER 17

PROOFING

In the Preface I posed the question, "How can an owner be certain the dog will defend on command?" That's what proofing is all about.

One

Wearing a Tyrollean hat, quartz-thick glasses and a faded beige topcoat, the little, white-haired man tottering toward Cupcake and me seemed 200 years old and as harmless as air.

"Hello, hello," he said in frail tones. "Oh, what a nice doggy." Lullaby soft, "Hello, doggy, hello."

With childlike gentleness, the old gentleman patted the huge German Shepherd (I didn't name the dog, by the way) and made cooing sounds of enjoyment. Delighted by the stranger's affections, Cupcake licked the offered hand.

"I once had a dog like this, a long, long time ago," the old man sighed, looking wistfully at Cupcake. "Well, bye, bye, doggy. Good-bye now." He patted the animal's head a last time.

With slow wags of his tail, Cupcake watched the old gentleman dodder away, and I reflected it was too bad the dog had to lose this illusion. Cupcake liked people, especially kind folks who liked him. But he was headed home soon and I had to be sure he'd trigger in situations that aren't what they seem.

The elder toddled to a large oak tree 30 feet away, one that had shed most of its leaves. He rubbed the back of his neck. I pointed at him. "Action!"

Cupcake hesitated for just a second. Mike had given a bravo performance. He had never agitated Cupcake, thus the animal harbored no memories that the visitor might be a bad guy.

The dog devoured the distance to the "old man," who shucked his coat as he ducked behind the tree and reappeared wearing a hard sleeve and wielding a cardboard tube, screaming curses. The Shepherd struck like a maddened thing. Cupcake didn't like being fooled.

Having followed the dog at a run, I grabbed a length of the 30-foot lead trailing from his leather collar.

"Out! Back!"

The dog released and scooted to my side.

"Watchim!"

Cupcake was a responsive barker.

Mike, magically gifted with the agility of youth, departed in great haste.

I patted the dog. "Moves good for an old timer, doesn't he, Cupcake?"

Now, please, before you attempt this proofing scheme, have your agitator reread the Warning in the front of this book. Several times. Then know that you do not have to use this technique. If your pet has done well to date, there's no reason to suspect he would not respond like Cupcake. I make my living training, teaching and writing about dogs. I have to look an owner in the eye and say, "On command, your dog will nail a seemingly friendly person not wearing a sleeve." You don't have to do that. Because this is a book about training techniques, I'm obligated to report this proofing method to you. But at the same time, I hope you'll listen as I attempt to talk you out of trying it.

Yes, I had a long leash on Cupcake. No, he was never so far from me that I couldn't have landed on the lead with both feet to stop him in an emergency. Yes, Mike and I had rehearsed this scene many times without a dog present before we ever tried it for real. He was within touching distance of the tree when "he rubbed the back of his neck," his signal that he could see the sleeve and the cardboard tube behind the tree and was ready. No, I don't even want to think about the consequences had Mike slipped, fumbled the sleeve, been clawed or—use your imagination.

If you choose to try such training, know that it is done but once during a dog's life. Cupcake would never again be aimed at a "nice" stranger (at least, not in practice), especially one so benign as the persona Mike portrayed.

Q. So why do it at all?

A. Do you remember the "well-tailored gentleman" Greta flattened in Chapter 1? Recall that the grinning glad-hander became a knife-wielding assailant in a heartbeat. The world can be like that.

Two

The church parking lot that Greta and I walked across was as empty as a politician's promise. From behind a tree, Jenny approached us menacingly. She wore boots, heavy jeans and a tired denim jacket, but no sleeve was visible.

She stopped six feet away and withdrew a short, inch-thick cylinder from a pocket. A flick of her wrist expanded the baton to almost two feet in length as its metal tubes telescoped and locked into place. Jenny shrieked, raised the weapon and ran toward us.

I dropped Greta's leash. "Action!"

Greta raced at Jenny with fearsome imperative. Jenny jerked an arm up to protect herself. Though Greta had never before bitten a hidden sleeve, which is worn

Which arm wears the hidden sleeve?

under clothing, she didn't hesitate to nail Jenny's nearer forearm. Jenny yelped and dropped the club. She cursed the German Shepherd as she smacked the palm of her free hand between the dog's ears. Greta bit harder.

"I quit! I quit!"

"Out!"

Greta released.

"Back! Watchim!"

She hopped to my side. Clacking her teeth, her muzzle jabbed toward Jenny.

"Get hold of that damn dog. Don't let it bite me again."

"Take off while you still can."

Jenny left, with dispatch.

"You did good, Greta." I patted her neck as she stared after the fleeing figure. "You're about ready to go home, babe," I said, smiling, thinking to myself, "Dammit."

Hidden-sleeve agitation is not for the squeamish. Depending on the equipment's quality and the dog's jaw pressure, the job can be painful. No, I've never seen stars, but I have come away with horrendous bruises. The work is also riskier, because you can't easily slip a hidden sleeve.

Q. How is that riskier?

A. Imagine a dog has knocked you to the ground. The trainer's feet are dug in and the lead is tight. The animal couldn't pursue if you could roll away, but you can't because the dog's jaws are locked on a sleeve you can't slip—and his eyes just switched to your face.

Two basic types of hidden sleeves are open- and closed-end. Because open-end sleeves expose the helper's hand, a slipped bite can result in amputation. At the same time, closed-end sleeves leave an

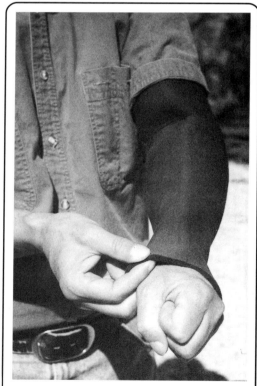

Gauntlets are much thinner than a sleeve but can provide extra protection.

agitator without the use of her sleeved hand, which reduces her ability to defend herself if things go wrong.

Q. Aren't artificial hands and similar devices available?

A. Yes, but most are not much more realistic in appearance than closed-end hidden sleeves. With hard-biting dogs like Tank, wear extra padding, often termed *gauntlets*, under the hidden sleeve.

Look back at the line, "She cursed the German Shepherd as she smacked the palm of her free hand between the dog's ears." Recall from Chapter 8 that Jenny is "hummingbird quick." I'm not kidding. Jenny's hands are faster than a Las Vegas dealer's. Before your agitator tries something like this, make darn sure the person is every bit as fast, because the dog is very quick and can come off a sleeve like a bat, and can bite infinitely harder than one.

Three

Chattan snoozed while I fished from a creek bank. Resident trout were as safe as in God's pocket, since my line had no hook. Twenty feet downwind Mike, wearing a hard sleeve, jumped from behind a tree and shrieked a sentiment about a Yankee general named Grant that was as unkind as the act it described was improbable. The Doberman leaped up.

"Action!"

A heartbeat later the handsome dog had thundered to within a bound of Mike, and I yelled "Out! Watchim!" Chattan slid to a stop inches from the sleeve and set off a canine cacophony, saliva flying from his jaws. I walked to his side, said "Out!" and heeled him away. When we were 10 feet from Mike, I spun around and sent the dog in to get his daily bite.

Some trainers don't use this technique, claiming it reduces the dog's fire and teaches hesitancy. My answer is, if you'll indulge an archaic word, balderdash. Like the lesson involving Cupcake, we practice aborting a rush only once during the dog's life, unless the animal ignores the "Out" command and takes a cheap shot at the agitator. Should that happen, the dog and I have words, and we repeat the test a few days later. Just as I have to know a manstopper will fight a non-threatening stranger, I must be certain the animal will stop on command in mid-charge.

Q. But don't you always have a leash on a guard dog? Couldn't he be stopped that way?

A. Sure, but leashes can break. Rock-solid control in regard to your commands should be the key to safety, not equipment.

Four

I was minding my own business, sitting in my living room, when Travis burst through the front door like he owned the place, radiating cop-like authority.

"You! On the floor! Now!" he said, pointing a gun at me.

Just then Smokey, my German Shepherd, raced into the room.

"Dog, don't give me no static!" Travis yelled. Unsure, Smokey stood in place.

Although I had arranged the evening's entertainment, Travis just about had me convinced he had turned terrorist and should not be messed with. Truly, it was an Oscar-caliber performance.

"SIT! STAY!" he commanded Smokey.

But Smokey did neither of those things. He stared at Travis, quivering. Fear? Or anticipation? We'd soon know, for a second later I said "Action!"

I had never seen Travis knocked backward before, during his football days or by a 90-pound German Shepherd. And Travis cut the animal no slack. None. For a moment it was war. He lunged at Smokey as the dog went for him, and the collision was Super Bowl quality. As he later said, shaking his head, pondering the bruises on his arm despite having worn a stout hidden sleeve, "Man, when that dog decides to rock 'n' roll, Gawd!"

"Well trained, thanks to Jenny and Mike. And now, to you."

"And there he was," Travis went on as if I'd said nothing, "licking your damn cheek two minutes after blowing my doors off!"

"Smokey's got good taste."

"Hell of a dog. Hell of a manstopper."

A Seldom-Mentioned Point

During hidden-sleeve work, the agitator should wear a sleeve on *each* arm, not just the one she intends to present to the dog. Given Murphy's Law, protecting only one arm guarantees that someday an animal will hit the other.

Five

The usual suspects had assembled: Jenny, Mike and Travis. Each wore hidden sleeves. It was understandable that Chaska was enamored of none of them, because they were taking turns making hostile gestures and yelling at me.

"Watchim!"

Chaska let everyone know she was there. The trio started to back off, but then Jenny ran at me, a raised club in one hand.

"Action!"

Jenny screamed in pain and dropped her weapon as Chaska nailed her arm.

"Out!"

Jenny staggered away, simpering and holding her arm. Then Mike and Travis rushed us.

"Action!"

Chaska picked one—Mike, as it happened—and fastened onto his arm like a talon. Travis had seen enough. He changed course and hurried after Jenny. Mike screamed, "Get it off me!"

"Out!"

Chaska released, Mike took off. The Doberman was breathing hard. The triad held a fast conference and began slinking toward us.

"Watchim!"

If a dog's bark ever said "Make my day," Chaska's did that afternoon. The wrecking crew backed off, then loped away. "You did Rotty good, Chaska."

"Better than any damn Rott," the Doberman's glance shot back.

Contending against multiple bad guys is the program's final aggression element, and it is as much training as proofing.

Q. When Mike and Travis rushed you, did you point at which one Chaska should bite?

A. No. Guardians usually react to the nearest target.

Six

I heeled my Doberman, Chattan, across the deserted football field's goal line. He didn't think much of the idea because Smokey, my German Shepherd, was being handled by a friend and was busy hitting bad guys at mid-field and greatly enjoying himself.

Moments later, after running Chattan through his obedience repertoire, I played switch with him and Smokey. While Chattan flattened agitators, Smokey had to prove to me that his obedience was first rate, despite the supreme distractions occurring 50 yards away.

I worked each dog in obedience, on-leash, only for as long as it took me to make certain that their responses were acceptable. In a real situation, a fight between man and dog, I would get my own pet out of there. But until a manstopper is reliable regardless of the nearby agitation of another animal, his training is incomplete.

These two photographs depict another kind of proofing: That a manstopper won't lunge at someone just because the person is wearing a sleeve. Note that the leash is loose; I wasn't restraining the dog—she did that herself.

Did You Notice?

You shouldn't conduct proofing sessions at the training site. Once the lessons have taken, practice them in other settings. Still, note the foregoing accounts made no mention of passersby. That's because there were none. For safety reasons, each session was and should be set up in areas with no uninvited guests.

Q. Once I've finished my dog's training, how often should I work her to keep her sharp?

A. With my pets I taper off: once a week, then every couple of weeks. A canine seldom forgets what she learns. I've seen dogs perform flawlessly during practice, even though they had not been worked in months. Manstoppers come to like their craft, so much so that I stage outings for their enjoyment. Things a dog likes and has worked hard for should not be denied her.

Friendliness

One might infer that manstopper training imbues a disdain for humans. Not true. Throughout the program I frequently expose each animal to numerous non-threatening, friendly, love-to-pet-you people. This shows the dogs that all humanity has not become a potential threat, and it provides contrasts between folks like us and the bad guys.

Reflection

A dog is like an eternal Peter Pan, a child who never grows old and who therefore is always available to love and be loved.

Aaron Alexander

CHAPTER 18

POISON PROTECTION

This chapter's title may be somewhat ambiguous, because poisoning is not the only way a sicko can murder your pet. I remember a Doberman who was offered beef impregnated with tiny shards of glass. A Great Pyrenees was slipped meat laced with metal shavings. It took both of them a long time to die.

Dog killers often function with relative impunity. Such cowards are hard to catch, and even when brought before the bar of justice, the punishment seldom fits the crime. Often classed a misdemeanor, killing someone's pet should be a felony and retribution should be swift and terrible.

The ideas behind poison-proofing are twofold: The dog should learn to eat only from his food dish, and should spurn tidbits offered by strangers or tossed into his yard. Don't subject a puppy to this training, however. A pup, having no frame of reference, could misapply the lesson's point and refuse to eat at all.

If the proofing technique I offer seems harsh, remember we are protecting your dog's life. We need a method that will unmistakably say, "Don't touch it unless it's in your dish," and will work whether or not you are present should temptation arise.

First, consider some ancillary guidelines. Always feed your pet in an area inaccessible to strangers. Place the water bowl near the food dish, so that by association he may learn not to take water from unfamiliar sources. Run your hand through the food before feeding your dog. This makes the meal safe, as it imbues it with your scent (the practice also reminds the animal that his food comes from you).

When boarding your dog, furnish the kennel operator with your pet's dish and bowl, or else the animal may not eat or drink until you return. Bring an adequate supply of food, too—be sure to scent it first, as described above—as

166

a dog can learn from this training to accept only the type of food to which he is accustomed.

Never allow strangers to give tidbits to your dog. That's bad technique for two reasons. It runs counter to the mindset we're trying to instill—take no food from strangers—and once the dog has internalized the lesson, a well-meaning stranger could be bitten.

Training

To poison-proof your dog you need an electric-fence charger (a device that electrifies a wire fence with mild current) and several feet of insulated wire. Fence chargers come in varying strengths, and while you want equipment that will get the job done, you don't want something with enough power to knock a bull over backward. Explain your intent to a product-knowledgeable salesperson and seek recommendations as to which model would be safe yet suitable. Then get your veterinarian's opinion.

Conduct the first session in the morning before feeding your dog; delay the meal until after the lesson. With your pet not in attendance and with the charger turned off, run an insulated wire from the charger to a location in the yard that your dog frequents (when a dog is let into his yard, he travels a specific route, checking for evidence of visitors). Use leaves or a few inches of dirt to conceal the cord. Strip away enough insulation to jab an end of bare wire through a piece of meat, and bend the wire around itself so that, should the charger fail, the dog cannot easily pull the meat from the wire. Wear rubber gloves so as not to put your scent on the food. Either arc the wire so it holds the bait just off the ground, or place the meat on a non-conductive surface, like heavy cardboard, lest it ground out.

Activate the fence charger. Let your dog into the yard. Alone. You stay in the house. Your pet has to learn this one on his own. We can't allow him to conclude that the upcoming event had anything to do with you. Not only might such an association cause hard feelings, but the lesson might seem to apply only when you're home, and a poisoner would be more likely to go after your pet when you aren't around.

Q. Won't my dog scent that I have been in the yard?

A. Sure, but I'm presuming that you spend enough time in your dog's yard that finding your scent there won't be unusual. If your setup is such that you seldom visit this area, walk about it thoroughly before letting your pet out-side, to scent the entire area rather than just the location of the meat.

Watch from a window. Your dog will soon discover the bait, will try to grab it and will likely yip when the current bites. Stay put. He may go back for a second try, or even a third or fourth. Eventually he will abandon the idea of grabbing the meat. Once you are certain this is the case, immediately bring your pet into the house and—acting as though nothing unusual has hap-pened—feed him. I say "immediately" because we want to provide your dog with a quick contrast: Edibles found outside the bowl are dangerous, but food in his dish is safe. While the animal partakes of breakfast, turn off the fence charger and remove the bait and the wire from the yard.

Using another type of meat, set up the same temptation the following day but at a different time (afternoon or evening) and at a new location in the yard. If you initially used beef, try boneless turkey next. (Be sure your dog is not allergic to any of these foods.) Try lamb the following day when you again create the setup, and vary the time and location of the event once more.

Watch for avoidance behavior: Your pet discovers food in the yard and not only does he not mouth it, he retreats from it, perhaps barking at it. Once this response is established, you can give the training a rest.

Still, you must periodically verify that your dog's memory is operating by recreating the temptation. A week after you see your pet avoid the bait, con-trive the situation once more. Presuming that your dog still shuns the food, turn up the heat: Have a non-threatening stranger offer meat over or through your fence. Again, you should not be present. Your assistant should be new to your dog—and, not incidentally, should never be seen by the dog again—and should wear insulated rubber gloves for protection against the current. Hide the cable under your accomplice's jacket. When offering the food, your helper should seem friendly, not at all threatening. Moreover, he should entice the dog in affable, kindly tones, as a real poisoner might.

If your pet refuses the food, good. If he tries to take it, also good, because if his inclination is to do so, better he should learn from fiction than from wondering "What happened?" as his light winks out. In either case, once the dog's reaction is clear, the helper should depart without agitating your dog in any manner. We don't want the animal to become aggressive toward strangers simply because they are strangers. In fact, we don't want the dog to be hostile toward a poisoner—that's for the owner to handle—we just want the animal to refuse food offered by outsiders.

That said, be aware that this type of training can lead some dogs to show defensive aggression when offered food by an outsider. My practice is not to let anyone give my dog treats, because I don't want to enable the animal to take food from strangers. This would run counter to poison-proofing, and I don't want anyone undeserving to be bitten.

Reflection

Until man extends the circle of his compassion to all living things,
man will not himself find peace.

Albert Schweitzer

PART III

EXTRAS

CHAPTER 19

PUPPY, PUPPY

In the way you select the puppy, you begin to train the dog. That piece of profundity crystallized as I watched Karen kneel to pet her new pup, a male Rottweiler.

Though I couldn't say who was more fascinated by the other, the nature of an eight-week-old attention span soon came into play and the pup departed at full romp to explore the perplexing world in which he'd found himself.

Notice Karen knelt; she didn't loom over the pup by bending at the waist. Remember, things above a canine seize his attention and can inhibit. A towering human can impart negative memory traces—vague, indistinct yet troubling feelings that resonate when someone bends over the mature dog. A manstopper doesn't need that kind of blind spot.

For an insight into the power of associative learning, consider that many professionals elevate food bowls to habituate a "heads-up" carriage. Dishes on the floor can create a habit of holding the head down, not in a conscious search for food but because that's where it is found. As mentioned in Chapter 9, "Dogs exist at a primitive level."

The pup soon discovered he couldn't plow through chainlink fences or uproot trees, when he ran at birds they leaped impossibly high and danced on air, and Karen was always right where he'd left her. After another flurry of petting and being told, "What a good little-big guy you are," he again toddled off in quest of adventure.

"Karen was always right where he'd left her." I've heard owners chuckle when speaking of tricking a pet into going out in bad weather by walking outdoors with the pup, then ducking inside when the little one's attention was elsewhere. That's an excellent way to instill insecurity, illustrate human unreliability and highlight a truth better left unlearned: No dog needs a person for survival.

Recall from Chapter 4, "Evaluation and drive stimulation of puppies can be started as soon as the little ones can puppy-run and show interest in bump-crash play with one other." You've studied drive concepts and training of mature dogs. Now consider foundational puppy lessons.

Karen plucked a burlap sack from the porch railing where she'd draped it earlier to air. Holding the six-foot cord she'd tied to one end, she walked past the pup, trailing the burlap on the ground, peripherally watching the young one's reactions.

Do the job right and a juvenile canine mind won't connect the sack's mysterious movements with you. The puppy will notice the article, investigate and a confluence of play, prey, dominance, protection and fight drives will take over.

The pup heard Karen's footsteps and ran-bounced after her and—"What's this?" (mentally I wrote a canine script). "It's moving away from me. I should stop it! I'll put a foot on it!" Plunk. "That didn't work—it's still moving. Maybe if I jump on it, bite it." Leap. Dive. Crash. Bite. "Yay! It stopped! I got it!"

Flicking her hand, Karen fluttered the sack, making it seem to be trying to get away. As the puppy sank his teeth in and gave the burlap a murderous shake, Karen released it. The young animal thrashed the cloth once more, then trotted to Karen, who had knelt a few feet away. She clapped her hands and said, "C'mere, pupper." Again the young Rotty delighted in being petted and fussed over. Then a passing leaf seized his attention, and he flounced away in earnest pursuit.

Moments later, the leaf vanquished, the pup again saw the sack rippling across the lawn. Nose down, butt up, tail fluttering, body aquiver, he stared and stared— then burst forth, fell over his own feet, landed in a heap, leaped back up, pounced on the burlap and bit it into submission.

He dragged his slain dragon to Karen, who sat on the ground and applauded the young fuzzy as he strode toward her. Battle weary, he sprawled across her legs.

She picked him up, carried him into the house and set him on the kitchen floor. Seeing me, his feet were churning before he touched the tile. I knelt as he ran toward me. His front paws against me, he mouthed my shirt while I rubbed his shoulders.

"She picked him up" says a lot. That she stifled a groan of effort says even more. When this Rott became a duppy (not yet a dog but no longer a puppy) he was humongous, big enough that Karen would need a forklift to hoist him. But what the puppy learns the dog remembers, and Karen knew that he would probably always think she could scoop him up like a feather, even when his

Sherri Sullivan demonstrates the correct way to hold a puppy, making sure to support his back legs. Letting them hang free could cause a feeling of helplessness when being held. When picking up a pup, do so slowly. Lifting too quickly can cause the blood to rush from his head. That can trigger dizziness, motion sickness or fainting, any of which can make him fear his owner.

age would be measured in years; a handy mindset should push ever come to shove over human-canine dominance issues.

Q. Doesn't that conflict with your earlier statement that dogs think?

A. No. I never said they think like humans. Many a puppy raised behind a fence that was insurmountable then won't try to clear it as an adult, because he learned at an impressionable age that it's too high.

"Well, what do you think?" Karen asked, glowing.

"You got a good one," I told her. "Have you named the little colossus?" Even as a pup he had a chest as deep as a James Joyce novel.

"No, the right idea hasn't come to mind. He makes me think of a—oh, what's that word?" Karen scrunched her brow. "I mean, did you see him try to walk through the fence, pushing it with the top of his head? And how amazed he was that he couldn't rip out that sapling and carry it off?"

"Uh-huh. He didn't just fool around with the sack, either. He ran over it, flattened it." In my mind I'd already named the big little guy.

"Like"—flashing a thousand-watt smile, Karen snapped her fingers—"Like a tank!"

Tank soon developed a healthy taste for burlap. Then one day Karen gave him an old sleeve cover and he discovered that jute was even better. She played with him as before, and jute, being tougher, was a tougher foe, much to Tank's delight.

Q. Did she withhold the sleeve cuff during teething?

A. Of course not. Biting can make a teething pup's mouth hurt less. Similar to the lasting effects of associative learning with elevated food bowls, Tank found that when he chewed jute, his gums felt better and thus it was good to bite the material.

Q. So you taught the dog at an impressionable age to enjoy biting jute?

A. Yes, that's the method.

Some trainers put the kibosh on the notion of owners playing tug-of-war with their young dogs, saying the animals can get the wrong idea and learn to fight their food-givers. I grant you, this can happen if the activity is conducted improperly; and no dog should ever perceive the owner as a rival or, worse, an adversary. The animal should sense that he and the owner are together fighting the sack, but a person can inadvertently send signals that say he is fighting the dog.

Q. I shouldn't roughhouse with my puppy?

A. Don't even think it. Recall "Your perception of reality differs from your pet's." Markedly. What you view as playful your dog may see as the real thing. He can decide that you are fighting him, and will try to get better at it. The result can be an emotional basket case torn by conflicting desires: to be your buddy on one hand, to shred you on the other.

However, tug-of-war with a sack is not roughhousing with an owner—it is roughhousing with a sack. You are a facilitator, not an aggressor. The sack is a third party, a focal point for the dog. It is a barrier that attracts her attention, diverting her focus from you to it. The concept is similar to ball play: You hold the ball, you throw it, the dog grabs it. The animal does not nail your hand while you are holding the toy. The essential difference between ball and sack play is that you hold rather than throw the sack for the dog to bite. However, the sack is still not you or part of you, any more than the ball is.

Roughhousing involves behaviors I don't recommend, such as rolling around on the ground with pooch, slapping at her and encouraging her to jump against and bite at the owner. That is crazy-making. It sends all the wrong signals by teaching the dog to fight her human. I know a gent who, against my advice but on the urging of a local "expert," roughhoused with his German Shepherd. One evening, after a few weeks of practice, the owner wound up stitched like a baseball and the dog had to be put down. The animal had been taught too well, and the resultant confusion had turned to anger that fed upon itself until it mushroomed into rage.

Sack play with a young Doberman.

A next step after sack play is to replace the burlap with a lightweight sleeve.

Playtime

Every day Karen rolled tennis balls for Tank. She didn't throw them until he was older, as a puppy cannot follow the flight of a tossed article. Given his size, she later switched to larger toys (motorcycle tires and junior-size basket-balls among them), lest the animal swallow smaller objects. These "training periods" heightened Tank's drives and provided regular exercise, which is as important to canine well-being as proper nutrition. Lacking either, healthy physiological and psychological development suffers.

Another plus: Play with a resilient toy builds jaw muscles. A dog who grabs a tennis ball mouths it while returning to the handler, to force submission onto the object, which, being springy, stimulates the dog's fire by seeming to resist. A ball carried 10 times per play session figures to at least 50 compressions per day multi-plied by several outings a week, which produces extensive isometric jaw exercise.

Don't use hard toys, however. I knew an owner who preferred baseballs, but the toys' hardness habituated a hesitant bite. Because the dog couldn't sink his teeth in, he learned a light bite. Worse, if the ball took a bad bounce and struck him, he could have learned to fear it.

Q. When throwing a toy, should I say "Action" to get my dog to associate the word?

A. No. Play is play, but "Action" is business. Reserve it for contention against human aggressors. Besides, "Action" commands defense, and tennis balls seldom waylay anyone.

I do use a two-syllable command ("Get it!") in cueing my pet to grab a toy, just for the mental linking that can occur between it and other dual-syllable commands. Both are fun, both call for intensity, and each can heighten attitude toward the other.

Socialization

As I mentioned in Chapter 3, *socialization* refers to the quantity and quality of situations, people and events a puppy encounters during his first months. They will affect him all his life. A dog raised in isolation, one who knows only the owner, wilts like a hothouse plant when exposed to the real world. Likewise, a dog who meets only gruff, harsh or emotionally bankrupt people is ill-equipped for guard training. He has learned—indeed, he has been taught—that anyone other than his owner represents a threat.

This pup delights in play with a ball . . .

. . . or an old sleeve cover.

Puppies can learn a powerhouse attitude at an impressionable age.

Q. At what point has socialization done its work?

A. Nine out of 10 sound dogs beyond four months are too old for socialization to be effective. For the remaining one out of 10, the period extends to five months. If that sounds very young, remember the focus is *Canis familiaris*, whose larger members' life span seldom exceeds 12 years, not *Homo sapiens*, who often lives six times longer. Things must happen at an earlier age for dogs, because their time here is shorter.

Also, socialization applies to canine perceptions of humans, not of other dogs. We're examining the canine-human relationship here, not the canine-canine. Learning about dogs occurs between littermates during the fifth to seventh weeks of life. This is why a pup should stay with the litter for the first seven weeks. It may not seem a great difference in time, but pups sold at six weeks, as many "breeders" do to avoid vaccination costs, lose for life the chance to learn to get along with other dogs.

Q. You're saying certain learning is meant to happen at certain ages?

A. Right. Keep in mind, too, we are talking about dogs slated for fightwork. Their temperaments must be unfailing. Genetics contribute, but so does learning. Improper socialization can skew an otherwise sound personality.

Q. Can an unsocialized dog be brought around, made amicable, reprogrammed?

A. As a companion and pet, maybe. It depends upon his genes, how much neglect occurred and the owner's skills. As a guardian prospect, though, I wouldn't even consider the notion. Would you like to share your days and nights with a bite-trained dog who harbors a deep-seated wariness of humans?

Bonding

You met this concept in the Preface, when I discussed the importance of your pet knowing "he is a genuine member of the family." It popped up again in the first chapter: Greta "saw Tim and almost came unglued." The two-way nature of this relationship was suggested a few lines later: "a stream of joyful yips and hops (by both owner and dog, incidentally)." The crux of a healthy human-canine relationship is bonding, an endless process born of giving your dog a sense of security and belonging. It derives from feeding, approval, disciplining, petting, grooming, shared travel, playtime, training and the simple act of talking to your pet.

Q. These are things the dog's mom did during puppyhood, aren't they?

A. That's why they're effective, and necessary. In puppy perceptions the owner becomes the parent.

Consider this simple act: Your pet scratches at the door, you open it for him. This adds one more piece to bonding's mosaic as your response says you not just hear him, you listen to him.

Karen heightened bonding with Tank by ensuring he had lots of playtime with her. This also gave birth to the idea in Tank's mind of him and Karen as a team. Play, an enjoyable drive heightener that helps to draw the dog out of the puppy, was something they did *together*.

Karen also talked to Tank a lot. She never baby-talked to him—as a friend once observed, "That makes the dog silly"—and she didn't deliver long, rambling monologues, but "Let's take a walk," "Thank you for bringing me such a nice leaf," "Want a cookie?"

Some folks liken human-canine bonding to love. Though the importance of affection varies among species, consider "research" performed upon young primates. Experimenters took healthy baby monkeys from their parents and housed the young animals in separate, spacious, well-lighted rooms. In each was an appropriately sized, man-made parent, a furry, big-eyed substitute engineered so the orphans could nurse at will.

But there was no communication, no affection, no cuddling. Love and the opportunity for bonding had been withheld from the equation.

After a few days the young primates began to cling to the surrogates' necks more than normal, as though seeking acceptance and touching. Finding not

Bonding is key to successful training, and can be enhanced even when you're not directly occupied with your pet . . .

. . . and it can pay life-long dividends with a manstopper, who should be stable, intelligent, friendly.

even acknowledgment, the little ones soon regressed, curling into the fetal position at the replacement parents' feet for long periods. Interest in play withered. Lethargy set in. Chaos ensued.

This was predictable, as radically stressed animals often retrogress to the last emotionally safe place. It's a survival mechanism. Sometimes it works, but often it just weakens the system further by fighting a delaying action.

Within weeks, despite the availability of wholesome food in a protected environment, the results were those that any knowledgeable animal trainer could have predicted: Over half the young animals had died.

Now, while that image of so-called science resonates, consider human-canine bonding. Dogs trapped without a family may not expire, but often they develop the canine equivalent of a thousand-yard stare, always looking, seeking, trying, sometimes frantically, at least at first.

Puppy Picking

Karen found Tank by dealing with a breeder she trusted and by spending a good deal of time around the litter, observing and evaluating, when the pups were seven weeks old. She had met and approved of both the sire and dam, their structure and temperament, and knew that neither animal had hip dysplasia. Not incidentally, German Shepherd and Doberman parents should also be certified free of hip dysplasia, and Dobes should be clear of von Willebrand's Disease (vWD) and cardiomyopathy.

Keep in mind, "pick of the litter" is relative. It depends on who is doing the picking and the qualities sought. Was Tank a show dog? Not to my eye, as he exceeded the dimensions described in the breed standard. Would he have been right for most retirees? No. He was too active, too powerful. A guide or therapy dog? I doubt it, given his innate dominance level.

Our concern, however, is how to pick a manstopper candidate. And "spending a good deal of time around the litter, observing and evaluating" is the best way to do that. Karen didn't "Ooh!" and "Ah!" for a few minutes and then say, "That one!" She spent hours with the pups. She knew that the support each puppy draws from the litter can mask traits, and that she'd learn more about each wee beastie once her own newness wore off. She also knew that what you see in the puppy you get more of in the dog.

And she knew not to simply grab the "best" pup available. That's another relative concept. She was prepared to go home with no puppy if the right one wasn't there.

Karen's first observation concerned responses to her, a stranger. The litter showed curiosity and varying degrees of dominant and submissive behaviors. Had any of the pups displayed little interest in her, she would have scratched them from contention. She wanted sociable, not contentious. A pup exhibiting chronic fear or excessive aggression over a newcomer's arrival would also be a washout. However, if an entire litter is uninterested—or should the puppies flee from someone—the problem is the person, not the pups.

Karen had long known the breeder and that he cared well for his puppies. She had also met and approved of the sire and the dam. If you don't know a breeder, note the conditions the litter is kept in. You want to see clean, roomy and safe surroundings, not dirty, packed into cages, or mutterings akin to, "One's been missing for a day or so but I imagine it's around here somewhere." Yes, that's an extreme characterization, but that's what you're trying to identify and avoid: extremes in any respect, in the pups' temperament or the breeders'. Many such people are out there, and to call them *breeders* is like labeling drug dealers *entrepreneurs*.

As a rule, I won't consider a pet store puppy, or one from anybody who raises more than two breeds or often has several litters on the ground. The phrase *puppy mill* leaps to mind, where pups are bred for quantity, not quality, and socialization is a word nobody knows.

Puppy tendencies vary within certain tolerances, but one inviolate factor concerns canine attitudes toward cleanliness. No, it isn't strike one if a pup delights in playing in mud. Puppies do that sort of thing. But one who sleeps atop droppings or ingests them is out of the running. At the very least, he may prove difficult if not impossible to housebreak. For a puppy to dash through an unnoticed pile is neither unusual nor alarming; but one attracted or indifferent to filth is unacceptable. Likewise, a pup who evacuates two inches from his sleeping area or food dish is less desirable than one who first moves well away.

An important manstopper attribute is curiosity. He explores the unknown and is seldom uninterested in or intimidated by newness. Spirit, élan, reverence of self—all are smoky concepts that are difficult to quantify. It can be trickier to define a puppy who feels good about himself than to identify one who doesn't, who suffers from the plastered-tail syndrome. The latter looks at you without turning or raising his head, which he often holds down, while the former lowers his head only for a purpose, such as eating, scenting or playing.

Karen noticed one puppy was underweight, listless and unwilling to compete at the food pan, choosing instead to make do with meager remains. A pup who cares little for sustenance seldom has much interest in learning. When motivation toward life's basics is lacking, an owner has scant inducements to promote bonding. Karen crossed this pup off her list.

She rolled a ball amid the litter to spot individual degrees of play and prey drives as well as dominant or submissive tendencies. Some pups showed more interest than others, but none responded with fear toward the toy's motion. If one had, Karen would have eliminated him from contention.

Karen asked the breeder to walk among the litter, to spot pups drawn to the human companionship of someone they knew. Curious, they all approached and remained. They were people pups. One who flees to a hiding place is not. Those who bounce away to pursue other activities may not be loners; perhaps they were just distracted for the moment. Puppies are like that.

In any litter, some members shine brighter than others. Karen wasn't concerned if one seemed a trifle slow. Sure, she wanted intelligence, but she knew that perseverance is what counts and was more concerned that a young animal tries to learn. A pup uninterested in acquiring knowledge has problems.

How a puppy responds to older dogs can indicate how he will relate to humans, because social behavior is the common denominator. As the breeder had a mature dog he could trust not to maul the little ones, he brought the adult to the litter area, and Karen noted the pups' reactions. The puppy who wouldn't muscle in at the food dish took a bug-eyed look and fled at full yelp with tucked tail. Although this is a one-strike-and-you're-out game, that was strike two. The pup wasn't manstopper material. Neither was a puppy bitch who launched an all-out attack at the visitor. Karen noticed that, while the first pup was apathetic toward his littermates, the second one had war in her heart, worrisome conditions both.

Again, Karen knew to avoid extreme behavior patterns, not slight or infrequent exaggerations. Some pups are rowdy, others are reserved. Either condition is acceptable. Constant indifference is not, nor is endless, neck-ripping aggression.

Petting is a simple check. A pup who dislikes being petted, one who responds with a sideways, lowered-head look as he slinks away, isn't companion material.

Conduct a similar test by picking up a puppy. Affectionate licking, light nibbling of hands or relaxed acceptance are all acceptable responses, but major struggling, screeching or fearful shaking or snapping are not.

Note which pups enjoy play. Puppyhood is a self-testing time during which healthy pups, through play and other drives, discover their capabilities. A young dog who seldom participates may harbor a temperamental weakness. Also, there is a difference between a playful pup and a controller. Karen wanted a dominant dog, yes, but not one so domineering as to present training problems.

At a moment when none of the pups were occupied with Karen, she dropped a sealed coffee can containing a few pebbles several feet from the litter. This one-time test of reactions to sudden noise and movement reveals stability. Some pups reacted with curiosity, others flinched. Karen left the flinchers there. Other unacceptable reactions are remaining frozen in place, trembling or fleeing. Of equal concern would be a pup who attacks the object. Either reaction indicates unstable temperament and suggests a fear-biter.

Karen had narrowed her search to two pups. One was a bitch of light structure and winning ways, the other a male of daunting proportions and scant reticence. She subjected each to one final test. Using the fleshy part of thumb and finger—*not* the fingernails—she compressed the webbed area between two front toes, counting to 10 while increasing the pressure. The test is completed and must stop *the instant* the pup shows any discomfort, such as whining or pulling the foot away. Extreme readings either way suggest an animal difficult to obedience train. One who yelps at the first hint of force won't be able to handle corrections (physical discipline); one who yawns as the count is

Karen and her full-grown friend.

finished won't notice them. The puppy bitch whined at four; the pup who would be christened Tank showed distress between seven and eight, which is about right.

Take care not to be bitten when testing an older canine. Further, don't use this test if the animal hasn't done well so far; don't stress a dog who is already out of the running. Whether testing a puppy or a dog, follow up with petting to show you weren't trying to make an enemy.

Homecoming

Karen nestled her pick in her arms, said, "Hi there, puppy, puppy," and drove him to her veterinarian, who checked the not-so-little one from top to bottom. The time to discover your pet has a heart murmur, for example, is not months after acquiring him.

Before bringing Tank home, Karen had stocked up on nutritious food and had acquired bowls, toys, an airline crate (for housebreaking purposes), grooming tools and other trinkets. Also, Karen took Tank home on a Friday afternoon so she would have the entire weekend to spend with him. She didn't want to leave him alone during his first days in his new environment. She brought him home during the day, too, not at night, so he would feel more secure when night came.

Sunday morning Karen phoned and invited me to stop by. She introduced me to Tank, took him outside, I watched them through the kitchen window, and you know the rest.

Reflection

Puppies are such a tremendous source of joy, and their personality is so easily influenced in a positive, or a negative way, that the dedicated working-dog owner will almost always acquire his dog at a very young age. Seven- to 10-week-old puppies are the best prospects.

Dietmar Schellenberg

CHAPTER 20
PROCEDURES AND TACTICS

I'm comfortable in telling you how to train your pet; it's how I train my own. But I'm not at ease in presuming to tell you how to use your guardian. I don't know you, your dog or your situation. At the same time, I'd be less than forthright if I left you hanging, as though such questions don't exist. My best and most proper solution is to report how I handle my dogs. To a degree, I have already done this.

Think back to Chapter 1, "Command Performance." Did you notice that after Greta dealt with the well-tailored gentleman, she met no other strangers?

First she encountered Mr. Strangeways. Next up was the woman asking directions. Then came the children, then the Toy Poodle, next the guy looking for a handout.

Then she met the bad guy. Following that encounter, "Greta was ready to go home."

Message: After a training period or a real defense, keep your dog away from strangers for several hours. Let him cool. The canine mind goes into another dimension during combat. He enters that plane in a flash but needs time to resurface. Prevent a mental case of the bends by making sure he's all the way back before letting anyone near him.

Use a different collar and leash for outings, too. To amplify that last caution, *don't* harness your dog when taking him for a stroll. The animal could associate a harness with impending fightwork.

As a corollary, never set up a socialization session involving children at a training site or soon after agitation. Don't ever risk the possibility your dog might link kids with combat. If you've ever seen the degree to which a dog can harm a child, you know it's a chilling, heartbreaking sight.

Q. You're saying that I shouldn't expose my dog to friendly people soon afterward, for contrast?

A. Yes. Doing so can get someone bitten. You have to appreciate that a dog, one who has just fought a person, has just been in a war zone, even if the skirmish appeared minimal to you. Recall that dogs see such matters as all or nothing. For them, few gray areas exist. Besides, you are the best contrast and, in any case, are all the animal needs. Understand that distinction: He not only needs no one else, he needs only you.

Q. After Greta hammered the well-tailored gentleman, you didn't simulate detaining him for police. Why not?

A. I answered that near the end of the same chapter: "Her role is to shield her human from scoundrels, not to chase or apprehend them. That's the cops' job."

Now, consider a terrifying instance: What if an assailant has a gun? Would you send your dog against someone holding a firearm? Might this not be a death sentence for your dog, and for you in retaliation for triggering the animal? Consider, too, a dog's rush might cause shots to be fired accidentally, striking God knows who. If someone points a gun at me, that person is in charge, calling the shots, if you will. And since neither my dog nor I am bulletproof, I'd not do anything to irritate that person.

This strategy can raise the question, "Why not teach the dog to go for the weapon hand?" I want my dog to bite the closer upper limb. This makes for a very quick, successful fight—the assailant feels pain so fast that he may forget he is armed. Training the animal to target a specific hand (or arm) can have an adversary controlling the dog just by keeping the hand holding the weapon out of reach. Then the dog bites no one.

Don't devalue the notion of a "quick, successful fight." In a real situation, that concept is key to survival. A dog who clamps down and is there to stay creates terror, which often wins the battle. Now take this a step further: Suppose the fight isn't fast. "The logic of terror reaches its logical conclusion: a humble rabbit, cornered by a fox, has nothing to lose by striking out, and rabbits have teeth, and sometimes the rabbit gets lucky."[1]

Q. Should I keep my dog's nails long and pointed for combat purposes?

A. My dogs' nails are normal length and aren't sharpened. Though a guard dog's nails assist in defense, their main function is in achieving traction. Also, excessively long nails can cause lameness.

Q. Should I teach an "Action" hand signal?

---

[1] *Executive Orders*, Tom Clancy, G.P. Putnam's Sons, 1996, page 123.

A. No. Signals are too risky and are bad tactics. The danger is that the dog might misunderstand a hand motion and wipe out the nearest citizen. The tactical flaw is that I do not want my dog looking at me for guidance during an escalating situation. I want him staring at the problem, which—as stated earlier—may cause the problem to slither away.

Collars and Leashes

Are you familiar with quick-release collars and leashes? Both cut the dog loose with a flick of the wrist. Does the idea sound good? It isn't. Too much can go wrong. A dog can learn to key on equipment instead of commands. Appearing to reach for a quick-release snap can trigger an animal, when the handler intended just to adjust a leash or collar. Such equipment may have a place with military or police K-9s, but not with personal protection dogs.

Q. How would you release your dog during a real conflict?

A. I would either unsnap the leash or, if there wasn't time, just let go of it.

Q. But couldn't an assailant use it to yank the dog away?

A. It's possible, but so is political integrity. Someone beset by a large, powerful dog probably wouldn't notice a leash, let alone grab it. Besides, a person yanking away from himself cannot generate much power—the leverage is wrong—and trying would just make the animal bite harder.

Q. How come?

A. Remember, when someone pulls a dog in one direction, his natural response is to go the other way. Besides, we've trained the dog to fight harder when the target fights back.

Leather collars with sharp, protruding metal points are another controversial type of equipment. Proponents assert no one could grab the dog's collar without injury. And that's true. No one could. Including the owner. I recommend against such equipment.

Q. Do you ever have your dog off-leash in public?

A. No. Never.

Q. Not even at a vet's office?

A. Especially not at a vet's office.

When taking my dogs for outings, I favor a steel, fur-saver collar or one of heavy-duty leather, and a four-foot leather leash strong enough to be unbreakable. I don't use a pinch or choke collar. An assailant could use either type to thwart the dog.

The popularity of chain leashes derives from their strong appearance. But appearances don't just deceive in this instance, they lie. Often made of weak pot metal, these leashes can pop where the wrist loop joins the chain, and their snaps are dime-store quality.

Retractable leashes are another trendy type. While the concept sounds good—excess lead disappearing into a handle at the flick of a button—the lunge of a powerful dog could snap such a leash like string.

Q. I've heard of a device called a Halti, which fits on the dog's head and muzzle. Opinion?

A. Forget it. Such devices restrain rather than train, and as such are totally inappropriate for a guard dog.

A fur-saver collar provides control while enhancing a dog's visual deterrence.

Housing and Transport

When your pet is home alone, what should he do if someone tries to enter the house? A person would have to be as quiet as a shadow to enter a dog's territory without alerting him. Canine hearing far exceeds ours, to say nothing of dogs' scenting abilities. If my pet senses someone nearby, he barks, which is sufficient to dissuade most people from entering. Should someone try to get in despite my dog's warning, that individual would be in for a hard day's night.

A related question is whether to leave the dog unattended in the yard. I do so with my pets, but the area is fenced in such a way that the animal cannot escape, no one can stick a hand or fingers through and gates are locked to prevent intrusion.

Q. What about posting signs warning that the dog is guard trained?

A. I've heard of a court ruling that held a "Beware of Dog" sign meant he was so vicious that he constituted a threat even to the owner. Go figure. A realistic objection is such a sign may be ineffective: Not everyone can read, and not everyone reads English.

Q. How about tying out a guard dog?

A. I won't routinely tie out any dog, protection trained or not. Tying can make a canine paranoid, as it negates his main defense: the ability to flee. It can also hamper the animal's trust in you, since you did the tying.

When traveling with my dog, across town or across the country, I leave him unattended in the car only during trips to a rest room or while registering at an inn. During those brief moments, the car's windows are up and its doors are locked. (Notice I said *brief* moments; a dog can suffer from heatstroke in a locked car in a matter of minutes.)

Children

Do you have kids? If so, when their friends visit what should you do with your dogs? I isolate mine from them. Sure, the animal might never misunderstand; he might know it's normal for *kinder* to knock one another flat while playing football, for instance. But should he ever think a family member is being threatened when that isn't the case . . . need I say more?

Q. Should my children be able to command the dog?

At 10 years old, Ashton Mayes has atypical maturity and understanding of guard dogs. Her parents trust her with Wolf and, equally important, him with her.

And when the photographer made a quick forward move that Wolf didn't care for, Ashton was able to control the situation, much to the shutterbug's relief.

A. Right away we have a problem. I mean, what's a child? I know prepubescents who are more mature than some teenagers and middle-aged people who are going on 11. If my child has the maturity and knowledge to handle a dog, I allow it. Keep in mind, though, that a court of law might take a dim view of the practice.

Company

Upon discovering that my dogs are protection trained, students in my obedience classes often say, chuckling, "I'll bet you don't get too many visitors."

"Few unwanted ones," I reply, but there's more to it. Most folks who drop by my digs are dog people. They know how to act around a guard dog. More to the point, they know how *not* to act. If a visitor shows fear of my dogs, I either put the animals in another room or run off the visitor. As mentioned earlier, "A canine's sensing of human fear can catapult her responses to the boil-over point." This is especially true of a manstopper.

Q. Do your dogs wear collars when company stops by?

A. Only if they were wearing collars when the visitors arrived. Earlier I recommended your dog be obedience trained before protection schooling, and I mentioned a favorite training manual, *Dog Logic—Companion Obedience*. Another book you should consider is *Advanced Obedience—Easier Than You Think*, specifically Chapter 4, "Off-Leash/Off-Collar Obedience." Unless you bring your pet to that level of reliability, his obedience will always be contingent upon equipment rather than thoroughness of training. Moreover, if you're ever hauled into court, demonstrating your dog's impressive off-leash/off-collar obedience might help your case.

Lights Out

If you are temporarily incapacitated, how should your dog respond to the approach of strangers? Example: You fall unconscious. How should your pet react to an emergency medical technician's approach? This is a paradox of guard dog ownership: In attempting to defend you, your best friend might unknowingly cause you harm.

Many protection dogs, given the above situation, would not let a stranger near the owner. Others, if approached properly, could be handled. The difference is sometimes less a function of training than of the dog's temperament, personality and bonding. Be aware, though, that a police officer might be called upon to shoot the animal so medical personnel can help the owner.

Vehicle Protection

Training a dog to protect a car or truck can cause problems. Even without specific training, many guardians won't let a stranger into their territory, including a vehicle, unless the owner shows approval. Not only do some dogs trained to protect automobiles take license to bark at anyone within hailing distance, but a child's fingers stuck through a window can be nipped off. That's why the only scenario worse than a guard dog left in a vehicle with the windows open is leaving a protector in an open truck bed.

Semantics

Throughout this book I have referred to guard dogs, protectors, guardians and manstoppers. I have avoided the phrase "attack dog." The difference between the two concepts is similar to that of offensive versus defensive military hardware: Both can serve either purpose; the key to characterization is in usage.

One could argue that a bite-trained dog is attack trained. From the dog's point of view, that may be accurate. But the reality is that the animal's action is no different from that of a human who fights someone assaulting him. From our perspective, the dog is a defender—his proper use is as a defensive option, not as an offensive weapon. In that sense the dog is like a gun: It depends on how he is used.

Reflection

The average dog is a nicer person than the average person.

Andrew A. Rooney

CHAPTER 21

Q & A

This chapter covers bits and pieces not addressed elsewhere in the book. Much of the material derives from questions asked by my seminar students.

Q. Can I show a guard dog in AKC obedience, tracking or breed competition?

A. I've done it and have never had a problem. Before entering a show I have shopped the judges, however. Many are good with dogs and know how to approach animals; some are overbearing fusspots who could easily trigger fight-or-flight in any dog, bite-trained or otherwise, and a manstopper has forgotten what flight means.

Q. In several of your books you talk about the importance of play toys and play time. Does this hold true for a guardian?

A. You bet. Guard trained or not, a dog is still a dog. One who enjoyed play before protection training likely still does, perhaps more than before, as the work raises drives (play, prey, retrieve, homing) related to chasing a toy.

Take care, though, not to confuse bitework with fightwork. Bitework can range in activity from chasing a ball to biting a sleeve playfully. Fightwork is the real McCoy. Message: Don't tease your pet with a toy—throw it for him.

Q. Can I teach my pet to be a watchdog—not to bite, just to bark on command or when strangers come around?

A. You can train a dog to show partial aggression (to bark but not bite), but the result can be like being a little bit pregnant. A dog can learn just to bark but the odds are, given the right circumstances, the animal will progress to biting.

Q. I've heard of a concept known as muzzle training, yet you don't use it in *Manstopper*. Why not?

A. One, it's too dangerous. Two, it's overly expensive. Three and four, it's both unnecessary and inappropriate for a personal-protection dog.

In such training, a muzzled dog is set against a sleeveless bad guy. Since the animal can't bite, he learns to use his paws and momentum to contend against a human.

Too dangerous: Note the phrase "sleeveless bad guy." Then envision the results should a muzzle come loose.

Overly expensive: Price a basket-weave muzzle (which is the only style I would use). Have a friend nearby with smelling salts when making this inquiry.

Unnecessary: Muzzle work frustrates the dog by restricting his ability to bite, thereby making him a more solid biter when not muzzled. At least that's the theory. In any case, we have already used sufficient frustration. "Too much of a good thing" is the phrase that comes to mind.

Inappropriate: We are training a family pet, not a war dog. Muzzle training can tap into higher levels of aggression than I would care to have lurking around my house. Also, if the work is handled incorrectly—which is easier than one might suppose—it can contribute to creating the "distrustful biting machine" mentioned in the first chapter.

Smokey, shown here with his first owner, Connie Deutsch, was flattening agitators long before earning his CDX (Companion Dog Excellent) AKC obedience title.

Q. Don't you feel you should at least provide guidelines for proper muzzle training?

A. No. Leave it alone.

You will also not find extensive outlines of certain common training techniques, such as line, circle and kennel agitation (see Glossary) in *Manstopper's* pages. All come under one or more headings: too dangerous to the agitator or the dog, or too risky *vis-à-vis* the effect upon a canine's perception of strangers.

Q. I know a trainer who knots his long leads every five feet, so he can feel how much leash is left. Comment?

A. Knotted leashes often snap at a knotted point.

Q. Is it true that feeding a dog gunpowder will heighten his aggression levels?

A. It's true the practice will eat away his stomach lining. Whoever originated the gunpowder myth must be depraved.

Q. I own two large dogs I'd like to guard train, but they don't get along well with each other. Your thoughts?

A. Ask yourself, "Would I like to try to stop a fight between these animals?" Then ask, "What if both were bite trained?" Perhaps sufficient bonding exists between you and your pets that none would ever turn on you. But during a dog fight, a combatant's mind can slip into another dimension. A canine engaged in a fight is an animal engaged in a war. He can wheel around and nail an owner before you can blink; and one dog biting someone can stimulate others to join in the fray.

Q. Nowhere have you outlined what an agitator should do when a dog has knocked him onto his backside, like the well-tailored gentleman Greta battled in Chapter 1.

A. You're right, I haven't. We don't practice it. It's too dangerous. It happens sometimes, is called an accident, and the agitator and trainer have to make do as best they can.

Q. My dog does well in obedience and protection. I would like to use him in search and rescue work. What do you think?

A. Don't. Handlers work S&R dogs off-leash, or on a very long lead, to provide space and maneuverability. Given that lost people often become disoriented, stress can cause them to take temporary leave of their senses. A missing, crazed camper could react badly to the sight of a large dog (who might appear to be a wolf), enough that the animal might nail the individual before you could move.

However, for cops reading this book, my thought is that a dog used to search for criminals should be guard trained. Whether the K-9 should bite or bark upon finding the target depends upon departmental policy, but the animal should have the training to protect himself (and you) against attack. Also, a dog should not be used against a barricaded suspect. The common result is a dead dog, as some departments have found out the hard way.

Q. What about training a manstopper for drug detection?

A. Were my dogs drug sniffers, you can bet they would be guard trained so they'd know they may protect themselves if some scurrilous druggie-type tries to harm them (as such miscreants are wont to do). I've known of drug dealers who offered bounties on drug-detection dogs—bounties that could provide retirement for you, me and several of our friends.

Be aware, however, of two points. One, to use drugs (either synthetics or the real stuff) in dog training requires federal and state permits. A person lacking proper documents could be arrested on possession charges, possibly even on an intent-to-distribute warrant, which is a felony in most jurisdictions. Two, during training or actual searches, a dog can overdose. Fatally.

Q. Some people claim, "My dog would protect me without training." True?

A. Some would. Heaven knows the dog is *semper fidelis* on four feet. Many, however, if given the opportunity, would not. Sensing they could avoid a threat, they would flee. The dog seeks his own advantage, and while he is man's best friend, he is his own best friend first. This is one of myriad ways in which dogs epitomize mental health.

Q. I've heard that trainers should hold the leash with one hand and extend the other with downward pressure along its length to prevent a dog from jumping toward an agitator's face. Comment?

A. Don't do it. The consequence can be to dump a dog on his butt for doing what you want him to do: bite the agitator. Accidentally bringing a dog down too hard or at a bad angle can result in injury, and the animal could decide it's to his advantage never to bite anyone again. The agitator should battle the dog with the sleeve, hoping that in time the animal will turn his fire against it.

Though some folks never think this through, it is not the trainer's job but the agitator's to teach the dog what to bite—the arm, under my system. Agitators must be adept enough to see an attempted face-bite coming and fast enough to jerk back from the dog's line of fire or block the animal with the sleeve, in either case denying the dog a bite until he targets the right area. Helpers too slow for such maneuvers obviate the point that bad-guy work isn't for everyone.

Q. Sometimes my dog ingests small quantities of burlap or jute during a working session. Can this hurt him?

A. I've known trainers who added minute burlap or jute shavings to their pups' food to build the animals' taste for the material. Check with your vet, but I'll go with a twinkle-eyed comment made to me by an aged, elfin nurse when I was hospitalized and experiencing the joys of a kidney stone: "This too shall pass."

Q. Have you heard of a technique that has the agitator kicking at the dog, the idea being to teach the animal to spin the bad guy, to dizzy him?

A. Yes. It can teach leg biting and can get a helper's leg ripped. Let it be.

Q. My dog is aggressive toward children. I don't have kids myself, so is it safe to guard train him?

A. No! That dog, perhaps through no fault of his own, is already unsafe around children. He could kill one. Bite trained, he could kill one easier.

Q. Do you ever use full-body suits in training?

A. Just with police K-9s. I want personal protection dogs to target just an arm, and body suits facilitate bites anywhere. Besides, have you ever priced such equipment? We're talking some serious bread here.

Q. Does neutering negate a guard dog's effectiveness?

A. It can have just the reverse effect. A bitch comes in season twice a year, during which time her head can slip into another zone, causing her to be listed *Out of Commission* for several weeks annually. Males are in heat 365 days a year. A friend once told me that the presence of a bitch in estrus within a block of his protection-trained male Rottweiler meant all bets were off. "Someone could have beat me to death, and I don't think the dog would have noticed."

A neutered animal can better concentrate on other matters when sex-drive hormones don't periodically flood the system. Have I ever owned a neutered guard dog? Several.

Having said all that, know that neutering, if it is to occur, should happen *after* the animal is trained. In the dog the line between sex- and violence-aggression drives is razor thin, and to neuter too young can be to diminish those and corollary drives.

Q. How about having a novice agitator use a lightweight radio with earphones to take directions from an experienced observer?

A. On paper, yes. In practice, no. A beginner awaiting instructions could hesitate, ignore his instincts, and be hurt. Plus, by the time a director reacts and transmits, the helper could be bleeding.

Q. Is it okay to use commands other than those you prefer?

A. Sure, so long as the cues don't sound like any other words you often use and are not words that could negatively influence a judge. To cite an extreme, if absurd, example, "Kill!" would not be a prudent choice.

Q. Did I miss a photograph of Greta somewhere in here?

A. Greta

Q. In the photograph of the three sitting Dobermans in Chapter 2, which one wasn't guard trained?

A. At the time the photo was taken, none were. Before long, all were.

Summary

I hope this chapter has raised enough topics to make you think of others germane to your situation. The answers presented reflect decisions I've made for myself. Consider your choices now, rather than after an incident that makes you wish you had.

Reflection

We are two travellers, Roger and I.
Roger's my dog.—Come here you scamp!
Jump for the gentlemen,—mind your eye!
Over the table,—look out for the lamp!
The rogue is growing a little old;
Five years we've tramped through wind and weather,
And slept outdoors when nights were cold,
And ate, and drank—and starved—together.

J.T. Trowbridge

CHAPTER 22
LESSONS FROM THE BEST TEACHER

Readers of my books know that each concludes with Lessons From the Best Teacher, containing anecdotes intended to teach and reinforce. The series continues in *Manstopper*, with the hope you will find the stories both instructive and enjoyable.

Deterrence

One evening years ago, before I got good sense and pulled away from a career in law enforcement, circumstance found me sharing a patrol car with another deputy sheriff. Hawkeye, my German Shepherd K-9, occupied the back seat.

Midway through the shift we stopped a van for speeding. The driver popped out, grinning like a used-car peddler, and I opened a rear door on the cruiser. Hawkeye sat, as I'd trained him, to keep an eye on things.

Soon the driver's two compadres emerged, despite the other officer's admonition that they should remain in the van. The driver, bolstered by his friends' presence, began running his jaws. Soon his buddies were throwing in their two cents' worth. A fuse was burning. I signaled Hawkeye to join us.

Instantly the two-year-old Shepherd was standing at my side, gazing at the three ne'er-do-wells. He didn't bark, growl or flash his teeth. He just stared. That was enough. Though by nature a gentle animal, Hawkeye radiated a muddy aura that people chose not to dwell upon.

Larry, Curly and Moe quieted in mid-yap. Their demeanor underwent an astounding change, from hostile body language and abusive verbiage that would never get past my editor to "Yes sir, no sir, you betcha." I believe any or all of them would have gleefully washed and waxed the patrol car, had the idea been put forth.

An effective manstopper may never have to bite anyone. As I said earlier, "In many instances the dog's presence alone may be deterrent enough."

Non-Think

Trainers receive a common type of inquiry, similar to one I received an hour ago.

"I want to train my dog to attack," the caller said. "She's already mean as hell."

"'Mean as hell' meaning. . . ?"

"Shoot," the man chuckled, "my friends can't even get near her that she don't try to bite them."

In years past I would ask what made the dog mean as hell, but I've discontinued the practice, having heard all the horror stories I want to hear.

"I'd like to help you," I said, "but I don't work with mean dogs." Or with their five-watt owners, I thought to myself. "Improper conditioning has made them too dangerous. I suggest you forget about guard training this animal."

Silence hung like a heavy fog.

Then, "Well, listen you (bleep), if you ain't (bleep) man enough to—"

Click.

I mean, why waste my time listening to a string of redundant, unimaginative bleeps? I used to try to reason with such people, but have found it pointless.

Are some of the dogs in question trainable? Maybe. But in truth, the owner worries me more than the dog. I get this vision of some yo-yo triggering his dog at a pub to impress his friends, and some poor soul whose only sin was taking a snootful, making a furtive move and being mauled.

As a retired protection trainer once commented, "The human element is what always bothered me. I knew the dogs I trained were steady, but some owners I've met. . . . "

Some People I've Met . . .

Baron, an undersized male Doberman, was a pure delight in protection work: bright, tough and intense. Near the end of his training, we visited Carl and Jeanne, rancher friends, to remind the dog that most folks pose no threat.

When we arrived I noticed a stranger perched on the porch railing. I remembered Carl saying, "My nephew's in town for a spell," but something about the guy didn't seem right. As Baron and I stepped onto the porch, the nephew, a child in his 20s, leaped from the railing, slammed hard onto the wooden flooring, said, "Aha! A killer Doberman," and crouched and slapped his palms on the floor while growling at the dog.

Q. Did he know Baron was being guard trained?

A. Yes. He'd been told.

Q. Was the state mental institution missing an inmate?

A. If not, the local zoo may have been.

Baron roared and lunged at the joker. I restrained the dog, and Carl, reposed on a glider, said, "Nephew, don't be a full-time dimwit." I told Baron, "C'mere." As the Dobie turned toward me, Dimwit smacked him on the butt.

My first impulse was to toss the guy off the porch. I mean, a dog should only have to put up with just so much, and—while not all that bad an idea in the abstract—I couldn't let Baron square things himself.

Then an inner voice whispered, "The fool is eight feet from you." Baron was on a six-foot leash. An evil glint may have flickered in my eyes. I released the slack.

Dimwit wound up off the porch. In jumping away from Baron's flashing teeth, he toppled over the railing and landed with an appropriately dull thud in Jeanne's flower bed. Just then, Jeanne, carrying a tray of iced tea, came through the front door, said, "What the hell's going on?" and Dimwit's troubles began in earnest. Jeanne was partial to her flowers.

I sat next to Carl, who commenced to rub Baron's ears, and we listened in rapt awe as Jeanne verbally skewered the nephew, characterizing him in salty terms that would have made President Harry Truman weep in admiration.

Moral: If some jerk puts bad moves on your dog, get the animal out of there. Should someone strike your pet, well, what happens next is your call. No, I wouldn't have let Baron sink his teeth in, but "a dog should only have to put up with just so much."

Provocation

A friend, Luís, was enjoying a late-night stroll with Lucy, his guard-trained Rottweiler, when three gangbangers accosted them.

"Hey, man, what you doin' on our walk-along here?"

Luís ignored the hoodlums.

"Hey, dude, I be talkin' at you!"

Luís and Lucy kept walking. Seeing my friend wouldn't play their game, the three harlequins fell in step a few feet behind the pair and continued their heckling. Luís disregarded them. A block later the mouthy leader rushed at Luís' back and reached for him.

I had long thought *Lucy* a synonym for *powder keg*, one devoted to Luís. Their reunion at my kennels had outshone even Tim and Greta's—at one point the howling, hopping dog had tried to crawl inside Luís' shirt.

Luís heard the punk coming and started to turn to face him, but Lucy was already moving. She went airborne an instant before Luís commanded "Out!"

Lucy's teeth clacked together like a pistol shot, inches from the creep's raised arm. He froze, his bravado a wilting weed as his mind raced through options (one seemed to be immediate location and use of bathroom facilities). Lucy rumbled at him, her anger radiating like steam from a boiling kettle.

"*Madre Dios!*"

"Don't be scarin' my dog!"

"What?"

"Don't scare my dog, fool!"

Fool presented placating palms and cloaked his mouth with something that tried to imitate a smile. Then, sounding like Mickey Mouse on helium, "Hey, homey, we was just . . . "

Luís told Lucy to heel, turned and left the three clumps of city crabgrass, all trying to look cool.

Two points: First, provocation. Many untrained dogs will react to it. A trained protector almost always will. Luís didn't trigger Lucy, you notice. She had registered hostile vibrations—dogs are good at that—and reacted to a shot at blindsiding her human.

Lucy wasn't trained to defend on provocation, but neither was she trained not to. To condition for provocation can create a four-footed grenade. To train a guardian to ignore provocation is to corrode her spirit by taking the dog out of the dog.

I handle the issue by leaving it alone: I neither train my dogs to react to provocation nor to ignore it. I don't draw attention to the matter one way or another, my intent being to leave relevant canine instincts intact, as they far exceed ours. I've trained manstoppers since somewhere in the '70s and have yet to see this approach backfire on me. I also know I can read and control untoward canine impulses.

Can you? That's point two: awareness. Yours. It ties into the provocation concept. Not only must you be able to read your pet, you must be a reader of situations. Innocent circumstances can ignite a dog. A jogger can do it. So can someone wearing an arm cast (because it resembles an agitator's sleeve).

Even a package-laden shopper, two moving legs protruding from bulky, noisy paper bustling toward you, can be a trigger.

Why? Because such images are unusual, and the canine survival instinct demands dogs heed the abnormal. Recall Tim's response when he saw the aged, cane-wielding soul: "Mindful that Greta might misread the moment, Tim altered their route so as not to intersect Mr. Strangeways' path." In a similar situation, divert your dog's attention or move her from the area.

Be alert to what occurs around you and your dog. Cover thine.

Knockout

A sidebar to the preceding tale could be developed from the fact that Lucy "had registered hostile vibrations—dogs are good at that." I've lost track of the number of times I've seen dogs act on input from their sixth sense (or maybe it's their 16th).

Of course, part of what alerted Lucy was the noise of sudden movement. Consider the canine sound and sight sensitivity and scent-discrimination capabilities portrayed in the following tale.

Jason was not just handsome, the black-and-rust Doberman was as bright as the breed gets. Despite a pronounced sense of territoriality, he was also a lover. He gave me unwavering affection and never met a human or another animal he didn't like.

Among his greatest friends, in fact, was Shadow, a neighbor's barn cat. The two often groomed one another, and their play sessions together obviated the myth about dogs and cats being natural enemies.

An Indiana thunderstorm was making a delightfully horrendous roof roar that nearly overrode my hacking at the keyboard. Jason, snoozing on the couch, suddenly leaped up and ran to a window, his abbreviated tail at full flutter. I walked to his side and peeked through the noisy gloom. I patted the young Doberman's neck. "What do you see, pupper?" His eyes tracked from left to right as his nostrils twitched more in confirmation than curiosity.

All I saw was silver rain streaking through the yard light's glow, and the only sound I detected above the torrent was Jason's excited whine. Then lightening flashed and I saw Shadow, moving from shelter to shelter, left to right, some 60 feet from the window.

I had known for years that dogs can hear a bug burp, that their night vision far exceeds ours, and that we can only wonder at their scenting abilities. Still, Jason's demonstration of all three that evening stunned me, such that moments later, while stroking the Doberman's sleeping form on the couch, his head in my lap, I caught myself muttering a word Mike had taught me. "Sho'nuff."

"To Err Is Human, to Forgive Canine"[1]

Mistakes can teach. Consider one made by a novice trainer-handler. I was the agitator, and the handler sent his dog at me without first checking that the leash, a 20-footer, had not tangled around his boots. It had, and one bound later the harnessed Akita hit its end with a jolt severe enough to take the trainer off his feet.

Of course, that the handler had been dumped on his derriere was of little concern. Confused, the dog had stopped.

"Get up! Send him again! Hurry! Hurry!" I yelled, knowing if we didn't reignite the animal and get him on the sleeve right away, he might internalize hesitancy for life.

This is an easier mistake to make than you might think.

[1]*Remembering Farley*, Lynn Johnston, Andrews & McNeel, 1994, page 37.

In a rush the trainer leaped up, patted the dog's shoulder, said, "I'm sorry, Jeb," pointed toward me and screamed, "Action Action Action!" I made moves to attract the dog, and the Akita blew in like a hurricane, as he always had. Weeks later no negative carryover problems were seen. After the session, though, the handler cursed a blue streak, aiming the invectives at himself and his carelessness.

"It isn't just that I could have jammed up his training. Jeb might have been hurt," he said.

"You got a big lesson," I told him.

"Yeah, but my dog had to pay for it," he said, and spewed another stream of self-depreciating oaths.

Though a beginning handler may make mistakes during the learning process, dogs are forgiving creatures by nature. The occasional inept correction won't subvert a sound training program. As author and dog-lover William Diehl wrote in *Show of Evil*, "Dogs'll forgive anything."

Be careful, but don't work nervous. Scared money never wins.

Persuasions

Despite the declarations of some, there is no "right" way to teach every dog every lesson. Were an ideal method available, we'd have one training book, not the many in print.

Training is art, not science. As art is a projection of the artist, trainers tend toward individualism regarding method and technique.

With those thoughts in mind, imagine a bull session involving several experienced trainers and you'll see how the discussions can range from calm to heated. Evening had fallen and the day-long seminar had served to stimulate a good deal of "Well, here's how I see it" among the dozen or so of us gathered at a tavern.

A topic that split the group was arm-and-hand versus leg biting. The words *if* and *but* were getting a royal workout.

"If a dog comes in high, he can injure his neck."

"But some leg biters tend to slam on the brakes just before striking, and that weakens impact."

And so forth. Then a wizened, somewhat inebriated soul who had said little, made converts.

"Look, most of us train for a living. We know the main use of a guard dog is deterrent, that setting him on some [censored] may land the owner in court." *Nice serve*, I thought.

Agreement was general, as was grumbling about the latter lamentable truth.

"We also know if we send the dog at someone, we want the fight short. We want the target to give up fast. The longer the fight, the less chance the dog has." *Good footwork.*

Again, no arguments.

"Okay, then look at two things. One, leg biters often come in below knee level and that can get a dog's head kicked in."

"Yeah, but . . ." someone began.

"Hold on, now. The floor's still mine." *Great backhand.* "Now," he said, "think of all the things you can't do without a hand."

No one spoke. *Game, set and match.* A baddie whose hand, wrist or forearm has just been engulfed by a hard-biting dog doesn't reason all this out at the moment, of course, but the emergency part of the brain sends the message, "Give up now or lose something vital."

Hair Trigger

In Chapter 1 I recommend against prefacing commands with the dog's name, especially protection commands. "Repeated linking of the dog's name with the Go word can develop a response where the dog goes target shopping upon hearing his name. Its sound can switch the animal's mind to cross-hairs mode."

In Chapter 4 I mentioned that some trainers experienced in obedience but not in protection labor under the illusion of forced reliability. One conclusion is, unlike obedience methodology, force is not an option.

Consider an incident in which these two concepts came into play.

When a name-link difficulty occurs, a trainer has to confront a Hydra: curing anticipation while not hampering the dog's edge. This is made trickier because the animal has by then established a low boiling point. The trainer who phoned me had just such a problem, among others.

During his initial foray into guard training, he had routinely preceded his "Action" cue with his dog's name, Saber (the trainer's background was AKC obedience competition, where exhibitors routinely use their pet's name). Saber, who delighted in protection work, had developed the habit of firing in response to her name. Once the problem was manifest it was also ingrained. The trainer had attempted to cure it through severe pinch-collar corrections when the dog reacted as she had been taught.

"As she had been taught" is not a slip. A dog's reservoir of knowledge consists of genetic information with which she is born, plus what she learns. In the context of training, trainers—not their dogs—are responsible for what the animals learn. To claim otherwise is merely an attempt to blame the dog for trainer ineptitude. This gentleman should have discerned the problem when it was developing, not after it had taken hold. Failure to do so and to take immediate corrective steps told the dog that her response was acceptable.

The training sessions became a routine of heeling the animal to within a few feet of an agitator, saying the dog's name and if she reacted with any form of aggression toward the helper, the trainer yanked the critter into last week. Finally, predictably, Saber took him.

Some days afterward, the trainer came upon a copy of *Advanced Obedience—Easier Than You Think*, read it and tracked me down. The young man minced no words. "I've screwed up my dog something fierce, her training is in the toilet and she's afraid of me. I'm a bit nervous around her now, too. What should I do?"

Before continuing, check out your own dog-think skills. Consider what you would recommend in this situation.

I mean it—set *Manstopper* aside and ponder a bit. I'll wait.

I made four suggestions. One, suspend protection work. Go back to basics, starting with making friends with the dog again. What happened was not her fault, not in the sense of first cause. Saber was a bite-trained canine who had been taught a faulty lesson, and there came a day when her frustration boiled over just as she reached the fight-or-flight stage in the stress cycle. Most children know not to corner a dog, yet that's essentially what the trainer had done. The animal's survival instinct took over, and the rest is history.

Suggestion number two relates to regaining the dog's trust: Change her name. Never use the former name again and make sure the new name doesn't sound anything like the previous one, even to the point of choosing a name with a different number of syllables. The old name was damaged beyond repair. It harbored ghosts no one could exorcise.

Likewise, when and if this animal continues in protection training, teach a new Go command. Like the name, previous associations with the old cue are tainted, like rotten meat.

Last, never use the dog's new name in conjunction with commands. Avoid the usage not just with protection cues but with obedience commands as well. This comes under the heading *Don't create a problem where none exists*. As with most aspects of dog training, keep things simple and direct.

The approaches worked. The trainer contacted me several months later to say that he and his dog were best friends once more and the animal was doing great protection work.

Pat-Pat

"Don't do that," I told the student.

"Don't do what?"

"Don't pet your dog during sleeve work."

"What?! It's basic to praise a dog for doing things right. I thought you were an expert."

It had been a long, trying seminar. I asked the group, "How many of you think it's a bad idea to pet your dog during agitation?"

Only the agitator raised his hand.

"Look," I said to the student, "petting during agitation is distracting . . ."

"No, it is not!" Some people would argue with a signpost.

". . . and can get you bit."

"My dog would never bite me." I remembered Saber.

"It can get an innocent person hurt and you sued."

"Might get your dog put down, too," the agitator said.

The silence was electric.

"How?"

I took the leash from the student's hand and walked his American Stafford-shire Terrier 20 feet from the agitator, an ancient soul who knew as much about dogs and training as I, perhaps more, and whose elfin expression said he knew what was coming. The Am Staff and I spent a few moments getting to know one another, then we walked toward the agitator, who stood death still.

We passed him without incident, walked 20 feet past him, turned and headed toward him again. He remained motionless as we strolled past him a second time.

"Hey, I can take my dog for a walk," the student yelled as the Am Staff and I started our third advance toward the helper, at whom I nodded almost imperceptibly. He caught the signal and grinned. The student went on, "If you're not going to do anything with my dog, just bring him here and. . . ."

I patted the Am Staff's neck twice. He flew at the helper and hit the sleeve with a resounding whump. After a few seconds I called the dog off, told him to sit, and stared at the owner. He wouldn't meet my eyes. You could almost hear dust fall.

After a long 10 count, the owner made an improbable reference to the Deity. Twice. Then, "I've taught my dog a Go signal, right?"

"Something like that," I said.

You could see that most of the other students had picked up on what had happened, but one said, "I don't get it."

"It's a variation on signal training," I said. "The owner got in the habit of patting the left side of his dog's neck twice just as he gave the 'Action!' command. Today, after making sure the dog wouldn't take the helper due just to proximity"—I made eye contact with the owner—"I patted the left side of the dog's neck twice. Pat-pat. You saw the dog's reaction."

This is the third reason why I told you earlier, "For heaven's sake, don't pet the animal during agitation!"

Linda Brown

That was the Doberman's name, and the day I met her . . . it was a memorable encounter.

The two-year-old German import had arrived at her new owner's home untrained. The gentleman had contacted me, saying "I need to get some manners in this dog. She's a handful."

So I drove to the man's home, a mansion, really, and a butler directed me to wait in the kitchen. I turned a chair toward a window and plunked myself down to watch deer feeding on the lawn. Then I met Linda Brown.

The black uncropped dog pranced into the kitchen (which approximated the size of my house), took one look at me and froze. I was new and wasn't supposed to be there. Her hackles rose, she bared her teeth and I thought, "I don't think I like this."

"Hi, babe," I said, in squeakier than normal tones, "C'mere and talk to me." I patted my leg but remained seated. Standing would have been the wrong tactic. Movement could have triggered her.

The Doberman wasn't buying my subtle attempt at domination, and in any case needed no invitation. She walked toward me on stiffened legs, staring at my face. If she blinked I missed it.

She swatted her front paws onto my thighs. A moment later she added her rear feet. Her beak was a foot above mine and her stare was riveting. I remember my inane thought that her mesmerizing eyes were the darkest I'd seen in years, the color of strong coffee.

I kept my feet on the floor and my arms at my sides, my left hand open, my right clinched. We were down to inches. I hoped that if she took a shot, I could counter by standing, slugging and using my momentum to throw her off me long enough to get the chair betwixt us. I grinned a lot.

I wrote in *Teaching Obedience Classes and Seminars* that in a tense situation, "Inner calm is crucial. If I feel it I may be able to send it; and if I can send it the dog may adopt it." I did, and—thank Whomever—the Doberman did. As the heat left her eyes I eased her onto the floor, stood next to her with knees of taffy and petted her. Pretty soon we were becoming friends.

A chilling moment? You bet. I mean, have you ever experienced an unknown adult Doberman sitting on you, breathing into your face, staring out the back of your skull? It can age a person.

But if you train dogs long enough, you'll find yourself in a similar situation. I don't know what will bring it about, or what the specifics will be, but I do know it will happen.

Lesson: Keep your cool. Then you have a chance. Lose it and the dog owns you.

Too Close

I've mentioned, "Manstopper ownership requires full-time attention." You must always be conscious of the animal's potential and aware that he may perceive innocent circumstances as threatening. Consider these two accounts.

While tossing a Frisbee for one of my guard-trained German Shepherds, a friend asked if she might throw the toy for him. Since the dog knew and liked her, I said "Sure," intending to hand her the disk when the animal returned it.

But the Shepherd decided to take five. He hit the ground and commenced to gnaw the Frisbee. My friend stepped forward and reached for it. A front paw on the toy, the dog shot her a sideways look of warning that sailed past her. I yelled "Out!" Everyone froze. I walked to the animal, interposing myself between him and my friend, took the disk and threw it for him. The dog flew away in happy pursuit.

"What was the problem? He wouldn't have hurt me." Bright laughter.

Another inch and he would have been on her like stripes on a tiger. My friend was intelligent and more of a dog person than many. She knew the animal and had spent much time around him, but his message of "Don't! It's mine!" sailed right past her.

Like I said, your radar must operate constantly. My worry is not that a dog might turn on his owner. Sound animals do that only in response to abuse.

My concern is a dog might nail an innocent before the owner senses trouble developing. That's a lead-in for the second tale.

While visiting my Dad, he drove me and Chattan, my Doberman, for a visit to a friend's house. It was a cool day and we had parked in the shade, so I opened two windows a few inches and left Chattan in the vehicle while we went inside for some "Good to see you."

Several minutes later my Dad mentioned he needed to get something from the car and would be right back. Engrossed in conversation, I didn't make the connection. I could give you all sorts of reasons, but the fact is I missed the obvious.

My Dad returned moments later, as pale as candle wax. "Chattan won't let me in the car," he said in shaky tones. In a blink I imagined what had happened, and felt I had won "Idiot of the Year." I could just see my trusting father, who moments earlier had petted Chattan, reaching for the door handle and the Doberman making the car rock as he roared and slammed against the door. The good news was my Dad didn't get the door open. If he had, I shudder to think. . . .

"Manstopper ownership is a full-time job."

Look Out!

The leash broke. I had tested the brand new, inch-wide, six-foot leather leash and it seemed all right to me; but when Slammer, a police K-9 candidate, lunged toward the helper, the lead snapped like a strand of spaghetti.

The agitator was about 15 feet away and bereft of sleeve—we were doing sack agitation—and the situation developed faster than my ability to recount it.

The helper froze, thank God. Running would have been the worst thing he could have done, as that would have further attracted the dog. I saw that in two bounds the Rottweiler would be on him and did the only thing I could think to do: I leaped at the animal and screamed "Platz!" (lie down) at the top of my lungs with enough fire to melt steel.

Guess what? The dog hit the ground. He was amazed by his own reaction—you could see the wheels turning: "Why am I lying down? I had planned on dining alfresco on agitator *au jus*."

I attached my reserve leash—I always carry one in a hip pocket—told Slammer what a good Platz he had done, suspended the session and heeled the Rotty to his run. When I returned, the helper, once he quit babbling, avowed a newfound attraction to the drink.

This incident illustrates another reason why I insist that obedience training should precede protection work. As in any endeavor, accidents can happen, things can go wrong. A dog's reflexive response to commands can make all the difference.

"Why Train Dogs for This?"

That's what Jim asked me. He was a man of the cloth, a gentle soul to whom anything more violent than a heated game of poker was anathema. Knowing it would be pointless just to say that sometimes it's dealer's choice, I told him a story.

The young man seemed scared to death. Awaiting transport to state prison, the skinny kid wore handcuffs looped through a belly chain, and ankle manacles. Another deputy sheriff entered the holding room accompanied by his five-month-old German Shepherd, a dog who had never met a stranger.

The convict appeared to melt at the sight of the pup. He had been regaling several deputies with macho statements about his toughness, but the animal's presence seemed to touch the softer side many people have.

"Deputy, could I pet your dog?"

"Naw, I don't think so."

"Please, man. I grew up around dogs. They were about my only real friends. I won't see one for a helluva long time. It would sure mean a lot to me to touch this little guy before I go."

Just then the prison's driver entered the room. He had caught the drift of the conversation and wasn't impressed. "I wouldn't let this [noun removed] touch my dog," he said.

"Aw, please, deputy. Hell, the way I'm trussed up I couldn't hurt the pup, and I wouldn't anyway. Please?"

Several of us were new to the job. We would soon learn a valuable lesson.

The deputy relented, said "Okay," and walked his tail-wagger to the felon. Later the deputy ruminated, "The kid wasn't up on a violent rap. He was just a nickel-and-dime burglar, so I figured. . . ." His voice trailed off as he looked at the floor.

The driver shook his head in disgust as the convict extended his cuffed hands as far as the waist chain would allow. He slipped his fingers alongside and under the pup's muzzle, and placed his thumbs atop it. For a moment he massaged the soft fur.

Suddenly the dog squealed and bucked backward. The punk was compressing the animal's muzzle so hard that his hands shook. We quickly got the guy to release, never mind how, and stared at one another as the driver led the laughing—laughing!—bully away.

Fortunately the goon was as weak physically as morally—he didn't injure the dog in any permanent sense. Moments later an attorney waiting to see a client tarnished the day further. "If the pup had bit the kid, he could have sued the county. And won. He was bound and in your custody, so you were obligated to protect him." The lawyer wasn't kidding.

After I finished the story, Jim slowly shook his head. Then, "The Lord must have had an off day when he made that one."

"To Ward Off Evil"

Do you recall those words from Chapter 2? "All you may ever need to ward off evil intentions is a sizable, responsive dog at your side."

Laurie was cashiering on the graveyard shift at a convenience store when a stocky Asian gent approached the counter. With one hand in his jacket pocket, suggesting a weapon, he gestured at the register.

"You're robbing me?" Laurie said.

The man nodded sharply.

Laurie said, "Ready." Perhaps the thief thought that meant cooperation. It didn't. Next to her a black-and-white apparition periscoped up, saw the intruder, and, saying nothing, stared at him. The man, expressionless, looked back at the dog. He put his arms at his sides, gave a slight, sharp bow toward Laurie, and left "in dignified haste."

The animal seemed disappointed as he watched the door close. Looking wistfully toward it, he lowered himself from sight and was soon chasing the rabbits of slumber once more.

The dog was not protection trained. He knew basic obedience and a few tricks, like "Shake" and "Catch" (a food treat) and "Ready," which meant that when he sat, the nearest visitor would give him a tidbit.

It was appropriate the dog was not guard trained, for seldom is the work compatible with the nature of an Afghan Hound.

Cabbages and Kings

We all know that the farther some folks proceed along any path, the more some of them decide they know all there is to know about their profession (or, in some cases, about any subject you care to name). They can't hear the words of others. Their own opinions are too loud.

In dog training, this bent can appear when obedience trainers progress to protection work. It can also show up when a protection trainer becomes a badge-heavy cop. In either case the attitude can rig a self-defeating trap.

Police K-9 seminars are among my favorite events. I get to exchange war stories with trainers who deal with real-world working dog problems and applications. However, during one clinic I attended, the speaker's hubris sullied the event. The man knew dogs but only up to a point: His self-proclaimed superiority had rendered him blind and deaf. He had lost the abilities to listen and learn.

Earlier that day we watched his department's dogs do bitework. They acquitted themselves well enough but had a problem with non-responsiveness to the "Out" command. Handlers had to repeat it several times and often had to pull dogs off the agitators.

Later, when someone in the audience asked about this, the speaker rationalized his dogs' selective hearing. "I don't want to accent the release phase of training, as that could knock down the dogs' drive." I could appreciate the sentiment but felt it was only a partial truth.

Certainly, no police dog trainer wants to abbreviate his dog's fire for commanded aggression. In that line of work, the animal may someday be called upon to keep the handler alive.

But when a handler tells a police dog—or any canine protector—to quit, he must quit. Now. Not when he gets around to it. Encouraging a contrary attitude risks needless injury. It could also incur the wrath of a judge, who might rule handler negligence due to lack of sufficient control of the dog. Besides, pulling a biting canine off someone can rip flesh.

During a break I approached the speaker, introduced myself, said I was enjoying his presentation and, once I was sure no one could overhear, mentioned that a dog can learn to release without loss of enthusiasm.

"Oh, can he now?" he said in booming tones. So much for discretion.

"Sure, and I'd be glad to show you a technique. . . ."

That was as far as I got.

"You?! You show ME?!"

Some people overestimate their own abilities and underestimate everyone else's. The arrogance in this bird's attitude glowed neon, and I have never catered to small minds. Those in the room who had yet to tune in to our conversation were now on-line.

"No, now that I study on it," I said, matching him glare for glare, "I probably couldn't teach you a damned thing, pal."

Ah, vanity. It can be infectious. I returned to my seat and gave myself hell for letting the clown get to me.

In any profession someone always knows more. When you meet someone knowledgeable, listen up. Narcissism is a soul killer.

Liquid Courage

The agitator arrived drunk. Not just tipsy or mildly gassed: hammered.

But, not to worry. "I just had a couple, Joel. I can handle whatever you throw at me. Bring 'em on!"

Yeah, right.

I dismissed him. Permanently. If you're ever faced with a similar situation, I suggest you do the same.

Q. Permanently? Isn't that a bit strong?

A. I've found that addicts only try to parlay second chances into thirds, fourths, fifths and so on. Until they see their behaviors bring consequences, they have no motivation to change.

Besides, the individual might sue you for injuries sustained during a training session. Ask an attorney. When you boil the polysyllabic answer down, you'll find that allowing someone under the influence to participate in hazardous endeavors is to take responsibility for the person's safety.

Always A Dog

Nikai of Marks-Tey[2] was the registered name of one of my dogs, a striking red-and-rust Doberman who had a lion's heart and a stare that could melt glass. His call name was Nick, and his *nick*name (if you'll forgive that) was The Red

---

[2]Marks-Tey is the kennel name of Joanna Walker (*The New Doberman Pinscher*, Howell Book House, 1981, 1977). Chattan, mentioned earlier, is another of Joanna's dogs.

Blur. In terms of quick, sudden bursts of movement, Nick was as fast a Dobe as I've known, but that alone didn't lead to his name.

It had been a stormy evening, both within and without. Within: I had confronted Nick about the reality that a roast chicken on the counter does not confer permission to purloin. Without: Thunderstorms were prowling the darkness. When I went to turn in, the Doberman, still miffed over having to make do with kibble while I fanged down the festive bird, decided to crash on the couch rather than on my bed, his customary berth.

"Hasta la bye-bye," I said and padded to the three-acre bed, leaving Nick to deal with his case of the sulks.

Now, Nick also topped the charts in hardness. Truly, he was tougher than Chinese algebra and a scrapper of the first order. He hit like a savage wind, and even such prosaic pursuits as chasing a ball elicited his full intensity. As one helper put it, "You couldn't knock that dog off a sleeve even if you hit him with a brick."

So the fast, tough manstopper was asleep on the sofa as I was tumbling toward the place where they keep the dreams when thunder exploded right over the house, about one foot above the chimney, flash-boom, ground zero, the kind that shakes foundations, rattles windows, and leads to nicknames like The Red Blur.

As one movement Nick sproinged off the couch and over the coffee table, touching the floor just once in his beeline to the bedroom, and the next thing I knew there was this trembling, bug-eyed, furry mass curled by my neck.

A few days later I recounted the incident to an acquaintance, a trainer possessed of meager talent but ample certitude. He commented in down-the-nose fashion, "Humph! Some guard dog!"

"True," I said. "If I'm ever attacked by a thundershower, Nick may let me down."

Some folks never get the idea. They may know this, that and the other technical aspect about dogs and training, but they have neither the wit nor the compassion to see the implications of any of it.

But that's a sidebar. A chapter title in my dear friend Carol Lea Benjamin's excellent book, *Second-Hand Dog*, is "The Good Life—What Your Dog Needs." I embrace that sentiment. Your pet deserves "The Good Life." So does mine. The concept includes providing your dog with love and security on demand. He won't ask for anything frivolous (save for an occasional drumstick)—just to be with you whenever possible, good nutrition, fresh water and an understanding friend to lean on when the roof seems about to fall in.

When your buddy gets on in years, remember that he still needs you.

Wrap Up

We are near the end of this book. Have I told you everything there is to know about guard dog training and handling? Of course not. I've covered way more than the essentials, but the subject is too vast and encompasses too many variables for anyone to know or elucidate every nuance. As mentioned earlier, things happen from second to second. Change one variable, like breed, gender, bloodline, stance, stare, ear or tail positioning and an event that means one thing in a given situation can mean something quite different in another. That's why you must be able to read your dog.

That can sound mysterious—reading the dog. But all it means is hearing her, what she is saying, either to you or to a bad guy, or to herself. Then you have to react properly. Once you can do these things, anything I might add would be commentary.

If this chapter has triggered memories, good. If it has led you to ponder some what-ifs or stimulated your imagination, even better. If it has moved or motivated you, frosting on the cake. If it has taught, bingo!

Reflection

Dogs are our link to paradise. They do not know evil or jealousy or discontent. To sit with a dog on a hillside on a glorious afternoon is to be back in Eden, where doing nothing was not boring—it was peace.

Milan Kundera

POSTSCRIPT

Be careful.

Guard dogs have been likened to loaded guns. Though some parallels exist—either can go off accidentally, both have a muzzle—the analogy is flawed. Guns have one ultimate function: to kill. But a manstopper has multiple gifts and is not a killing machine.

Besides, a bullet cannot be halted or called back. Guns are impractical in the dark and can't be fired around corners or used by the blind. The noise of firearms insults the ears more than a dog's cautioning bark. Guns cannot think or solve problems.

Or lick your face or chase a toy or sense that faraway look in your eyes and pass the hours with you. A guard dog can do all these things, and more. Unlike the craven among our species, a dog will never lie to or about you, use your own feelings against you, sell you out to preserve himself, attempt to build himself up by tearing you down, or project his own neuroses onto your motivations. As President Dwight Eisenhower observed, "The friendship of a dog is precious." In a changing world, canine companionship is a great constant.

Now and always a manstopper.

But the animal remains a manstopper. Once he has had a taste of bitework, the turned-on part of him may be sublimated but it will never go away, even if the training ends right then and there for all time. Remember, what the dog learns, he learns for life.

Q. But can't any dog's training be reversed so that the animal will never again do what he was trained to do?

A. Consider the following. Many Americans donated dogs to the Army during World War II. After the armistice, some former owners wanted their pets back. However, the Army quite properly refused to release an animal who had undergone bitework until a panel of qualified officers judged it to be no longer dangerous to the civilian community. A program of de-training was organized.

What happened? "[A] trainer presented a Great Dane to the judgment panel, flung down a padded sleeve used in attack training and asserted that under no circumstances would the dog hit the sleeve, whereupon the Dane broke the trainer's arm."[1]

Be careful.

[1]*The Guard Dog*, Jerrold J. Mundis, David McKay Company, Inc., 1969, page 39.

GLOSSARY

Because the following lexicon pertains to guard dog training and related concepts, some entries bear scant resemblance to standard dictionary definitions. I have kept descriptions as nontechnical as possible and have included some terms not used in *Manstopper* because trainers at protection-dog level should be familiar with the terminology.

acceleration A event whereby an initially hesitant canine suddenly erupts, seeming to make up for lost time.

action The *Manstopper* command that means "Bite and hold the target's nearer forearm."

active resistance Overt canine defiance of trainer intent.

agitation A process by which a dog learns to become aggressive on command.

agitation whip A short-handled lash whose cracking sound excites a dog.

agitator One who agitates a dog; also known as a *helper* or *bad guy*.

alpha Pack leader, number-one animal, the boss.

Alsatian European designation for the German Shepherd Dog.

American Kennel Club (AKC) A governing body whose primary responsibility is maintaining purebred canine bloodlines in the United States.

angulation Canine skeletal angles.

animation Overt canine enjoyment.

anthropomorphism Assigning human traits and values to another species, such as comparing dog training to child rearing.

anticipation Performance of a command before it is given.

associative learning Powerful lessons derived as byproducts of other, seemingly incidental lessons.

attitude Canine behavior revealing the animal's feeling about a command's directive, a situation or event.

attraction The level of canine interest and trust in a handler; the degree of canine interest in an agitator.

automatic sit An obedience basic requiring a dog to sit because an event occurs: During heeling, the handler stops walking; during a recall or retrieve, the animal arrives in front of and facing the handler.

224

avoidance conditioning   A form of *instrumental conditioning*, this is aversive conditioning that allows a subject to avoid an unpleasant consequence by reacting properly to an environmental cue.

back   The *Manstopper* command meaning "Hurry to the handler's left side while keeping an eye on the bad guy."

backsliding   A short-lived phenomenon occurring in some dogs whereby the animal seems to have forgotten most lessons to date. This happens more often during obedience than protection training.

bad guy   Synonym for *agitator*.

baiting   A breed-ring technique for capturing and holding a dog's best attention.

bitch   A female canine.

bite bar   A stiff material three inches wide attached parallel to a sleeve's cylinder and angled toward the direction of a dog's bite, the purpose being to cause the animal to use her entire mouth when biting.

bitework   Specifically, training a dog to bite a defined area of human anatomy, and building bite compression; in general, protection training or play work.

bloodline   Refers to physical and psychological characteristics typically present among offspring of a dominant lineage.

bonding   A process that leads a dog to feel deep attraction toward another animal, either canine or human.

breed ring   Also known as a *show* or *conformation ring*, a dog-show area where canines are judged according to each dog's conformation to the written breed standard.

breed showing   See *conformation showing*.

burned out   Refers to a dog whose training has been so prolonged and repetitious that she has lost interest in the work and may have developed an aversion toward it and the trainer.

call name   A dog's around-the-house name, as opposed to his registered appellation.

Canadian Kennel Club (CKC)   A governing body whose primary responsibility is maintenance of purebred canine bloodlines in Canada.

Canis familiaris   The scientific designation of man's best buddy.

carryover effect   A positive or negative influence upon canine perception of one activity by another.

catch (a dog)   An agitator's method of accepting a bite.

catch stance   An agitator's posture assumed in readiness to catch a dog.

challenge the dog   A method that attempts to elicit a dog's best efforts by making tasks just difficult enough that she must work hard to perform them.

choke collar   A training collar fashioned from steel links that can restrict and even terminate breathing if misused.

circle agitation   A non-recommended technique during which dogs are arrayed several feet apart in a circle, facing inward, and the agitator fires each animal for a few seconds before moving to the next. Similar in concept to *line agitation*, circle agitation is far more dangerous, as there is no back door.

civil agitation   No-bites-allowed agitation by a sleeveless helper.

classical conditioning   Linking a natural biological response with an unnatural stimulus.

collar tab   A short length of stout cord or similar material attached to a collar's live ring to provide a ready handle.

command   A trainer's directive calling for a response from the dog.

communication   Imparting of information.

competition   Work performed against ideal standards.

compulsion   Correction; external force; pressure; punishment.

conditioning   1) Practicing lessons in varying environments. 2) Methods of teaching: see *avoidance conditioning, classical conditioning, escape conditioning, instrumental conditioning* and *operant conditioning.*

cone pattern   An agitation technique of following a tapering, cone-like pattern while moving toward a dog, who is at the point.

conformation showing   Competing of dogs against the written standard describing the ideal specimen of the breed. Also referred to as *breed showing.*

consistency   Relating to a dog in an unchanging manner.

contact   Any form of communication.

contention   Canine resistance to trainer intent.

correction   Physical and/or verbal pressure applied by a trainer in response to canine disobedience.

crossover conditioning   Similar to the *spillover effect*, this training encourages a dog to transfer a positive attitude he has about a given article or thing to another article or thing.

cue   Synonym for *command.*

cuff   See *sleeve cover (cuff).*

dam   A bitch who has produced offspring.

dead ring The choke-collar ring to which a leash is not attached. See also *live ring*.

decoy Synonym for *agitator*.

deflection Ignoring low-risk contention or minor misbehavior to prevent either from escalating.

desensitization Altering anxiety-producing responses through gradual exposure to increasingly stressful stimuli.

distraction proofing Exposing a dog to distractions, the purpose being to teach in a controlled setting that the animal must obey the trainer's commands despite nearby happenings.

distractions Stimuli that may entice a dog to break from command.

Dobermann European spelling and breed designation of the Doberman Pinscher.

dog Technically, the term denotes a male canine, but refers more often to members of *Canis familiaris* without regard to gender.

dog aggressive Strictly, this denotes a male who is hostile toward other males, but generally it refers to any member of the species who is aggressive toward others canines.

dominance The stance from which a trainer must operate to secure and maintain the Alpha role.

dominant Refers to an animal who would rather lead than follow.

double-leashing Attaching two leads to one dog.

double-sleeve technique Using a sleeve on each arm.

drive 1) Behaviors that seek to satisfy instinctual demands. 2) A training technique that capitalizes upon canine instincts. 3) A dog's degree of attraction to a stimulus.

escape conditioning Similar to *avoidance conditioning*, this aversive teaching method lets a subject avoid further unpleasant consequences without an environmental cue.

estrus Specifically, the sexual-cycle's peak, culminating in ovulation; generally, a bitch being in heat.

exercise A competition term that refers to an element of an obedience or protection repertoire.

extra-mile principle A proofing concept that requires more of a dog than the trainer actually wants.

fear-biter A dog who reaches the fight-or-flight state with no more provocation than occurs during normal contact situations.

fear training   A despicable training approach based on teaching a dog to respond correctly to avoid inhumane pressure.

feed a sleeve   Extending a sleeve toward a dog such that the article is the closest enticing object.

female aggressive   A bitch who is aggressive toward other bitches.

fence agitation   Similar to *kennel agitation*, this is agitation of a dog who is separated from the bad guy by a fence.

fence charger   A device that electrifies a wire fence with mild current.

fence fighter   A dog who habitually fights others through a fence.

fight or flight   Based in defense drive, this is the point in the stress cycle where a dog attempts to either fight or flee that which is causing the stress.

fightwork   Synonym for *agitation*.

finish   An obedience function by which a dog moves on command to sitting at the heel position.

fire   Canine exuberance.

flank   An extremely touch-sensitive area of loose skin located between the floating rib (the 13th) and the front of the rear leg where it joins the body.

flanking   A compulsion technique that teaches a dog to release her bite.

flew   The large, pendulous part of a dog's upper lip.

focus   Directed mental concentration.

forced-reliability illusion   The mistaken notion that any dog not trained through force cannot be dependable, that any dog subjected to enough pressure will prove reliable.

foundational   Refers to an exercise that is valuable not just for its own merits but that is a necessary element of a subsequent lesson.

full mouth   An expression referring to a dog's biting technique whereby the animal employs nearly all her teeth, not just the front ones.

fur-saver collar   A large-linked steel collar.

gender conflict   Refers to a dog who does not relate well with humans or canines of the same sex.

guard dog (guardian)   Synonym for *manstopper*.

gun shy   A dog whose central nervous system cannot cope with the sound of gunfire.

gun sure   A dog whose concentration is impervious to the noise of gunfire.

hackles   A defensive response involving the hairs on the neck and back of a dog that rise in anger to make the animal appear larger.

handler   1) Synonym for *owner* or *trainer*. 2) One who shows a dog in competition.

handler sensitive Describes a dog who is attentive *en extremis* to the handler, to the degree that the animal will shift her attention from a bad guy to the handler when the handler comes near.

hanging Suspending a dog by her leash. As a training technique, the concept is contemptible; its sole legitimacy lies in handler defense.

hardness The degree to which a dog is touch insensitive.

hard sleeve A padded sleeve that a typical bite cannot compress. Many such sleeves are designed for right- or left-arm use but not both and feature a bite bar.

heeling Canine synchronous movement with a handler to maintain the heel position.

heel position A dog's position at the handler's left side, the animal facing forward, her right shoulder adjacent to the person's left leg.

helper Synonym for *agitator*.

hidden sleeve A sleeve of minimal thickness intended for wearing under a shirt or coat, and which generally fits too tightly to be easily slipped out of by an agitator.

Homo sapiens The scientific designation of human beings.

hosing Striking a dog with a length of garden hose in the name of training, sometimes after first inserting wooden doweling therein. Unlike *hanging*, there is no justification for such abuse.

I and the Not-I A dog's view of herself in relation to other beings.

identifiers Terms a trainer assigns to objects, beings and conditions to create a language beyond commands with her pet.

independent A dog who would prefer to be alone and on her own.

in-out, back-out An agitation technique whereby the helper moves in (toward the dog), drawing the dog out, and the agitator reacts by moving back, thus drawing the animal out farther.

instincts General inborn urges to act in response to basic needs (survival, pack social structuring, etc.).

instrumental conditioning An educational method by which a canine develops habits by learning from the consequences of her actions.

integration A training phase during which exercises initially practiced separately are performed in sequences.

intelligence The ability to thrive and problem-solve in any environment.

jute A coarse, woven material often used in the manufacture of sleeve cuffs.

K-9 Synonym for *police dog*.

kennel agitation   Similar to *fence agitation*, in this method a kenneled dog is agitated from outside the structure.

lead   Synonym for *leash*.

learned-helplessness-syndrome   Canine acceptance of abuse as an inevitable, unavoidable consequence of contact with humans.

learning   A permanent behavioral change arising from experience.

learning rate   The speed at which a dog can absorb new material.

leash   A thong, cord, or strap by which a handler restrains a dog.

light lead   A leash appreciably lighter than the primary leash.

light line   A long, lightweight line used in off-leash training.

line agitation   A non-recommended method during which several dogs are positioned next to each other but several feet apart, and the agitator works up and down the line, firing each animal for a few seconds before moving to the next. Also see also *circle agitation* and *civil agitation*.

Listen   The *Manstopper* command meaning "Alert; focus on the person."

live ring   The ring of a choke collar to which a handler attaches a leash. Also see *dead ring*.

male aggressive   A dog who is aggressive toward other males. Also known generically as *dog aggressive*.

manstopper   A protection-trained dog who will not back down so long as she can contend.

manwork   Specifically, teaching a dog to deal with a person rather than a sleeve; in general, protection training. See also *bitework* and *fightwork*.

misdirected anger   Canine ire directed toward a person or object that is not the actual cause of the animal's resentment.

moment of recognition   The learning instant at which a dog's aspect communicates, "Aha! I understand what my trainer wants."

muzzle   A dog's snout; or, a device (usually leather) attached to said snout to prevent the animal from being able to bite.

muzzle agitation   A non-recommended technique whereby a muzzled dog contends against an agitator who is not wearing protective gear, like a padded sleeve.

name   A dog's appellation, which most canines see as more of a positively based attention-getter than an identification of self.

nose-tap   A dog's action of tapping her nose against a sleeve after releasing her hold on the object. Don't confuse this with a rebite.

novice   A trainer or dog new to training.

obedience training   Specifically, teaching a dog to perform a variety of tasks on command; in general, any type of dog training.

off-collar   Refers to a dog devoid of a collar.

off-leash   Denotes a dog not being controlled by a leash.

on-leash   Designates a dog controlled by a leash.

operant conditioning   Teaching an active behavior in response to positive or negative stimuli.

ostrich defense   One response of a frightened dog: Turning her attention from that which she fears—"If I can't see it, it can't hurt me."

Out   The *Manstopper* command meaning "Cease aggression but remain alert." This cue cancels the commands "Action," "Listen" and "Watchim." It is also used to stop a dog's reaction to provocation.

pack   All members of a dog's family.

pack hierarchy   A pack's social and ranking structure.

pack leader   See *alpha*.

passive resistance   Covert opposition to a handler's intent.

pedigree   A listing of a canine's ancestors.

personality   A dog's habitual manner of relating with her environment and those individuals she contacts.

personal-protection dog   Synonym for *manstopper*.

pet   As a verb (transitive), to show acknowledgment, acceptance, approval or affection. As a noun, your best friend.

pinch collar   A multi-linked metal training device that imparts the sensation of teeth grabbing the dog's neck.

playtoy   A toy that a dog enjoys.

playwork   Concentration-building exercises rooted in positive reinforcement using play-like techniques.

praise   Affirmation; approval; communicating to a dog that her behavior is as commanded.

pressure   Synonym for *correction*.

proofing   Ascertaining canine reliability.

protection dog   Synonym for *manstopper*.

puppy   A canine lacking physical or emotional maturation. Though there is no cut-off age, animals younger than six months are often more puppy than dog. In general, the larger the breed, the slower the maturation.

puppy sleeve   A soft, flexible sleeve designed for use with puppies that offers scant protection for the wearer against a mature dog's bite.

put down   Canine euthanasia.

rapport   An intangible that says "I seek that which I project: respect and oneness."

read a dog   A human skill for intuiting what a dog is feeling, thinking and likely to do in a given situation.

rebite   A dog's unacceptable action of biting after responding correctly to the release command. Don't confuse this with a nose-tap.

recall   A competition term that designates summoning a dog to a sitting position in front of and facing the handler.

recognition factor   The ease with which the general public can visually identify a breed and its tendencies.

registered name   A dog's "official" appellation registered with a governing body, such as the AKC.

reinforcement   A stimulus that can cause a behavior change.

replacement   A technique to halt destructive behavior by enabling a dog to vent natural urges acceptably.

resistance   Canine opposition to a handler's intent. See also *active resistance* and *passive resistance*.

response   Behavior elicited by a stimulus.

ring sport   Competition wherein a dog must excel at obedience and protection.

runaway   An agitator's act of running from a dog while extending a sleeve outward and level from the body.

run-by   An agitation technique whereby a sleeved helper runs past a dog at an angle (i.e., not directly at the dog) and comes close enough that the animal will barely miss or will be able to reach the sleeve, according to the helper's intent.

sack   As a noun, this term denotes a burlap bag measuring 21 inches wide by 36 inches long. As a verb, as in "to sack a dog," reference is made to a helper's use of a sack to stimulate play, prey, self-defense, fight and dominance drives.

schutzhund   Competition wherein a dog must be proficient at tracking, obedience and protection.

sentinel   A dog trained to guard an area and to work without a handler.

sharpness   A quality that refers to a dog's quickness to bite. The sharper the dog, the more she parallels a hair trigger.

shopping a judge   Refers to discovering the preferences and biases of a judge under whom a handler intends to show a dog.

show stance   A standing pose used in breed-ring competition.

sire A male parent.

sleeve A generic term referring to many types of padded sleeves, made generally from leather and/or synthetic material, worn by an agitator for arm protection. As a verb, to use a sleeve in protection training.

sleeve cover (cuff) Jute material that slides onto a sleeve, the purpose being to provide a firm biting surface while prolonging the sleeve's life.

sleeve happy Describes a dog who considers her possession of a sleeve to signify a confrontation's terminus.

sleeve slipping A helper's act of allowing the sleeve a dog is biting to slide from her arm, at which moment the agitator withdraws from the animal's striking range forthwith.

slipped bite A dog's accidental movement of his bite from one part of a sleeve to another.

sneak-biter A dog who bites for enjoyment but only after first projecting the lie that she likes the individual she intends to nail.

socialization Introducing a dog, usually during puppyhood, to various positive environments, individuals and experiences.

soft sleeve A compressible, marginally padded cylinder.

solid on the sleeve Characterizes a dog who craves only a sleeve (i.e., no other portion of helper anatomy).

spillover effect The effect of a seemingly non-structured lesson seeping into all areas of a dog's reliability.

stage A training phase.

stake agitation See *tie-out agitation*.

stimulus Perceived environmental information.

stop The indentation between the eyes where the nasal bones and cranium meet.

stress Sustained factors that create psychological and/or physiological pressure on or within a dog.

submission Acceptance of perceived dominant behavior.

submissive Denotes a dog who would rather follow than lead.

tab See *collar tab*.

tail-set The point where the tail extends from the body.

teachable moment A time when a dog is receptive to learning.

teething Emergence of adult teeth.

temperament Canine psychological soundness and stability.

temperament testing Systematic evaluation of genetically based canine traits.

throw chain A short, lightweight chain used as a compulsion device.

tie-out agitation   Agitation of a tied dog.

topline   The area of the back between the withers and the tail set.

topped out   A dog who hit a frustration peak but was not granted relief and slid into emotional apathy.

touch sensitive   A dog overly responsive to physical contact.

toughness   Synonym for *hardness*.

trainable   Refers to a dog responsive to instruction.

trainer   One who trains a dog.

training   A process through which one takes control of and enhances bonding with a dog by developing a basis for and means of communication.

typewritering   A dog's undesirable action of rapidly switching her bite along an arm or from limb to limb, or to other parts of a person's anatomy.

vehicle training   Agitation of a dog confined in a car or truck.

verbal bridge   Timing a word or phrase with a dog's actions, the trainer's intent being to thus teach the animal a command.

watchdog   A canine trained to bark at an outsider's approach but not trained to bite.

Watchim   The *Manstopper* command meaning "Threaten and show aggression by barking, growling, snapping jaws and/or showing teeth."

wham effect   Momentum generated by a guard dog during her rush and transferred to a bad guy at the moment of impact.

willingness   The degree of inherent and/or learned enjoyment a dog has toward working.

withers   Canine shoulders.

work concept   Teaching a dog that her obedience, including protection, contributes to her pack's welfare.

working   Teaching, practicing or applying knowledge.

FOR FURTHER READING

Anyone should do extensive study before attempting to train a canine protector. This list is not inclusive, as some guard books I don't recommend. Also, I do not agree with every training technique presented in certain of these manuals.

All About Guard Dogs, Howard H. Hirshhorn, TFH, 1976.

Basic Training and Care of Military Dogs, Department of the Army.

The Complete Guide to Dog Law, Deidre E. Gannon, Esq., Howell Book House, 1994.

Deutsche Schutzhundschule, Johannes Grewe, Quality Press, 1981.

The Dog's Mind, Bruce Fogle, DVM, MRCVS, Howell Book House, 1990.

Dog Owner's Home Veterinary Handbook, Delbert G. Carlson, DVM, and James M. Giffin, MD, Howell Book House, 1992.

Dogs for Police Service, Sam D. Watson, Jr., Thomas Books, 1963.

Dog Training For Law Enforcement, Robert S. Eden, Detselig Enterprises (Calgary), 1985.

The Guard Dog, Jerrold J. Mundis, David McKay Company, 1969.

How to Train Dogs for Police Service, Jay Rapp, Denlinger Publishers, Ltd., 1979.

Military Working Dog Program Training Manual, U.S. Air Force.

Obedience and Security Training for Dogs, Tom Scott, Arco Publishing, 1967.

Police Dogs: Training and Care, Home Office Standing Advisory Committee on Police Dogs, Her Majesty's Stationery Office (London), 1963.

The Police Service Dog, Johannes Grewe, Quality Press, 1989.

Rappid Obedience and Watchdog Training, Jay Rapp, Denlinger Publishers, Ltd., 1978.

Schutzhund Helper's Manual, Mark E. Leamer, Jr., MK Publications, 1981.

Schutzhund—Theory and Training Methods, Susan Barwig and Stewart Hilliard, Howell Book House, 1991.

Top Working Dogs (Revised), Dietmar Schellenberg, D.C.B., 1982.

Training Dogs, Colonel Konrad Most, Popular Dogs Publishing (London), 1951.

Training Guard and Protection Dogs, Joseph A. Dobson, Arco Publishing, 1984.

Training the Dog for Guard Work, Reginald Arundel, Denlinger Publishers, Ltd., 1952.

Your Dog and the Law, Murray Loring, DVM, JD, Alpine Publications, 1983.

Many breed texts are also available. At least 10 books are in print about the German Shepherd, over a dozen about the Doberman Pinscher, and so forth. There are also local and national clubs concerned with every breed.

ABOUT THE AUTHOR

Joel M. McMains, an award-winning Howell Book House author, has trained dogs professionally since "somewhere in the '70s." In addition to offering professional obedience and protection-training services, he holds public obedience classes and training seminars.

Certified by the State of Wyoming Peace Officer's Standards and Training Commission as a Police Service K-9 Trainer and Instructor, Joel served as Chief Trainer for the Sheridan County (Wyoming) Sheriff's Department, the City of Sheridan Police Department and search and rescue groups. He taught courses in K-9 selection, management, training and deployment for the Police-Science Division of Sheridan College, and has testified in numerous court proceedings as an expert witness on canine behavior and training.

Coordinator of Sheridan County's 4-H Dog Program for 12 years, Joel is a member of the Dog Writers' Association of America, and lives near Terre Haute, Indiana.

Other Howell books by Joel M. McMains
Dog Logic—Companion Obedience
Advanced Obedience—Easier Than You Think
Kennels and Kenneling
Dog Training Projects for Young People
Teaching Obedience Classes and Seminars

V

W